Ordnanc
Dor
Landranger Guidebook

Compiled by Andrew Bingham, B.A.
Series edited by Peter Titchmarsh, M.A., F.R.G.S.

How to use this Guide

Space has not allowed us to include every place on the relevant Landranger Maps in the 'Places of Special Interest' section (pages 22-89). The items have been selected, however, to provide you with a varied and interesting companion during your travels around the coast and countryside of Dorset. Places of exceptional interest have been highlighted by being printed in blue, and any place which has a separate entry in the 'Places of Special Interest Section' is identified in the text by this symbol: ★.

Each entry is identified first with the number of the Landranger map or maps on which it appears (eg. 193, 194, etc). This is followed by two letters (eg. ST) and by a four-figure reference number (eg. 07-37). The first two figures of this number are those which appear in blue along the north and south edges of Landranger maps; the other two appear in blue along the east and west edges.

Therefore, to locate any place or feature referred to in this guide book on the relevant Landranger map, first read the two figures along the north or south edges of the map, then the two figures along the east or west edges. Trace the lines adjacent to each of the two sets of figures across the map face and the point where they intersect will be the south-west corner of the grid square in which the place or feature lies. Thus Lulworth Cove falls in the grid square 82-79 on Landranger map 194.

The Key Maps on pages 4-7 identify the suggested starting points of our nine tours and twelve walks, and in the 'Tours' and 'Walks' sections, all places which also have a separate entry in the 'Places of Special Interest' section are in bold type. Each tour and walk is accompanied by a map, and there are cross-references between Tours and Walks on both the maps and in the text.

Acknowledgements

We would like to thank Miss Priscilla Houstoun, the Ramblers' Association Dorset Area Secretary, and her colleagues in the Association — Mary Baxter MBE, Ann Sayer, Marjorie Straton, Jack de Carteret and Cory Luxmoore — for their work on the twelve *Walks*. This work included walking over the routes concerned and provision of the detailed directions for walkers which will be found in the guide.

First published 1987 by Ordnance Survey and Jarrold Colour Publications

Ordnance Survey
Romsey Road
Maybush
Southampton SO9 4DH

Jarrold Colour
Publications
Barrack Street
Norwich NR3 1TR

Printed in Great Britain by Jarrold and Sons Ltd., Norwich. 187

Contents

KEY MAP INDEX

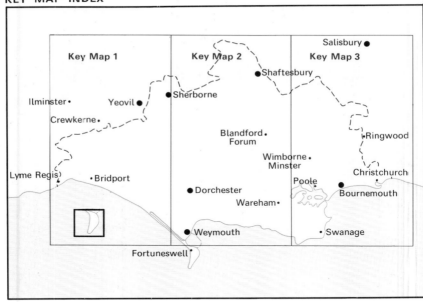

Motor/Cycling Tour start

Walk Route Start

Dorset County Boundary

LANDRANGER MAPS OF DORSET

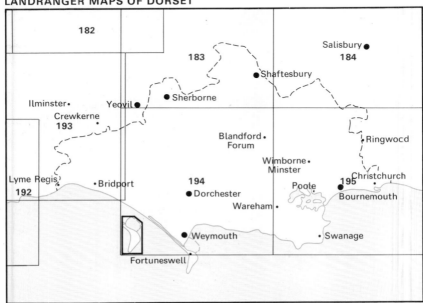

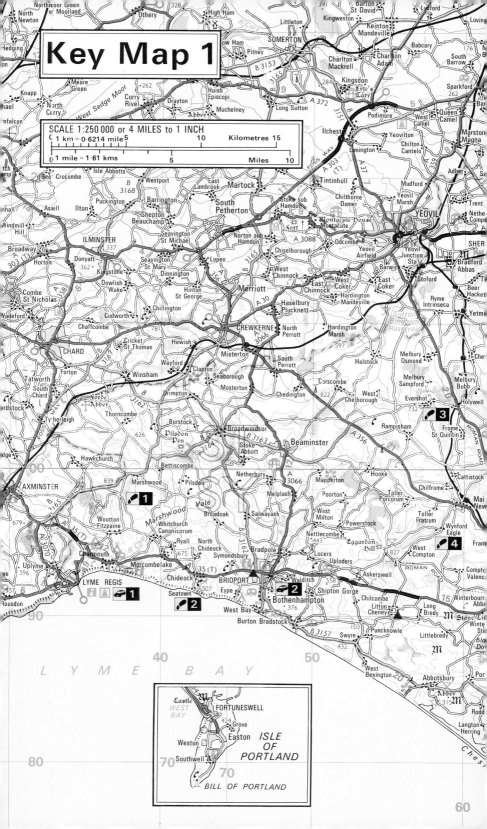

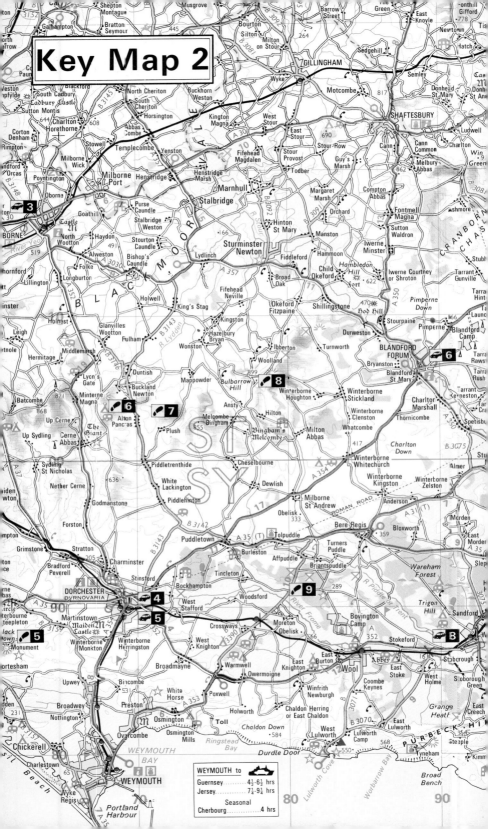

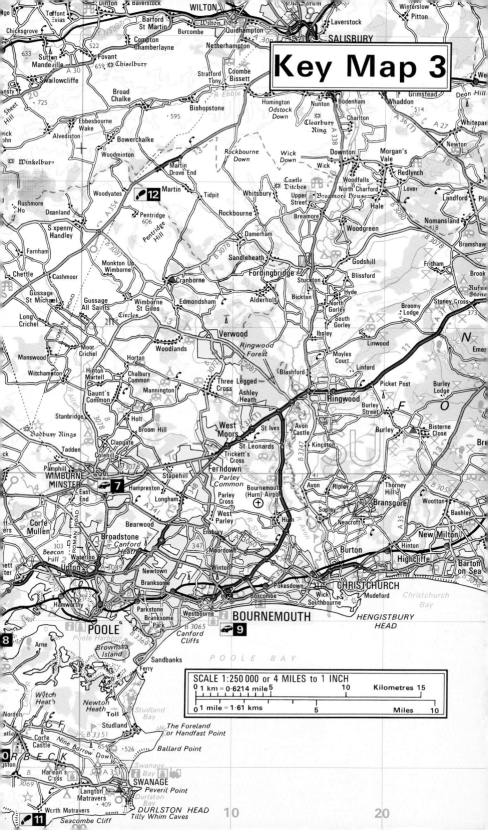

Key Map 3

SCALE 1:250 000 or 4 MILES to 1 INCH

0 1 km = 0·6214 mile   5 ... 10   Kilometres 15

0 1 mile = 1·61 kms ... 5 ... Miles 10

Introduction

This guide covers the entire county of Dorset and although not necessary for its enjoyment, Landranger Maps 183, 184, 193, 194 and 195 could go hand-in-hand with the book, to provide a companion without equal in the exploration of this delightful and varied county.

Heading westwards from the Hampshire border, along Dorset's splendidly diverse coastline, as if in an aircraft, we soon encounter the wide expanses of Christchurch Harbour, and the heathland of Hengistbury Head, before moving over the long, gently curving sands that have made Bournemouth one of Britain's outstanding seaside resorts. These are briefly interrupted by the narrow entrance to the great Poole Harbour, before continuing southwards around Studland and Swanage Bays to the cliff coastlands of the Isle of Purbeck.

Rounding the, great headlands of Durlston and St Aldhelm's, we head westwards, passing the little inlets of Chapman's Pool and Kimmeridge Bay, and over the army's tank ranges to arrive at popular Lulworth Cove. Westwards again along fine cliff country, before passing Constable's beloved Weymouth Bay, and the busy resort of Weymouth itself. And now with the mysterious Isle of Portland in view to the south, there is the start of the long pebbly Chesil Beach, backed by the brackish waters of the Fleet. Over low cliffs again at Burton Bradstock, cliffs which then run westwards on an ever more majestic scale, before ending at delightful Lyme Regis and the border with Devon.

Inland from Lyme Regis is clay-soiled Marshwood Vale, with its high-banks, and tall hills rising from quiet, close-knit farming country, with fine views out over small valleys to the sea. Beyond the hills well to the north-east of this, lies the rich clay farmland of Blackmoor Vale, Hardy's 'Vale of the Little Dairies',

with its charming stone villages, fine manor houses and quiet air of prosperity.

South again from here, stretching east and north-eastwards across the county, are the chalk uplands that cover half its area, and which are its outstanding feature. Here are great hills, like Bulbarrow, High Stoy and Okeford, miles of open rolling country, much of it rich in the relics of early man's life and death — field systems, stone circles, burial mounds, and many magnificent earthworks including Hod Hill, Hambledon, Badbury Rings and Maiden Castle.

Between the chalk country and the coast are the great stretches of sandy heathlands, Hardy's 'Great Heath'. Much of these heathlands have been built over, especially on the eastern fringes of the county, to the north of Poole and Bournemouth, while to the west, they are partly occupied by the military. However, in the broad valleys of the Frome and the Piddle, there are still fine stretches of unspoilt heath and woodland to be found.

Here then is Dorset in all its moods, and to guide you to the very best features that it has to offer, we have devised a series of nine tours. They are, like the guide as a whole, self-contained, but if you purchase the relevant Landranger map or maps you will be able to vary these tours to suit your own requirements. They have been designed primarily for motorists, but most are also suitable for cyclists.

We have also provided a series of twelve walks in widely varied countryside, and each of these link on to at least one of the tours. We cannot stress too strongly that your car is an ideal means to 'arrive' at an area, but to gain real enjoyment and satisfaction, it is infinitely preferable to explore the area on foot when you have arrived. So, if you do decide the use the Tour Section, please do so with discretion, and take your walking gear with you.

We do hope that you enjoy Dorset as much as we have done, and as we hope to continue so doing in the years to come.

History Revealed...
A Short Survey of the Area's Past.

Family ramble at Eggardon Camp.

Neolithic (or Stone Age) farming communities had begun to settle in eastern and central Britain by the mid-fourth millenum BC, and by 2500 BC they had firmly established themselves on Dorset's upland ridges. Relics of this era include causewayed camps at **Maiden Castle** and on **Hambledon Hill**, both of which were largely destroyed by subsequent occupation (see below), and at least forty burial mounds, or long barrows, the best examples of which are to be found near **Pimperne**, and near **Littlebredy**, the latter being delightfuly named 'The Grey Mare and her Colts'. The Dorset Cursus, a mysterious linear earthwork running over the downs near **Pentridge** also dates from this early period.

About 2000 BC the so-called 'Beaker Folk' moved westward from the Continent, heralding the Bronze Age, a culture that was to spread even further westwards than its Neolithic predecessor. This culture was characterised by worship at stone circles or henges, the most famous of which are at Stonehenge and Avebury in Wiltshire. The only circles of any significance in our area are to be found near **Portesham**, at Nine Stones, near **Winterbourne Abbas**, at **Knowlton Circles**, and Maumbury Ring near **Dorchester**, but although of great interest, they lack the drama of the great henge monuments in the neighbouring county. There are however many examples of Bronze Age burial mounds, or round barrows, to be found, especially in Dorset's high downland country. Good examples may be seen on Oakley Down, well to the north of **Pentridge**, at Winterbourne Poor Lot near **Winterbourne Abbas** and on Nine Barrow Down near **Swanage**.

A third wave of settlers, the Iron Age peoples, moved westward from the Continent between about 550 BC and AD 50. They organised themselves into larger and more cohesive groups, eventually banding together in this area to form a tribe known as the Durotriges. This formidable group was able to construct and maintain many large, well-sited settlements, such as those at **Badbury Rings**, **Eggardon Camp**, **Hambledon Hill**, **Hod Hill**, and the ousandingly impressive **Maiden Castle**. Many other fortified settlements were estabished in the area, and most may still be seen (for a fuller list, see page 20). They also started a process, to be continued later by the Romans and Anglo-Saxons, of extending their farming into the lower and more difficult valley country, and in some cases they built great enclosures for their animals.

The Romans landed in Britain in AD 43, and in that same year or early in AD 44, the Second Augustan Legion under Vespasian, the general who was later to become Emperor, occupied the area by force and ejected the Durotriges from their various fortified settlements in a series of small but savage encounters. Evidence of Roman military occupation is to be found at **Hod Hill** and at Waddon Hill near **Stoke Abbott**, and the many surviving stretches of the Roman **Ackling Dyke**, their road running from Badbury Rings to Old Sarum, are most impressive. Surviving civil remains include the earthworks of an aqueduct that ran from Notton, down the Frome Valley to **Dorchester**, a mosaic floor and foundations of a house in **Dorchester**, and the foundations of what may have been a temple on **Jordan Hill**. Several villas have also been uncovered in the county, but none have been left exposed for public viewing. At **Woodcutts**, on the northern edge of Cranborne Chase, General Pitt-Rivers, one of the founding fathers of British archaeology, carried out pioneer excavations on the site of a Romano-

British farming settlement, and many of his finds are imaginatively displayed in Salisbury Museum.

It is not surprising that the next period of history has become known as the 'Dark Ages', as our knowledge of what really took place in the centuries following the departure of the legions is still extremely scanty. However it seems certain that, despite the construction of such ambitious linear defences as **Bokerly Ditch**, the partly Romanised, largely Celtic inhabitants of our area were quickly overcome by Anglo-Saxons coming from the east, and that these vanquished tribesmen either moved further westwards, to Devon and Cornwall, or were subjugated by their conquerors. Fine examples of the art and architecture of these Anglo-Saxon invaders and of their descendants are to be found at St Martin's Church, **Wareham**, the abbey at **Sherborne**, the church at **Winterbourne Steepleton**, and the splendid font at **Melbury**

Norman font at Melbury Bubb.

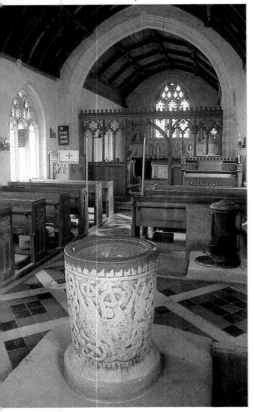

Bubb. Although the area was subjected to frequent raids by the Danes from the late-8th century onwards these seaborne predators made no lasting impact upon the Dorset scene.

However, the defeat of the Anglo-Saxon army at Hastings in 1066 lead to the rapid occupation of almost the whole of England, and Norman influence was felt as far west as Dorset in a comparatively short time. Consequently Norman work is to be found in many churches in the area, although not a great deal of it is up to the standard to be found further to the east, in Gloucestershire or Oxfordshire for instance. Some of Dorset's best examples are the great churches of **Christchurch** and **Wimborne**, the church at **Studland**, doorways at **Sherborne** and **Worth Matravers**, chancel arches at **Powerstock** and **Worth Matravers**, and fonts at **Stoke Abbott**, **Toller Fratrum** and **Puddletown**.

The round-headed Norman arch gradually gave way to the pointed, but still simple 'Early English' equivalent, and although this style predominated throughout most of the 13th century, there are few surviving examples in Dorset (but these include some excellent work at **Whitchurch Canonicorum**, and **Buckland Newton**). The emergence of English Gothic, heralding the 'Decorated' period, dates approximately from 1290 to 1350, and our favourite 'Decorated' church in the area is **Gussage All Saints**, with its ornately carved Easter Sepulchre.

The late 14th, the whole of the 15th, and part of the 16th century was an age of considerable prosperity, with large landowners, wool merchants and clothiers amassing considerable wealth. It was fortunate indeed that this prosperity coincided so closely with the final flowering of English Gothic, the style now known as 'Perpendicular'. There are a large number of churches in our area, that were either entirely rebuilt in this era, or were radically altered and improved. Our favourites are perhaps **Sherborne, Lyme Regis, Bridport, Bradford Abbas, Cerne Abbas,** and **Wyke Regis**, but there are many others. Thanks to this happy coincidence of prosperity and piety the Perpendicular period was also a great time for the detailed improvement and enrichment of many other churches. To name but a few, there are fine sets of bench-ends at **Trent** and **Bradford Abbas**, rood screens at **Trent** and **Winterborne Came**, and carved misericords at **Milton** and **Sherborne**.

Monastic remains in the area are limited, but the late-15th century 'Abbot's Hall' at **Milton Abbey** is very impressive, as is the massive 15th century tithe barn at **Abbotsbury**. **Forde Abbey** was founded by the Cistercians in 1141, and although converted into a mansion after the Dissolution many of its orginal features were incorporated and have survived to this day.

All these monastic institutions were swept away by Henry VIII in the years immediately after 1539, but in the centuries that followed, our parish churches contirued to reflect a strong religious tradition. Their content was often enriched in the 17th and 18th centuries with many splendid monuments. See espec ally **Wimborne Minster, Wimborne St Giles, Sandford Orcas**, and **Cranborne**.

In the 19th century, many churches were rebuilt or restored by Victorian architects who were often brilliantly inspired by the past in cold academic terms, but who seldom had any regard for the patina of age and character that they so often swept away. It was not until the closing years of the 19th century that it became clear to William Morris, his friends and some of his contemporaries, that steps should be taken to reverse this trend, and where restoration has been carried out after this time an atmosphere of the past can often still be savoured. See especially **Batcombe, Chalbury, Folke, Sydling St Nicholas** and **West Stafford**.

The 20th century has not witnessed many changes in the churches of the area, but there are a few worth visiting to appreciate what has been achieved. These include **Hazelbury Bryan** and **Wimborne St Giles**, incorporating respectively work by Sir Charles Nicholson and Sir Ninian Comper, two of our favourite 20th century restorers; and delightful Georgian Gothick **Moreton**, with its windows beautifully engraved by Laurence Whistler.

To return now to the secular front ...

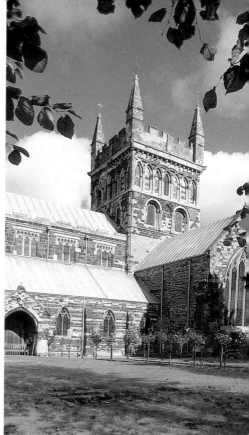

Wimborne Minster's Norman tower.

the Normans and their medieval successors built several castles in the area, and the most interesting survivors are the magnificent **Corfe Castle, Christchurch Castle**, Rufus Castle, on the **Isle of Portland**, the Old Castle at **Sherborne**, and **Woodsford Castle**. The earthworks of other medieval castles may still be traced at **Marshwood**, and **Wareham**. Mention should also be made of the chain of coastal forts established along England's southern coast by Henry VIII, the best Dorset example of which may be seen at **Portland**. By this time a series of busy market towns had grown up, and communications between them were gradually improved, sometimes by the building of fine bridges, the best survivors of which include Crawford Bridge, near **Spetisbury**, and the bridge at **Wool**.

Dorset is particularly rich in manor houses and these include **Athelhampton, Mapperton, Purse Caundle, Sandford Orcas, Parnham**, Smedmore, and **Wolfeton**, all of which are open to the public. The fortification of the 16th century manors was only minimal, and this was a reflection upon the strong central control now imposed by Tudor monarchs upon a land that had previously suffered so many centuries of feudal unrest. However, the Stuarts were not made of such strong stuff as their Tudor forebears, and in the middle years of the 17th century the country was torn apart by a bitter conflict between King and Parliament — the Civil War. While none of the major battles of this war took place in our area, the focal point of the struggle in Dorset was **Corfe Castle** which was heroically defended for many months by Lady Bankes against Cromwell's besieging troops before being forced to surrender. The escape of Charles II from the Battle of Worcester, and his subsequent flight across England, with Cromwell's troops in pursuit, provides a romantic postscript to the Civil War. The royal fugitive had hopes of leaving for France from **Charmouth**, but having hid at **Trent** and **Broadwindsor** he eventually headed eastwards, and crossed the Channel from Shoreham in Sussex. The latter part of the 17th century also saw the involvement of a number of Dorset folk in the Duke of Monmouth's futile attempt to secure the English throne, and the subsequent tragedies connected with the apprehension of Monmouth himself on **Horton Heath**, and with Judge Jeffreys and his 'Bloody Assize' at **Dorchester**.

However, all was not so gloomy as this in the county, and the 17th and 18th century produced many fine houses in the area, including **Kingston Lacy**, built by the Bankes family to replace Corfe Castle, which by then had been slighted by Cromwell, **Chettle**, Eastbury at **Tarrant Gunville**, the New Castle at **Sherborne**, Crichel House at **Moor Crichel**, Melbury House at **Melbury Sampford**, and St Giles House at **Wimborne St Giles**. In many cases fine parks were created, and most of the landscape, apart from the wilder hill and moor country, was now changing fast, with the acceleration of the enclosures. This was a process that had been started in the 16th century, and which was largely completed by the beginning of the 19th, as a result of those sweeping changes in agricultural methods, now known collectively as the Agricultural Revolution. It was as a direct result of the increasing dependence of the villagers upon rural employment that the 'Six Men of Dorset' met at **Tolpuddle** in 1834 in an endeavour to improve their lot, a move that was eventually to lead to their transportation to Australia, and their becoming known for all time as the 'Tolpuddle Martyrs'.

The Industrial Revolution on the other hand, did not have a great impact on this largely rural area, although the Bridport rope manufactory grew apace, and demand for stone from the quarries in the **Isles of Portland and Purbeck**, and for china clay from the heathlands to the south of **Wareham**, increased very considerably. By the end of the 19th century there was a network of railway lines carrying passengers and freight to and from most corners of the area, and these lines were also largely responsible for the growth of the area's greatest 'industry', the provision of holidays. Modest resorts like **Lyme Regis** had already grown up as a result of the inability of the leisured classes to holiday on the continent during the long wars with Napoleon, but it was the coming of the railways that led to the rapid growth of resorts like **Bournemouth, Swanage** and **Weymouth** in the latter half of the 19th century.

Now, well towards the end of the 20th century, light industry has expanded dramatically in the areas around **Poole** and **Bournemouth**, and there is even a nuclear reactor on nearby Winfrith Heath. Many of the 19th century railways have long been closed, and the roads, many of which started as turnpikes in the 18th century, have been improved out of all recognition, with several new bypasses having been built in the last few years. All the main roads through the area are busy with traffic, especially in summer, but once away from these no doubt essential arteries and the large conurbation that many of them serve, visitors will find that it is still possible to move quietly through most of Dorset's small towns, villages and beautiful countryside, and to appreciate the rich diversity of this splendid county's past.

Hardy's Dorset

Thomas Hardy was born in 1840 at **Higher Bockhampton**, near Dorchester, the son of a local stonemason. The thatched cottage where Hardy was born, now in the care of the National Trust, was built by his great-grandfather in about 1800. It is situated on the edge of deep woodlands overlooking quiet country, and it is no small wonder that while growing up here, he was soon embroiled in a life-long love affair with the Dorset countryside. The cottage is described thus in his earliest known poem, *Domicilium*:

> *It faces west, and round the back and sides*
> *High beeches, bending, hang a veil of boughs,*
> *and sweep against the roof ...*

He was a shy and introspective child, and certainly received encouragement from his mother to read and study to a higher standard than would have been expected of a normal country lad. His father led the choir of the parish church at nearby **Stinsford**, and it was no doubt due to him that the young Hardy, who also sung in the choir, owed his great love of music. He first went to school in the village and then to Dorchester, only to leave at the age of sixteen, to enter the office of John Hicks, a local architect involved largely in church restoration. At the age of twenty-two (1862) he went to London to work under the prolific and well-known architect, Arthur Blomfield, but his nostalgia for the simple Dorset life soon lead him to the writing of verse. These poems, however, did not find favour with the publishers, and so, as a means of expressing his intense love for the countryside that he had left behind, he turned to the writing of novels.

Although he continued to work as an architect for some years, either in London or in Dorset, Hardy increasingly relied upon writing for a livelihood, and for this reason his output at this time was of rather mixed quality, with a large

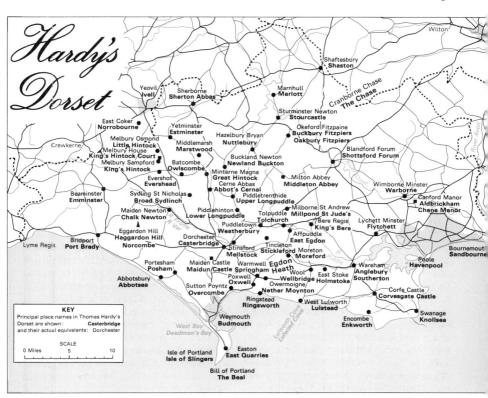

13

Hardy's beloved Stinsford Church.

number of lesser works, including many short stories, amongst his masterpieces. By almost general consent his greatest novels are *Under the Greenwood Tree* (1872), *Far from the Madding Crowd* (1874), *The Return of the Native* (1878), *The Trumpet-Major* (1880) *The Mayor of Casterbridge* (1886), *The Woodlanders* (1887), *Tess of the d'Urbervilles* (1891), and *Jude the Obscure* (1896). This last great novel was followed by one of lesser merit, *The Well-beloved* (1897) and from then onwards he turned to poetry and other works.

Hardy spent short periods of his life in other Dorset towns — he wrote most of *The Return of the Native* while staying in the rented Riverside Villa in **Sturminster Newton** in 1877, and also stayed in **Wimborne** between 1881 and 1883, when amongst other works he wrote *Two on a Tower*, in which Wimborne became 'Warborne', and also a poem entitled *Copying architecture in an old minster*, in which he referred to Wimborne's famous Quarter Jack. However, in 1885 he moved to Max Gate, a house on the Wareham road, about a mile out of **Dorchester**. He designed this himself, and lived here until his death in 1928. His ashes lie in Westminster Abbey, but his heart was buried in the grave of his first wife and near the graves of his parents, beneath a simple tombstone in the churchyard at **Stinsford**, outside the church in which he had been christened so many years before.

'Wessex' was the name of the ancient Saxon kingdom covering most of southwestern England, but Hardy first used it in *Far from the Madding Crowd*, and in the context of this and most of his other great novels 'South Wessex' was closely identified with the county of Dorset. Details of its towns and villages and its incomparable landscape were little altered by Hardy, whose concealment went little further than a delightfully transparent change of name — for example Dorset's Piddletrenthide became South Wessex's 'Longpuddle'. Hardy had a true countryman's understanding of the Dorset landscape and its peoples, and during his journeys through it, usually on foot, he noted not only the features of its often brooding landscape and the impact upon it of its ever-changing weather, but also the folklore and gossip that he was able to gather along the way. His great novels provide us with a unique picture of a rural England which has now all but disappeared. However, there is still a faint echo of Hardy's Dorset to be heard amongst the remoter hills and the broad valley farmlands by those who have read his splendidly atmospheric stories.

The combination of Hardy's consummate skill as a novelist, and his ability to relate to the landscape of this outstandingly beautiful county, has made Dorset almost as well-known as Shakespeare's Warwickshire. Many books, both scholarly and popular, have been written on the subject (see page 144), and readers of this guide would find particularly useful the special map based on the Ordnance Survey's Landranger Sheet 194, entitled *The Heart of Hardy's Wessex*, which has a wealth of Hardy place names shown and an index added. This is published by Wessex Heritage Tours, and is available from Longmans of Dorchester, 4, Cornhill, Dorchester, DT1 1BB.

Sturminster Newton Bridge ... Hardy wrote The Return of the Native *while living close by.*

Leisure Activities ...
A Brief Summary

The area covered by this guide provides a wide range of sport and leisure activities and we have listed some of those which we feel will be of particular interest to visitors.

Motoring. You will probably have arrived in your own car, but if you wish to hire a self-drive car or chauffeur-driven car, there is a wide choice available. Self-drive cars are available from the following organisations:
Avis Rent-a-Car, Bournemouth, *Tel: (0202) 293273*
B & C Self-Drive Car, Bridport, *Tel: (0308) 32451*
Guys, Sturminster Newton, *Tel: (0258) 72155*
Budget Rent-a-Car System, Poole, *Tel: (0202) 723343*
Hertz Weymouth, *Tel: (0305) 780404*
Loders Garage, Dorchester, *Tel: (0305) 67881*
If alternative services are required, or if you require a chauffeur-driven car, use the local Yellow Pages, or Thompson Directory, as there are many other services available.

Bus. Local bus services can be fun if you are prepared to fit in with their schedules, which in many parts of the country are governed by local transport needs. Timetables giving details of times and routes may be obtained from most T.I.C.s, or from the Wilts & Dorset Bus Co., Bus Station, Arndale Centre, *Tel: (0202) 673555,* Wilts & Dorset Bus Co., Bus Station, Swanage, *Tel: (0929) 422528,* Southern National, Bridport, *Tel: (0308) 22080,* South Dorset Coaches, Swanage, *Tel: (0929) 423622,* Stanbridge & Crichel Bus Co., Stanbridge, *Tel: (0258) 840355.*

Train. Details of British Rail's train services in the area may be obtained from most T.I.C.s, or from any British Rail Station, including Bournemouth, *Tel: (0202) 28216,* Weymouth, *Tel: (0305) 785501,* and Salisbury (for the Waterloo — Exeter line), *Tel: (0722) 27591.* The Southampton — Weymouth line runs through Christchurch, Bournemouth, Poole, Wareham and Dorchester, and there is a branch northwards to Yeovil, linking with the main line to Exeter, which also passes through Gillingham and Sherborne. The only non-BR line in the county is that operated by the Swanage Railway Society, which runs from Swanage to Harman's Cross, and which is hoped eventually to extend as far as Wareham.

Caravanning and Camping. There are so many suitable sites in the area covered by this guide, that it would be impossible, in a publication of this nature, to provide a list that could be judged to be adequately representative. There is a useful and inexpensive leaflet entitled 'Camping and Caravan Sites in Dorset', which is published regularly by the Dorset County Council and the two Tourist Boards, and all the T.I.C.s can provide further help. If you wish to plan in advance, there are a number of excellent countrywide booklets on sale nationally from early January each year. But if you wish to have the very best camping and/or caravan site information, you would be advised to join one of the national clubs covering these activities. These include: *The Camping and Caravanning Club, 11 Lower Grosvenor Place, London SW1W 0EY,* and *The Caravan Club, East Grinstead House, East Grinstead, West Sussex RH19 1UA.*

Cycling. This is a splendid way of looking around the area, and once off the main routes (which is the object of most of our listed tours) the little 'unclassified' roads (yellow on the Landranger maps) are relatively peaceful. If you do not have your own machine, these can be hired from: Ken Thursby Cycles, *152, Malvern Rd., Bournemouth. Tel: (0202) 529004,* Harveys, *58, Poole Rd., Westbourne, Bournemouth. Tel (0202) 761550,* J & J Corbett, *816, Wimborne Rd., Moordown, Bournemouth. Tel: (0202) 518844,* D & W Hire Services, *21-29 Spring Rd., Bournemouth. Tel: (0202) 296592,* Merry Cycles, *129, Alma Rd., Winton, Bournemouth. Tel: (0202) 523142,* Rayboulds, *579/581, Wimborne Rd., Winton. Tel: (0202) 529061,* Cycle Hire, *34, Irving Rd., Southbourne, Bournemouth. Tel: (0202) 431258,* Rent-A-Cycle, The Harbour Garage, *West Bay, Bridport. Tel: (0803) 22207,* Willoughby's, *179, Barrack Rd., Christchurch. Tel: (0202) 486278,* Charles Street, *Dorchester. Tel: (0305) 66750 or 62986,* Ray's Cycles, *The Two Wheel Centre, High St., Gillingham. Tel: (07476) 3195,* A1 Hire & Sales, *Newtown Industrial Estate, Poole. Tel: (0202) 736899,* Poole Cycles, *Grand Parade, High St., Poole. Tel: (02013) 676973,* Whittakers, *117, Commercial Rd., Parkstone, Poole. Tel: (0202) 744301,* Sherborne Cycles, *Cold Harbour, Sherborne. Tel: (093581) 5486,* Quikes & Bikes, *Cornwall Rd., Swanage. Tel: (092944) 295,* Wareham Wheels, *5a South St., Wareham. Tel: (09295) 6345,* Weymouth Cycle Hire, *Opposite Railway Station, King St., Weymouth. Tel: (0305) 787677,* Westham Cycle Hire, *114, Abbotsbury Rd., Weymouth. Tel: (0305) 76977.*
If you still have difficulty in making arrangements, the very helpful *Cyclists Touring Club,* of *69 Meadow, Godalming, Surrey GU7 3HS. Tel: (048 68) 7217,* may have other addresses and information. Why not become a member?

Walking. Walking is the ideal way of exploring the area, and may be combined with any of the above means of transport. You will find twelve walks described on pages 108 — 131 and we hope that these will provide a pleasant introduction to the pleasures of walking with map and guide in this wonderfully unspoilt countryside. Stout shoes and waterproof clothing are desirable, and during the wetter part of the year, walking boots, or even wellies can widen the scope of your journeys, taking in more of those sodden fields and footpaths than might otherwise have been possible. Small rucksacks are worthwhile, and while a compass is useful in this gentle, well-charted landscape, it is not essential. Do not always expect to find well-defined paths across this countryside's more pastoral corners. Rights of way are clearly shown on both the Landranger map and on the Pathfinder extracts, but these may not always show up too clearly on the ground. If in doubt, do try to ask locally regarding rights of way, and at all times do make sure that your dog is on a lead if livestock are anywhere near, and that all gates are left as you found them, which will normally be closed. The Dorset Coast Path ★ provides splendid opportunities for the walker, and its course is clearly marked on Landranger Sheets 193, 194 and 195.

Horse Riding. Details of the very wide range of available riding facilities may be obtained from any of the T.I.C.s, but here is a list of a few places offering this facility: Roke Riding & Trekking Centre, *Field Cottage, Bere Regis. Tel: (0929) 471181,* Colcombe Stables, *Broadwindsor. Tel: (0308) 68995,* Glebe Farm Riding Stables, *Church Knowle. Tel: (0929) 480280,* Ashtree Riding School, *Purewell. Tel: (0202) 482642,* Deer Park Riding Stables, *Blandford Forum. Tel: (0258) 53283,* Sutton Poyntz Riding Stables. *Tel: (0305) 833027,* Prospect Stables, *Cattistock. Tel: (0300) 20820,* Holtwood Riding Stables, *Holt. Tel: (0258) 840293,* Studland Riding Stables. *Tel: (0929) 944273.*

The Best of the Beaches. This is a brief list starting from the east of the area and heading westwards: Map 195: Highcliffe, Mudeford, Southbourne, Boscombe, Bournemouth, Sandbanks, Rockley Sands, Studland, Swanage, Chapman's Pool; Map 184: Lulworth Cove, Weymouth; Map 193: Burton Bradstock, Seatown, Charmouth, Lyme Regis.

Water Sports. This area has much to offer those who, in some way or other, love to 'mess about in boats'. There are several points along the coast where small boats may be launched, but the most popular areas are Christchurch Harbour, Poole Harbour, Kim-

Seatown ... one of Dorset's quieter beaches.

meridge Bay, Lulworth Cove, Weymouth Bay and Portland Harbour, West Bay and Lyme Regis. Dinghy sailing is especially popular in the more sheltered areas off Christchurch, Poole and Weymouth, but if you are inexperienced in matters concerning the sea, do ask for local advice, wherever you intend to go. Here are a few useful addresses: Poole Park Windsurfing, *16 Park Lane Rd., Poole. Tel: (0202) 686590,* Poole Harbour Boardsailing, *Slaterns Marina, Poole. Tel: (0202) 700503,* Windtek, *Weymouth. Tel: (0305) 787900,* Weymouth Sailing Centre, *Weymouth. Tel: (0305) 776549,* Studland Sailboards, *Studland. Tel: (0929) 425345.*

Golf. There are no fewer than 17 golf clubs in the area covered by this guide. They are: The Ashley Wood, at Tarrant Rawston, *Tel: (0258) 2253.* The Bridport & West Dorset, *Tel: (0308) 22597.* The Broadstone, *Tel: (0202) 692595.* The Bournemouth, Meyrick Park *Tel: (0202) 20307.* The Came Down, Dorchester, *Tel: (030581) 2531.* The Ferndown, near Wimborne, *Tel: (0202) 872022.* The Highcliffe Castle, near Mudeford, *Tel: (04252) 72953.* The Iford Bridge Municipal, near Christchurch, *Tel: (0202) 483199.* The Isle of Purbeck, Swanage, *Tel: (0929) 361.* The Knighton Heath, West Howe, Bournemouth, *Tel: (0202) 572633.* The Lakey Hill, Wareham, *Tel: (0929) 471776).* The Lyme Regis, *Tel: (029741 2043.* The Meyrick Park Course, Bournemouth, *Tel: (0202) 20862.* The Sherborne, *Tel: (0935) 814431.* The

Wareham, *Tel: (0929) 554147.* The Weymouth, *Tel: (03057) 773997.* Wessex Golf Centre, Weymouth, *Tel: (0305) 784737.*

Fishing. There is a wealth of fishing opportunities in the area covered by our guide. Much valuable information relating to coastal, river and reservoir fishing may be obtained from the various Tourist Information Centres, and the Southern Tourist Board publish an interesting fact sheet covering fishing in the eastern half of the county. There is good fishing from the quays at Mudeford, Christchurch, Poole, Weymouth and Lyme Regis, and from the various beaches, but only at the latter when there are no crowds about. Sea-fishing trips may be made from Mudeford, Poole, Swanage, Weymouth and Lyme Regis. There is also good sport to be had on the rivers Frome, Piddle, Stour and lower Avon. For details, write to Chief Fisheries & Recreation Officer, Wessex Water, Wessex House, Passage Street, Bristol, BS2 0JQ.

Sports Centres and other Sporting Facilities. There is a wealth of sports and leisure facilities in Dorset, but here is a selection: Blandford Sports Centre, *Tel: (0258) 55566,* Bridport Leisure Centre, *Tel: (0308) 27464,* Poole Sports Centre, *Tel: (0202) 675322,* Purbeck Sports Centre, *Tel: (0929) 56454,* Weymouth Sports Centre, *Tel: (0305) 813113,* Dorset Parachute Centre, *Bere Down Farm, Bere Regis. Tel: (0929) 471339,* Compton Abbas Airfield, *Ashmore. Tel: (0747) 811767.*

Christchurch Harbour from Hengistbury Head.

Wolfeton House, Charminster.

Places to Visit.... A summary list showing page number followed by map number/s and map reference.

Bronze Age Sites
Knowlton Circles (53) (195) (SU 02-10)
Nine Barrow Down (41,76) (195) (SZ 00-81)
Nine Stones Stone Circle (88) (194) (SY 61-90)
Oakley Down (62) (184) (SU 01-17)
Portesham Stone Circle (64) (194) (SY 59-86)
Winterbourne Poor Lot Barrows (88) (194) (SY 59-90)

Craft Centres and Craft Activities
Fontmell Magna Pottery (46) (183) (ST 86-16)
Holt Craft Centre (50) (195) (SU 02-03)
Parnham House (61) (193) (SY 47-00)
Place Mill, Christchurch (39) (195) (SZ 15-92)
Poole Pottery (64) (195) (SZ 01-90)
Sturminster Mill (75) (194) (ST 78-13)
Walford Mill Craft Centre (86) (195) (SU 00-00)
William Walker Glass Studio, Wimborne (86) (195) (SU 01-00)

Country Parks, Forests, Forest Walks, Open Spaces and Picnic Places
Avon Forest Park (25) (195) (SU 12-02 etc.)
Black Heath Nature Trail (99) (194) (SY 72-92)
Buckham Down Picnic Place (26) (193) (ST 48-03)
Bulbarrow Hill (34) (194) (ST 77-05)
Coney's Castle (89) (193) (SY 37-97)
Cull-peppers Dish Picnic Place (105) (194) (SY 81-90)
Durlston Country Park (44) (195) (SZ 03-77)
Fontmell Down (40,46) (183) (ST 88-18)
Golden Cap (47) (193) (SY 40-92)
Gore Hill Picnic Place (25) (194) (ST 63-03)
Hardy Monument, Blackdown Hill (48) (194) (SY 61-87)
Hengistbury Head (48) (195) (SZ 17-90)
Higher Row Forest Walk (50) (195) (SU 04-03)
Hod Hill (49 – 50) (194) (ST 85-10)
Lambert's Castle (57) (193) (SY 37-99)
Lewesdon Hill (33,73) (193) (ST 43-02)
Lodmoor Country Park (84) (194) (SY 68-81)

Maiden Castle (56) (194) (SY 66-68)
Okeford Hill Picnic Place (60,72) (194) (ST 81-09)
Povington Hill Picnic Place (45) (194) (SY 88-81)
Puddletown Forest (49,67) (194) (SY 73-92)
Ridgeway Hill Picnic Place (73) (195) (SY 90-81)
St Catherine's Hill (39) (195) (SZ 14-95)
Shatcombe Lane Picnic Place (45) (194) (SY 54-94)
Thorncombe Wood Nature Trail (99) (194) (SY 72-92)
Upton Country Park (79 – 80) (195) (SY 98-93)
Wareham Forest Nature Trail (81) (195) (SY 90-89)
Wootton Hill Forest Walk (89) (193) (SY 35-97)

Gardens and Parks
Abbotsbury Sub-Tropical Gardens (23) (194) (SY 56-85)
Blue Pool, The (28 – 29) (195) (SY 93-83)
Compton Acres (40) (195) (SZ 05-89)
Cranborne Manor Garden (41) (195) (SU 05-13)
Dean's Court, Wimborne (86) (195) (SU 00-01)
Edmondsham House (45) (195) (SU 06-11)
Kingston Maurward Manor (52 – 53) (194) (SY 71-90)
Minterne House (59) (194) (ST 66-04)
Poole Park (64) (195) (SZ 02-91)

Historic Houses, etc.
Athelhampton Hall (24) (194) (SY 77-94)
Bettiscombe Manor (26) (193) (ST 40-00)
Bloxworth House (28) (194) (SY 87-94)
Chantmarle House (47) (194) (ST 58-02)
Chettle House (37) (195) (ST 95-13)
Clouds Hill (40) (194) (SY 82-90)
Compton House (61) (183) (ST 59-16)
Edmondsham House (45) (195) (SU 06-11)
Forde Abbey (46) (193) (ST 35-05)
Kingston Lacy (NT) (52) (195) (ST 97-01)
Mapperton Manor (57) (194) (SY 50-99)
Moigne Court (61) (194) (SY 77-85)
Parnham House (61) (193) (SY 47-00)
Place Mill, Christchurch (39) (195) (SZ 15-92)
Purse Caundle Manor (68) (183) (ST 69-17)
Sandford Orcas Manor (68) (183) (ST 62-21)
Sherborne New Castle (72) (183) (ST 64-16)
Smedmore (51) (195) (SY 92-78)
Winterborne Clenston Manor (87) (194) (ST 83-03)
Wolfeton House (36,76) (194) (SY 68-92)

Historic Sites, including Castles
Christchurch Castle (38) (195) (SZ 15-92)
Constable's House, The (38) (195))SZ 15-92
Corfe Castle (40 – 41) (195) (SY 96-81)
Fiddleford Mill (45) (194) (ST 80-13)
Grange Arch (42) (195) (SY 91-81)
Melbury Abbas Mill (57) (183) (ST 88-20)
Portland Castle (65) (194) (SY 68-74)
Rufus Castle (65) (194) (SY 69-71)
St Catherines Chapel, Abbotsbury (22) (194) (SY 57-84)
Sherborne Old Castle (72) (183) (ST 65-16)
Woodsford Castle (78,88) (194) (SY 75-90)

Iron Age Sites
Badbury Rings (25) (195) (ST 96-02)
Bokerley Ditch (29) (184) (SU 05-18)
Bulbarrow (34) (194) (ST 77-05)
Buzbury Rings (77) (195) (ST 91-05)
Chilcombe Fort (37) (194) (SY 53-92)
Coney's Castle (89) (193) (SY 37-97)
Eggardon Fort (45) (194) (SY 54-94)
Flower's Barrow Fort (45) (194) (SY 86-80)
Gussage Hill (48) (195) (ST 99-14)
Hambledon Hill (48) (194) (ST 84-12)
Hengistbury Head (43) (195) (SZ 17-90)
Hod Hill (49 – 50) (194) (ST 85-10)
Lambert's Castle (57) (193) (SY 37-99)
Maiden Castle (56) (194) (SY 66-88)
Pilsdon Pen (62) (193) (ST 41-01)
Poundbury Camp (42) (194) (SY 68-91)
Rawlsbury Camp (34) (194) (ST 76-05)
Ringmoor (79) (194) (ST 81-08)
Weatherby Castle (58) (194) (SY 80-96)
Woodbury Hill (26) (194) (SY 85-94)
Woolsbarrow Fort (28) (194) (SY 89-92)

Museums, Art Galleries, etc.
Barney's Fossil Museum, Charmouth (36) (193) (SY 36-93)
Big Four Railway Museum, Bournemouth (30) (195) (SZ 1-91)
Blandford Museum (28) (194) (ST 88-06)
Blandford Camp Signals Museum (27) (195) (ST 92-08)
Bovington Tank Museum (30 – 31) (194) (SY 82-88)
Bredy Farm Old Farming Collection (34) (194) (SY 50-89)
Bridport Museum & Art Gallery (31 – 32) (193) (SY 46-92)

'Butter-churning' at Bredy Farm Old Farming Collection.

Casa Magni Shelley Museum, Bournemouth (30) (195) (SZ 11-92)
Coach House Museum, Langton Matravers (50) (195) (SY 99-78)
Corfe Castle Museum (41) (195) (SY 96-81)
County Museum, Dorchester (43) (194) (SY 69-90)
Dinosaur Museum, Dorchester (44) (194) (SY 69-90)
Dorset Military Museum (44) (194) (SY 68-90)
Gillingham Museum (47) (183) (ST 80-26)
Lyme Regis Museum (56) (193) (SY 34-92)
Milton Abbas Farm Museum (59) (194) (ST 80-02)
Poole Lifeboat Museum (64) (195) (SZ 00-90)
Poole Museum, Scaplen's Court (63 – 64) (195) (SZ 00-90)
Portland Museum (65) (194) (SY 69-71)
Red House Museum, Christchurch (39) (195) (SZ 15-92)
Russell Coates Art Gallery & Museum, Bournemouth (30) (195) (SZ 09-91)
Salisbury Museum (45,88) (184) (SU 14-29)
Shaftesbury Museum (70) (183) (ST 86-22)
Sherborne Museum (71) (183) (ST 63-16)
Tithe Barn Museum & Art Gallery, Swanage (75) (195) (SZ 02-78)
Tricycle Museum, Christchurch (39) (195) (SZ 15-92)
Tyneham Exhibition (79) (194) (SY 88-80)
Weymouth Museum (84) (194) (SY 67-79)

Roman and Romano-British Sites
Ackling Dyke (23) (184,195) (SU 01-16 etc.)
Cerne Abbas Giant (35) (194) (ST 66-01)
Dorchester Aqueduct (42) (194) (SY 67-91 etc.)
Hod Hill (49 – 50) (194) (ST 85-10)
Jordan Hill Roman Temple (51) (194) (SY 69-82)
Maiden Castle (56) (194) (SY 66-68)
Roman Town House, Dorchester (42) (194) (SY 69-90)
Waddon Hill (73) (193) (ST 44-01)

Stone Age Sites
Dorset Cursus (48,62) (195) (ST 98-13 etc.)
Grey Mare and her Colts (Long Barrow) (53) (194) (SY 58-87)
Hell Stone (64) (194) (SY 60-86)
Maumbury Rings (42) (194) (SY 69-89)
Pimperne Long Barrow (62) (195) (ST 91-10)

Wildlife Parks, Farm Parks, Nature Reserves, etc.
Abbotsbury Swannery (23) (194) (SY 57-84)
Arne Heath Nature Reserve (23) (195) (SY 97-88)
Brownsea Island Nature Reserve (33 – 34) (195) (SZ 02-88)
Burton Mere (34) (194) (SY 50-87)
Dorset Heavy Horse Centre (80) (195) (SU 08-09)
Godlingston Heath (74) (195) (SZ 01-82)
Merley Tropical Bird Gardens (58) (195) (SZ 02-98)
Natural World, Poole (64) (195) (SZ 02-00)
Radipole Lake (68) (194) (SY 67-80)
Sea Life Centre, Weymouth (84) (194) (SY 68-81)
Stanpit Marsh Nature Reserve (39) (195) (SZ 16-92)
Studland Heath (74) (195) (SZ 02-84)
Weymouth Butterfly Farm (84) (194) (SY 68-81)
Worldwide Tropical Butterflies, Compton House (61) (183) (ST 59-16)

Special Events
For a list of events, dates of which change annually, see the relevant leaflets which are available from the various Tourist Information Centres listed below.

Poole's handsome 18th century Customs House.

Further Information

Tourist Information Centres
Blandford. *Ham Car Park. Tel: (0258) 51989*
Bournemouth. *Westover Road. Tel: (0202) 291715*
Bridport. *32, South Street. Tel: (0308) 24901*
Christchurch. *Saxon Square. Tel: (0202) 47180*
Lyme Regis. *The Guildhall. Tel: (02974) 2138*
Poole. *The Quay. Tel: (0202) 675151 ext. 3550*
Shaftesbury. *County Library, Bell Street. Tel: (0747) 2256*
Sherborne. *Hound Street. Tel: (0935) 81534*
Swanage. *The White House, Shore Street. Tel: (0929) 422885*
Weymouth. *The Pavilion Theatre Complex. Tel: (0305) 72444*
Wimborne. *Cook Row. Tel: (0202) 886116*

Other Useful Addresses and/or Telephone Numbers
National Trust, *Stourton, Warminster, Wilts, BA12 6QD. Tel: Bourton, Dorset 840224*
Dorset Naturalists' Trust, *Dorchester. Tel: (0305) 64620*

Nature Conservancy Council, *Dorset Office, Slepe Farm, Arne. Tel: (0929) 56688*
Southern Tourist Board (covers East Dorset), *Town Hall Centre, Leigh Rd., Eastleigh, Hants*
West Country Tourist Board (covers West Dorset), *Trinity Court, Southernhay East, Exeter, Devon*
A.A. 24 Hour Breakdown Service, Bournemouth *Tel: (0202) 25751*
R.A.C. 24 Hour Breakdown Service, Bournemouth *Tel: (0202) 766697*
Police, *Blandford. Tel (0258) 52101*
Police, *Bournemouth. Tel: (0202) 22099*
Police, *Bridport. Tel: (0308) 22266*
Police, *Christchurch. Tel: (0202) 486333*
Police, *Dorchester. Tel: (0305) 63011*
Police, *Poole. Tel: (0202) 22099*
Police, *Sherborne. Tel: (0935) 812101*
Police, *Swanage. Tel: (0929) 422004*
Police, *Wareham. Tel: (0929) 52222*
Police, *Weymouth. Tel: (0305) 63011*
Police, *Wimborne. Tel: (0202) 882345*

Ordnance Survey Agents
Beales, Old Christchurch Road, Bournemouth *Tel: (0202) 22022*
Martin the Newsagent Ltd., 12, East Street, Bridport *Tel: (0308) 22639*
Thatcher & Co, 17 Durngate Street, Dorchester DT1 1UP *Tel: (0305) 64977*

Places of Special Interest

Places of outstanding interest are printed in blue. Places referred to in the text which are also covered by a separate entry in this section are identified with the symbol ' ★ '.

Abbotsbury (194) (SY 57-85) *8m SW Dorchester.* Squeezed into a deep valley encircled by magnificent hills, this delightful village of thatched yellowstone cottages lies less than a mile from the sea, where Chesil Beach joins the mainland. One of the oldest centres of Christianity in Britain, a church was reputedly here in Roman times. The Benedictine Abbey was founded in the 11th century by Orc, King Canute's chief steward, and flourished for 500 years before being demolished during the Dissolu-

tion. Except for the tithe barn the abbey ruins (EH) are disappointing. Only the outer and inner gatehouse remain, the latter now incorporated into a house. The splendid 14th century barn, 270 feet by 31 feet, stands to the south of the village. The great thatched timber roof, half of which no longer exists, was originally stone tiled. The mainly 15th and 16th century church of St Nicholas lies immediately to the north of the barn and has some excellent features within, including an unusual plastered and barrel-vaulted chancel ceiling, some beautifully painted 15th century glass of the Virgin from a crucifixion, and an early 13th century marble monument of an abbot. Note also the fine 17th century oak canopied pulpit containing two bullet holes, possible evidence of the fighting that occurred here in the Civil War. A short distance from the church stands Abbey House, a late 17th century replacement for a house destroyed during a skirmish between the Royalists and the Parliamentarians. A footpath close to the Ilchester Arms leads to St Catherine's Chapel (EH), standing like a giant

Abbotsbury and St Catherine's Chapel.

stone outcrop at the summit of 250-foot Chapel Hill (SY 57-84). The mighty buttresses and four-foot-thick walls of this imposing 15th century building hold up a stone tunnel-vault, an architectural feature are in the south of England.

The Swannery, three quarters of a mile south of the village, dates from the 14th century and is probably the largest colony of managed swans in the world, the number of birds varying from between 450 and 700. The swans come here because the Fleet contains an abundance of their favourite food, a type of seaweed known as Zostera marina. Take binoculars if possible as there are always many other sea-birds to be seen. West of Abbotsbury are the beautiful *Sub-Tropical Gardens*, first planted by Lord Ilchester in about 1760. Magnificent azaleas, camellias, magnolias and other sub-tropical plants flourish here, protected from frost and sea-winds by the gardens' sheltered position *(tel: Abbotsbury 871387)*.

A path north from the village ascends a steep hill before bisecting a footpath which runs along the ridge. Turn left to join the Dorset Coast Path ★, which cuts inland at Abbotsbury. Swing right and it is possible to walk to Abbotsbury Castle (SY 55-86), a triangular Iron Age hill fort superbly sited on a desolate, treeless slope. It is likely that the Romans used part of this fort as a signal station, for it commands spectacular views across the whole of Lyme Bay.

Ackling Dyke (184,195) (SU 01-16 etc.) This is the local Dorset name for the Roman road running north-eastwards from Badbury Rings ★ to Old Sarum, both important junction points on the extensive network of roads covering Roman Britain. It is particularly evident in the downland area to the south-east of Sixpenny Handley ★, and apart from a short stretch which is common with the busy A354, it makes a fine walk almost all the way from Badbury Rings to the outskirts of Salisbury.

Affpuddle (194) (SY 80-93) *8m E Dorchester.* Long picturesque village pleasantly situated in the green valley of the River Piddle, its name derives from the Saxon Aeffa. The church stands on the river bank next to a disused water-mill, and with its chequered ashlar and flint pinnacled tower and fine mid-13th century doorway is most appealing. The notable features inside are the exquisite bench-ends and pulpit both carved in the mid-16th century by Thomas Lyllington, a monk from Cerne Abbas who became vicar here after the Dissolution. It is clear that he did not hold his fellow monks in high regard

for he carved them into the pulpit, half-monk and half-fool. To the south is Affpuddle Heath, part of the Great Heath which stretches across south-east Dorset, and which Thomas Hardy renamed Egdon Heath in his Wessex novels. A delightful circular walk through the heath passes an official picnic place (SY 80-92) and leads into Briantspuddle before returning back to Affpuddle. (See also **Walk 9.**)

Almer (195) (SY 91-98) *7m W Wimborne Minster.* The Elizabethan manor house and ancient church dominate this small village which lies just to the north of the A31. The eight-foot-high wall bounding the south side of this busy road extends for more than two miles and encloses the park of Charborough House, a large mansion built in 1661 and extended early in the 18th century and again in the 19th. It is not open to the public. St Mary's church has Norman arches, 15th century tower, early 18th century nave and Victorian chancel. The stained glass in a chancel window, depicting the Last Judgement, was fashioned by Swiss craftsmen in about 1610 and in the churchyard stands the shaft of a 14th century preaching cross.

Ansty (194) (ST 76-03) *4m W Blandford Forum.* Lying on chalk uplands, just south of Bulbarrow Hill ★, are the four Ansty villages; Lower Ansty, Higher Ansty, Ansty Cross and Little Ansty (also known as Pleck). The Fox Inn at Lower Ansty is one of Dorset's best-known inns, and is particularly noted for its fine cold buffet and large collection of Toby jugs.

Arne (195) (SY 97-88) *4m E Wareham.* A very isolated hamlet lying at the centre of a large, heath-covered peninsula projecting northwards from the Isle of Purbeck into Poole Harbour ★. The miniature 13th century church, the interior of which is charmingly lit by candlelight, was greatly altered in the mid-19th century and again in 1952. Do not miss the magnificent vista of Poole Harbour through the altar window. The drive or walk from Stoborough to Arne is splendid in all seasons but particularly in late summer when the heath is in bloom.

Arne Heath is the home of two rare British species, the Dartford Warbler and the Smooth Snake. A nature reserve of about 1,200 acres is open to visitors, but certain parts can only be visited by permission of the RSPB warden at Wareham *(tel: Wareham 3360)*. A mile-long nature trail leads eastwards to Shipstal Point where evidence of a Roman salt-making industry has been found.

Ashmore (184) (ST 91-17) *5m SE Shaftesbury.* Centred on its lovely round duck pond this exceptional Cranborne Chase village of thatched cottages and handsome 18th century homes is Dorset's highest village at 700 feet above sea level. The large church was harshly restored by the Victorians but does contain an unusual set of 20th century stone corbels shaped as various animals. To the south-east, the Roman road crosses Murdoak Wood Dyke (ST 92-17), a bank and ditch 45 feet across. Walks from Ashmore offer superb views across Cranborne Chase but for the finest panorama, walk north to Win Green Hill (ST 92-20), a 910-foot hill just inside the Wiltshire border. The walk south-westwards to Washers Pit and through Stubhampton Bottom (ST

Pond at Ashmore.

magnificent, mainly 15th century building of creamy limestone ashlar and golden Ham Hill stone. Home of the Martin family for 400 years, the present house was built for Sir William Martin, Lord Mayor of London in 1493. The interior has two splendid features; the open timber roof, and the inside of the oriel window. Note also the elaborate plaster ceilings, the rich panelling and the newel staircase, its solid wooden blocks set into the stonework. The

89-16) to Stubhampton is also particularly delightful. Wild flowers, butterflies and deer are all to be found in this enchanting woodland.

Askerswell (194) (SY 52-92) *4m E Bridport.* Though the busy A35 road runs less than half a mile to the south this compact village is extremely peaceful in its quiet downland setting. Standing next to a farmhouse is the church of St Michael, completely rebuilt in 1858 save for its medieval tower, under which is a massive stone with the clear impression of what must have once been an elaborately foliated cross of the 13th century. The French inscription indicates that it came from the abbey at Abbotsbury. Walk northwards, past Eggardon farm, to Eggardon hillfort ★.

Athelhampton (194) (SY 77-94) *5m NE Dorchester.* Thomas Hardy's Athelhall and the reputed site of King Athelstan's palace, this main road village would have little to recommend it, did it not contain one of the finest manor houses in England. With its many mullioned windows, fine crenellated front, and lovely oriel window, **Athelhampton Hall** is a

24

beautiful gardens were laid out in 1891 by Inigo Thomas and take the form of three separate and enclosed gardens. Particularly impressive are the 25-foot yew pyramids and the great court, which has a water terrace reminiscent of the Villa d'Este in Italy. *(Tel: Puddletown 363).*

Avon Forest Park (195) (SU 12-02, etc.) *7m N Bournemouth.* This park consists of 580 acres of heath and woodland and is split into three separate areas; North Park, Matcham's View and South Park. There is an abundance of heather, which is best seen in mid-summer when it is in full bloom, and the woodland contains five species of Maritime Corsican and Weymouth Pine, Redwood and Noble Fir. Each of the three sites has a car park, picnic site and signposted walks.

Badbury Rings (NT) (195) (ST 96-02) *4m W Wimborne Minster.* Sited on a chalk knoll rising 327 feet, this is one of the great Iron Age hillforts of Wessex. Three great ramparts, the outermost of which is nearly a mile in circumference, encircle a tree-covered hill. It has been suggested that Badbury was Mount Badon, the site where King Arthur commanded the Britons against the invading Anglo-Saxons. One local legend even claims that Arthur lived in the wood in the guise of a raven. Two Roman roads, one running from Dorchester to Old Sarum (Ackling Dyke ★) and another from Bath to Poole Harbour, intersect just to the north-east of the Rings, and it is possible to walk almost ten miles north to Oakley Down (184) (SU 01-17), following the course of the Ackling Dyke ★ almost all the way. The great beech avenue that runs astride the

Badbury Rings.

B3082, to the south of Badbury Rings, was planted in 1835, but the story that there were once 365 trees on one side and 366 (for leap years) on the other has no foundation. As part of the Bankes Estate, Badbury Rings was bequeathed to the National Trust in 1982, and a massive restoration programme has returned the Rings to their former glory. (See map on Page 52).

Ballard Down (195) (SZ 03-81) *1½m N Swanage.* This lies at the eastern end of the Purbeck Hills which extend from Lulworth and which once continued to the Isle of Wight, though Old Harry Rocks. It is best reached by the Dorset Coast Path ★, either from Studland or Swanage. Over 200 acres of the southern slopes of the Down belong to the National Trust and due largely to its superb chalkland flora, is listed as a Site of Special

Scientific Interest by the Nature Conservancy Council. A large stone seat at the top of the Down allows visitors to rest and admire the magnificent views eastwards to the Isle of Wight and north over Poole Harbour.

Batcombe (194) (ST 61-04) *12m NW Dorchester.* A solitary place set at the edge of the mid-Dorset uplands and approached from a narrow twisting lane which drops steeply down Batcombe Hill. The church of St Mary nestles in an amphitheatre below the hill and above the vale, and although restored in the 19th century, remains little altered and largely unspoilt. The most interesting features inside are the nave's ancient timber roof, the fine 15th century screen of stone and the Norman font. One mile east of the church is an ancient monument known as the Cross and Hand (ST 62-03). A stone shaft whose origin and purpose is shrouded in mystery, it has become owner of many legends, one of which Hardy used in his book *Tess of the d'Urbervilles.* It is probably nothing more than a Saxon boundary stone. On nearby Gore Hill there is a picnic site with good views of the south-western reaches of the Blackmoor Vale.

Beaminster (193) (ST 47-01) *5m N Bridport.* One of the most perfectly sited of all Dorset towns, this small place sits in a partly wooded indentation of the high West Dorset hills. The town, centred on a pleasant square complete with market cross, is as attractive as its magnificent setting. Devastating fires in 1684 and 1781 enabled it to be rebuilt with the same consistency as Blandford, though in a very different, less urban style. Fortunately one building to escape the flames was the church of St Mary. The early 16th century tower, magnificently pinnacled and figure sculptured, is one of the most spectacular in Dorset. In 1685 James II used the yellow-stoned tower as a gallows, showing the townsfolk how their unpopular King treated disloyal subjects. Tragically the interior of the church fell victim to the Victorians' passion for renovation, and by ripping out the old roofs, pews and gallery, they destroyed much of its character. There are still a great many monuments including a particularly impressive one to George Strode (1753). The Strode family, owners of nearby Parnham House ★ for 300 years, founded the modest almshouses by the church in 1630.

The Manor House in North Street stands in a lovely 60-acre park complete with lake and grotto, but it is not open to the public. Bridge House, a late-16th century building at the foot of Prout Hill is

SCALE 1:25 000 or 2¼ INCHES to 1 MILE **Beaminster**

St Martin's Church, Beaminster.

worth looking at, as are 17th century Farrs House and Hitts House, both in Whitcombe Street. The best cottages, all of sombre local brown stone, are to be found in Church Street and St Mary's Street at the south-eastern end of the town. The Eight Bells Inn in Church Street is particularly attractive with its original stone-mullioned windows. Starting at St Mary's church walk southwards through the valley of the fast flowing River Brit to Parnham House ★. Alternatively walk north to the summit of Mincern's Hill, which has fine views over the town and where there is a pleasant picnic place (Buckham Down — ST 48-03).

One of Beaminster's most celebrated citizens was Thomas Hine, founder of one of the finest brands of Cognac. Born in the town in 1775 he went to France at the age of seventeen to make his fortune. Through marriage he eventually became the owner of a brandy business at Jarnac on the River Charente, and as time has proved, he prospered accordingly.

Belchalwell (194) (ST 79-09) *3½m S Sturminster Newton.* Until the late 13th century it is thought that this small hamlet, whose Saxon name means 'the hill by the cold stream', was two villages, Belle and Chadwell. The small battlemented church, standing alone on a mound at the end of a narrow, overgrown lane, though much restored by the Victorians was originally built by the Normans. Attached to the side of the short south tower is the porch, inside of which is the original late-Norman doorway. Items of interest within include a pretty Elizabethan pulpit, an oak eagle, and under a mat, a 17th century slab to the delightfully named Merry Bug, son of John Bug.

Bere Regis (194) (SY 84-95) *10m E Dorchester.* A large rather dull village that has suffered from being situated at an important road junction, although a bypass has now removed most of the traffic from its main streets. The Saxon queen, Elfrida, retired to a nunnery here, tormented and remorseful after the murder of her step-son Edward at Corfe Castle in 979. In medieval times Bere Regis was an important royal resort. Kings stopped here on their way to the hunting grounds of the south-west and King John had a house built in the village, the site of which sadly has never been identified. Simon de Montfort, founder of the English Parliament, is also believed to have lived here for a time. Severe fires, the last of which was in the 19th century, has left the village with no domestic buildings older than the 16th century.

The church of St John Baptist, substantial and impressive, recalls Bere's former days of splendour. Originally of the mid-11th century, it was enlarged and modified in the following three hundred years. The 15th century chequered flint and stone tower is among the most imposing in the county. The outstanding interior has a most remarkable and probably unique roof, given to the church by Cardinal Morton in about 1475. Massive life-size figures of the twelve apostles, unusually dressed in Tudor costume, stare down at the congregation from the ends of fake hammerbeams which form a part of this complicated, rather crudely carved and brightly painted open timber roof. See also the humorous carvings on the capitals of the late Norman pillars, one of which depicts the horrors of toothache, the 15th century carved bench-ends, the late-12th century font and the impressive monument to John Skerne (1596). In the churchyard lie the ravaged tombs of the Turbervilles, the family immortalised in Thomas Hardy's *Tess of the d'Urbervilles.* It was in this vault that Hardy's tragic Tess was buried.

One mile to the east of Bere Regis is Woodbury Hill (SY 85-94), a late Iron Age settlement renamed Greenhill in Hardy's *Far from the Madding Crowd.* In medieval times the hill was the site of an enormous fair that lasted five days — Wholesale Day, Gentle Folks Day, All Folks Day, Sheep Fair Day and finally a day when all the produce not previously sold was disposed of cheaply.

Bettiscombe (193) (ST 39-00) *12m NW Bridport.* Diminutive hamlet hidden away in a fold of the undulating West Dorset hills, and overlooked by Pilsdon Pen ★, the highest point in Dorset. A few hundred yards from the well-proportioned church, much restored in 1862, is the red-bricked Manor House, which was built for John Pinney, rector of Broadwindsor during the Protectorate. The house is still occupied by descendants of John Pinney, and is open to visitors by appointment only *(Tel: Broadwindsor 68239).*

From the manor walk east, and then head northwards, crossing the B3164, onto Filscon Pen ★. Alternatively walk south-east to the Shave Cross Inn, a delightful thatched 13th century public house which was formerly a monks' hospice. Besides stopping for refreshment the monks also had their heads shaved here, hence the inn's unusual name.

Blackmoor Vale (194,183) (ST 70-11 etc.) *E and SE of Sherborne.* Referred to as 'Blackmore', and 'The Vale of the Little Dairies' in several of Hardy's novels, this is a delightful area of gently undulating pastoral country extending eastwards from about Yetminster (194) (ST 59-10) and then curving north-eastwards to the Stour Valley in the vicinity of Gillingham (183) (ST 80-26). Much of the area is explored during the course of **Tour 3**.

Blandford Camp (195) (ST 92-08) *2m NE Blandford Forum.* Blandford's connections with the British Army date back to the early-18th century, when the 7th Hussars were stationed here to assist customs officers in their campaign against smugglers. During the Napoleonic wars a semaphore signalling station was constructed on Telegraph Hill as part of the Admiralty Shutter Telegraph System which ran from Plymouth to London.

Museum at Blandford Camp.

In the First World War the area was used as a training centre, and there was also a prisoner-of-war camp here. After the war the camp was closed down, but in the Second World War the area was again chosen as a suitable training ground for the military. In 1944 the camp was mostly converted into a hospital for American casualties from the Normandy landings, and in the 1950s and 1960s it became well-known as a site for motor cycle racing. After several bad accidents the circuit was closed, and in 1964 it was decided to move the Royal Corps of Signals from Catterick to Blandford Camp, and they still occupy it. The interesting camp museum contains items dealing with the history of army communications dating from the Crimean War to the Falkland Islands Campaign of 1982. *(Tel: Blandford 52581, extension 248).*

Blandford Forum (194) (ST 88-06). Lively country market town situated on ground sloping away from the River Stour at an important crossing point. It has one of the most complete and satisfying Georgian red-brick-and-stone town centres in southern England and in spite of considerable development, retains its Georgian flavour.

The suffix 'Forum' would suggest that the town has a Roman past, but this is misleading for there was never a Roman settlement here. The name is in fact a Latin translation of the old English name 'Chipping Blandford' — Blandford-with-a-market — and appears to have been given to the town in the 13th century by an over-pedantic monk. Little is known of mediaeval Blandford, but it had certainly become an important market town by the mid-16th century. The town's oldest building dates from these times. This is *St Leonard's Chapel (1)*, once a leper hospital but now used as a barn. In 1605 James I granted the town a Charter of Incorporation, thus confirming its status as a borough.

Always largely dependent on the farming community for its prosperity, Blandford has nevertheless had its own industries. In the mid-1600s the townsfolk began the manufacture of lace, and when Daniel Defoe visited here in 1724 he found it 'a handsome well-built town — 'chiefly famous for making the finest bone-lace in England'. The manufacture of buttons was another cottage industry that flourished here during the 18th and early-19th centuries. The introduction of machine-made buttons in the 1850's ruined the industry, but many of the children and women continued to make

1 St Leonard's Chapel
2 King's Arms
3 The Old House
4 Reyves's Almshouses

5 Greyhound House
6 Town Hall
7 No 34, Salisbury St.
8 Parish Church

9 Museum
10 Crown Hotel
11 Tourist Information Centre

Blandford Forum

SCALE 1:10 000 or 6 INCHES to 1 MILE

Georgian elegance at Blandford Forum.

the fine wires required by the button machines, while others turned their hand to glove-making.

Seven years after Defoe's visit, the town was devastated by a great fire, which began on the afternoon of June 6th, 1731, at a tallow-chandler's thatched house on the site of the present **Kings Arms (2)**. Fanned by a strong wind the fire spread so rapidly that by nightfall over 350 houses had been destroyed. The inhabitants made a valiant effort to preserve their church, but at around midnight the wooden building finally succumbed to the flames, its bells, according to one witness, dissolving and running down in streams. One of the few buildings to survive the fire was **The Old House (3)** in the Close. This massive mid-17th century structure has a great uneven hipped roof and a pair of tall polygonal chimneys. Other pre-fire buildings are **Reyves's Almshouses (4)**, erected in Salisbury Street by George Reyves in 1682.

The task of rebuilding the town was entrusted to John and William Bastard, representatives at this time of a well-known family of architects who had practised in the town since the end of the 17th century. Their work was completed by about 1760, and can best be appreciated at the junction of East Street and Salisbury Street. Stretching east is the **Market Place** flanked by elegant Georgian buildings and ending at the steps of the majestic church. Immediately to the south is **Greyhound House (5)**, one of Blandford's most handsome buildings, with a highly ornamented facade. The long north side of the Market Place is dominated by the **Town Hall (6)**, built of Portland stone and bearing the name of its creators on the curved pediment above the central window. A medallion on one of its walls celebrates the extraordinarily versatile Victorian artist Alfred Stevens, born in 1818 at **Number 34 (7)** in Salisbury Street, and best known for his fine classical monument to the Duke of Wellington in St Paul's Cathedral.

The **Parish Church (8)** is undoubtedly the Bastards' outstanding masterpiece. Of greensand ashlar it is among the largest and grandest Georgian churches outside London. The brothers had intended that the high tower should have a spire but instead it was topped with a small cupola. The spacious interior mercifully escaped Victorian restoration and retains its west gallery, elaborately carved square font, box pews, canopied mayor's seat, and pulpit. The organ is one of the few surviving works of George Pike England, and was said to have been donated to the church by George III after it was found to be too large for its intended home, London's Savoy Chapel. There are many interesting monuments recalling the notable figures of the town. Note especially those to the poet Christopher Pitt and George Vince who died on

Scott's Polar Expedition. Outside the church is the **Fire Monument**, a classical portico erected in 1760 to commemorate 'Gods Dreadful visitation by fire', and to give thanks to the 'Divine Mercy that has since raised this town like the phoenix from the ashes'. Opposite is the house where John Bastard is thought to have lived **(11)**. It is a beautifully proportioned building of red-brick with a grand central coaching gateway framed by two pilasters carrying a small pediment. The carriage entrance leads through to some old workshops and stables, which now house Blandford's small but interesting **Museum (9)**.

The finest post-fire dwelling is **Couper House(9)** in Church Lane. The front is particularly impressive with the Bastards making imaginative use of purple and red-coloured bricks. Church Lane opens out into **The Plocks**, a small square where sheep were kept before going to the market a short distance east in the triangular space known as **The Tabernacle**. There are many other fine Georgian buildings in the town, but do not be misled into thinking that the **Crown Hotel (10)** is one, for it was in fact built just before the outbreak of the Second World War. The **Tourist Information Office (11)** is in the Ham Car Park in West Street. *(Tel: Blandford 51989).*

Blandford St Mary (194) (ST 88-05) *½m S Blandford Forum.* In fact two distinct settlements lying south of the River Stour, and divided by the Blandford bypass. Lower Blandford St Mary hides from the main A350 road around a U-shaped lane and consists of a church, a manor house and a few dwellings. Inside the church there is a charming tablet to the architect Francis Cartwright. Blandford St Mary to the west of the bypass is dominated by the red-bricked brewery of Hall and Woodhouse, established here in 1882.

Bloxworth (194) (SY 88-94) *7m NW Wareham.* Close proximity to the conurbation of Bournemouth and Poole has resulted in much new building here, greatly altering the character of this once picturesque village. In spite of major alterations in the 19th century the church remains visually attractive and contains some interesting features within. Note especially the wide nave with its plastered wagon roof, the quaint manor house pew with its fireplace and the 13th century font, upon which is an unusual hourglass in its original wrought iron stand. In the 15th century John Morton, who was to become Henry VII's Lord Chancellor, was rector here. To the north-west of the church is 17th century Bloxworth House *(open to the public by written appointment only)*. Walk to East Bloxworth then south, crossing the main A35 road, into the heart of Bloxworth Heath. Here, ringed by pine trees, is Woolsbarrow Camp, Dorset's smallest Iron Age settlement (195) (SY 89-92).

The Blue Pool (195) (SY 93-83) *3m S of Wareham.* One of Dorset's most exquisite beauty spots, even at the height of the tourist season the Blue Pool has an atmosphere of extreme tranquillity. It is hard to imagine that this haven of peace was once a 50-foot clay pit supplying ball clay to the potteries of Wedgwood, Worcester, Derby, Minton and Spode. Abandoned in the early 20th century, the pit gradually filled with rainwater and water which seeped in from the surrounding clay. In 1934 the site was purchased by Mr Barnard and transformed into its present state. The extraordinary variation in colour, from turquoise blue to shades of green, is due to the light diffraction of the clay particles. A circular path allows visitors to walk through some of the 25 acres of heather, gorse, silver birches and aromatic Scots pine trees which surround the pool. Refreshments are available in a tea room and there is a gift shop and small aviary as well as a garden centre. There is also a museum showing details of the local history and how the expansion of the tea trade in the 18th century affected mining here. *(Tel: Wareham 51408.)*

Bokerley Ditch (184) (SU 05-18) *15m NE Blandford Forum*. Impressive Romano-British earthwork stretching for nearly four miles across the downlands of Cranborne Chase ★, and now forming part of the north-eastern Dorset-Hampshire border. Its flanks originally protected by woodlands, the ditch was presumably constructed to defend the farmland of the Romano-British *Durotriges* from the invasions of the Anglo-Saxons which took place from about AD 350 onwards. The ditch is at its most imposing on the Hampshire side where the rampart still stands 20 feet high. In fine weather there is a splendid walk along a footpath following the northern side of the eastern section of this great earth wall. (See also **Walk 12.**)

Bournemouth (195) (SZ 08-91) Dorset's largest town, and one of the leading resorts on the south coast, Bournemouth lies in a gap between high cliffs, where the tiny River Bourne flows into the sea. With its mild climate, superb sandy beaches, safe sea-bathing, and glorious landscaped gardens, it is not surprising to learn the town is invariably packed with holidaymakers during the summer months. For this reason it is best seen in the less crowded months of the spring or autumn.

As seaside towns go, Bournemouth was a late-starter. Until the beginning of the 19th century the land on which it stands was wild heathland. The first holiday villa was erected in 1810 on the deserted sandy shore at Bourne Chine by Lewis Tregonwell, on the site of what is now the Royal Exeter Hotel. Others soon followed the pioneering Tregonwell, and by the mid-19th century a thriving

1 St Stephen's Church
2 Town Hall
3 St Peter's Church
4 Casa Magni Shelley Museum (off map to east)
5 Pavilion
6 Pier
7 Russell Coates Art Gallery & Museum
8 Big Four Railway Museum
9 Langtry Manor Hotel (off map to east)
10 Royal Bath Hotel
11 Bournemouth International Centre
12 Winter Gardens
13 Tourist Information Centre

Bournemouth

SCALE 1:10 000 or 6 INCHES to 1 MILE

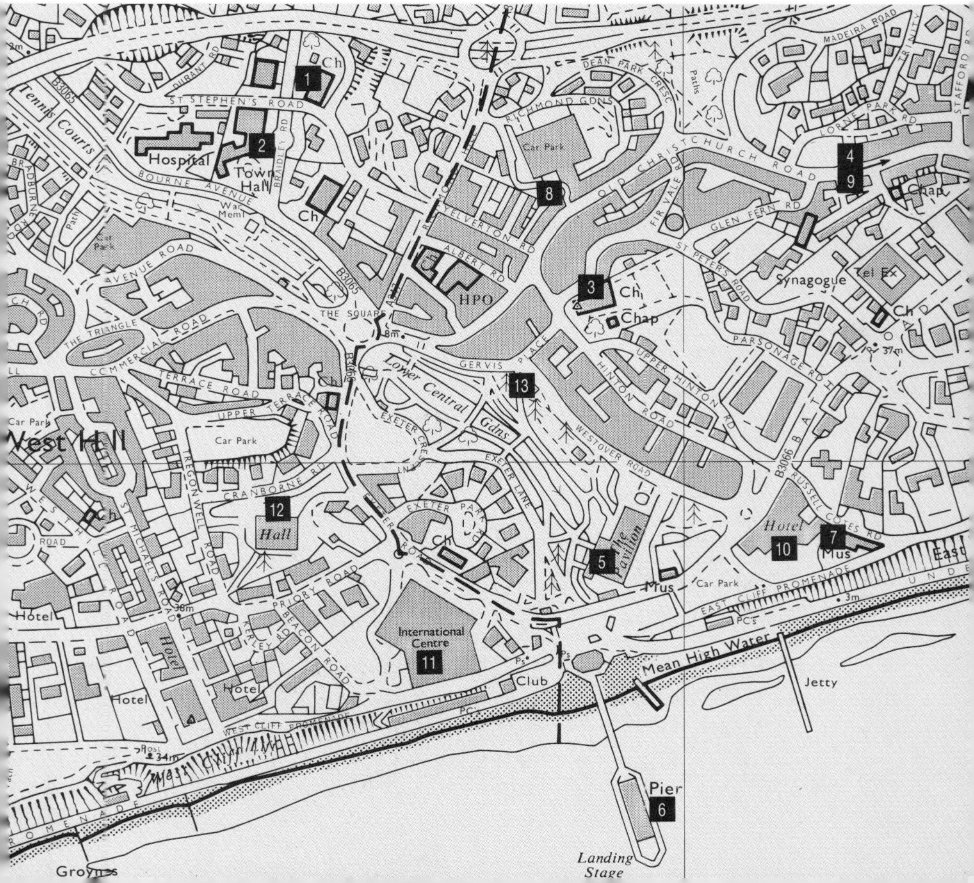

Bournemouth's attractive seafront.

village had sprung up. The arrival of the railway in 1870 further swelled the number of residents, and by the end of the century the population was over 37,000. The town has grown rapidly this century, and is now the centre of a massive conurbation stretching from Southbourne in the east to Poole in the west.

Bournemouth is not of outstanding architectural interest, and consists of a collection of buildings dating from the mid-1800s to the present day. However, there are a few interesting structures, notably the two large churches of St Stephen and St Peter. *St Stephen (1)* lies in St Stephen's Road, close to the uninspiring Victorian *Town Hall (2)*. St Stephen's was built in the late-19th century to the designs of J.L Pearson, whose most well-known work is Truro Cathedral in Cornwall. The interior is very spacious, with a great many pillars fashioned from Bath stone. Note also the fine modern glass by Clayton and Bell. *St Peter's church (3)* is another imposing building with a high 202-foot tower. The striking interior is decorated in typically late-Victorian fashion, with painted frescoes, mosaics, sculptures and much stained glass. Look out for the plaque in the choir stalls recording that the great 19th century Prime Minister Gladstone made his last communion in this church. Many celebrated figures are buried in the churchyard, including the religious reformer and hymn-writer John Keble; Mary Wollstonecraft, the late-18th century pioneer of the 'rights of women'; her daughter Mary Shelley, authoress of the horror-story *Frankenstein*, and the heart of daughter Mary's husband, the poet Shelley. The large house in Boscombe where Shelley's son, Percy, lived has been converted into *The Casa Magni Shelley Museum (4)*. It takes its name from Casa Magni in Italy, Shelley's home at the time of his death, and contains many items connected with the great romantic poet, including notebooks, letters, and poems. *(Tel: Bournemouth 303571.)* Another famous 19th century author who resided in the town was the Scotsman Robert Louis Stevenson. A memorial garden at the top of Alum Road in Westbourne marks the site of the house where he lived for three years, and where he wrote two of his best-known works, *Kidnapped* and *Dr Jekyll and Mr Hyde*.

Beautiful parks and gardens were established here almost as soon as the first houses were built. Lewis Tregonwell planted many aromatic pine trees on the cliffs and in the deep narrow fissures in the cliffs, known as chines. These chines, of which there are seven between the pier and Canford Cliffs, are idyllic places for walking. No less beautiful are the glorious Lower, Central and Upper Gardens which line the banks of the little River Bourne

almost up to the boundary with Poole two miles away. A path through the Lower Gardens leads past the *Pavilion (5)* to the seafront and *Bournemouth Pier (6)*. From here two wide tarmac paths run to the east and the west, beneath the high cliffs and in front of splendid sandy beaches. Running parallel to these pedestrian paths, on the cliffs above, are East Cliff Promenade and West Cliff Promenade.

The Russell Coates Art Gallery and Museum (7) is housed in a fine late-Victorian mansion at the end of East Cliff Promenade. This was the home of Sir Merton Russell-Coates, former Mayor of the town and an avid collector. The diversity of objects displayed is quite exceptional. There are paintings, silver and gold ware, swords, English china, furniture, sculptures, suits of armour from the Far East, items belonging to Napoleon and Sir Henry Irving, even a collection of 202 different rocks from all over Britain. *(Tel: Bournemouth 21009.) The Big Four Railway Museum (8)* off Old Christchurch Road *(tel: Bournemouth 22278)* contains a fascinating collection of railway memorabilia, including famous locomotive nameplates and station names.

One of the most interesting hotels in Bournemouth is *The Langtry Manor Hotel (9)* in Derby Road off the main Christchurch Road. This was the former home of Lillie Langtry, the beautiful actress from Jersey who was a great friend of King Edward VII. The *Royal Bath Hotel (10)*, a large all-white building erected in 1838, is one of the most luxurious hotels in the town. Equally impressive, is the recently opened *Bournemouth International Centre (11)* on the West Cliff. This has a massive concert hall, a swimming pool with wave machine, sauna suite, bars and restaurants. For information about the concerts and shows held here and at *The Pavilion (5)* and *The Winter Gardens (12)*, contact the *Tourist information Centre (13)* in Westover Road. *(Tel: Bournemouth 291715.)*

Bovington Tank Museum (194) (SY 82-88) *7m N Wareham.* This is situated in a large military camp, the home of the Royal Armoured Corps. For those interested in military memorabilia a visit to this museum will prove a delight, for it houses what is probably the most comprehensive collection of armoured fighting vehicles in the world. Many interesting displays, including a Centurion tank sliced in two to show its internal workings, models, and videos complete this most exciting museum. There is a cafeteria and picnic place outside. Every

At the Bovington Tank Museum.

year, on the last Sunday in July, the public are allowed to watch mock battles on the training ground to the north. *(Tel: Bindon Abbey 462721 Ext. 463.)*

Bradford Abbas (194) (ST 58-14) *3½m SW Sherborne.* Compact but expanding village lying in the broad and shallow valley of the River Yeo, and once owned by Sherborne Abbey, hence the word Abbas in the name. The glory of the village is the 15th century church, putting the visitor in mind of a miniature cathedral. The magnificent 90-foot medieval tower has eleven canopied niches on the west front but unfortunately only two are now occupied by figures. It is believed that the tower's north-west wall was once used as a fives court, the unusual notches on the north-west angle-buttresses being cut by players to enable them to clamber up the tower wall to retrieve balls from the roof. Before moving inside note the richly ornamented porch. Items to note within are the 15th century panelled roof, the handsome stone screen, the carved bench ends and the curiously ugly font. The remains of a 15th century preaching cross stand in the churchyard. Close to the church is the Rose and Crown Inn, formerly a rest house for the monks of Sherborne. It possesses an impressive stone fireplace with splendid panelling above. One mile east is Wyke Manor, a stately mid-17th century house surrounded by a lovely moat.

Briantspuddle (194) (SY 81-93) *9m E Dorchester.* Old-world village consisting of dumpy white-walled thatched cottages set in an idyllic rural landscape beside the lazy River Piddle. It took its name from Brian de Turberville, Lord of the Manor in the time of Edward III. At the east end of the village is the Ring, a linked group of thatched houses centred round an oval green which was constructed in 1919 by Sir Ernest Debenham, founder of Debenham's stores. A quarter of a mile west is *Blandon Valley*, a hamlet wholly created by Sir Ernest. The line of beautiful thatched houses with their wide grass verges remind one of the ordered layout of Milton Abbas. The impressive war memorial, shaped like a medieval cross, was designed by the talented sculptor Eric Gill. A footpath to the south of the farm shop leads to a picnic place on Briantspuddle Heath (SY 81-92). Note the strange hole opposite known locally as Cull-peppers Dish. This deep, tree-filled pit is a splendid example of what geologists term a swallow hole, and is caused by subsidence in the chalk below the gravel subsoil. Walk 9 starts from here.

Thatched cottages at Briantspuddle.

Bridport (193) (SY 46-92). Splendidly uniform town lying in the valley of the River Brit one and half miles above its entry to the sea at West Bay★. It has a distinct Georgian appearance but is in fact much older, for in Norman times it was already a sizable town, possessing its own mint, a priory and 120 houses. Long associated with rope-making, the first town records of the industry appear in 1211. However hemp has been grown in the surrounding area since Roman times and it is likely that the trade was well established by the 12th century. Henry III was one of the earliest royal customers, ordering a seine-net, and it was he who granted the first Charter to the town in 1253. By the 1500s Bridport was making 'for the most part all of the great cables, ropes and other tackling for the Royal Navy and the most part of other ships within this realm'. In the 17th century the navy started to make their own ropes in the naval yards of Portsmouth and Woolwich and for a while trade fell. But in the following century Bridport regained its prosperity by supplying the rapidly growing Newfoundland fishing fleet with nets and ropes. The town remains an important centre of net manufacture producing not only fishing nets but aircraft seat nets and the tennis nets for Wimbledon. At the bottom of West Street is the attractive stone building of the *Bridport-Gundry Company (1)*, the largest and oldest of the net manufacturers.

The character and layout of the town owes much to the rope industry, though it was not responsible, as is sometimes suggested, for the broad main streets; they are wide to accommodate the markets. Rope and twine making requires a 'walk', a long straight strip of land, hence the reason for the long narrow alleyways that stretch from the main streets. The great wealth generated by the trade in the 18th century enabled the centre of the town to be almost totally reconstructed, hence the predominance of Georgian buildings.

The red-brick *Town Hall (2)* stands at the crest of a steep hill, the place where West Street, East Street and South Street converge. Built in 1785, clock tower and cupola being added 20 years later, it occupies the site of a former chapel which fell into disuse after the Reformation. The charming Georgian *antique shop (3)* opposite was once the site of the George Inn where Charles II stopped during his flight from Worcester in 1651. *The Bull Hotel (4)*, with golden bull hanging above the pavement, was first recorded in 1593 but the present building dates from the mid-19th century. *Downe Hall (5)* to the north is the grandest 18th century monument in Bridport.

The *Unitarian Chapel (6)* stands back from East Street, a short distance from the junction with Barrack Street. It is a late-18th century building constructed in the classical style with Ionic pillars supporting a semi-circular porch. A line of tombstones in the garden have interesting neo-Classical designs. *Number 34 (7)*, on the south side of East Street, has a handsome Georgian front.

Running south from the Town Hall towards the sea is South Street, the oldest and most interesting of the main thoroughfares. The first building of note is the 19th century Methodist Chapel which now houses the *Bridport Art Centre (8)*. A short distance south is *'The Old Castle' (9)*, an elegant Tudor house which is now the town's museum and art gallery. As might be expected it contains many items connected with the rope industry including one of the last of the original net-making looms.

31

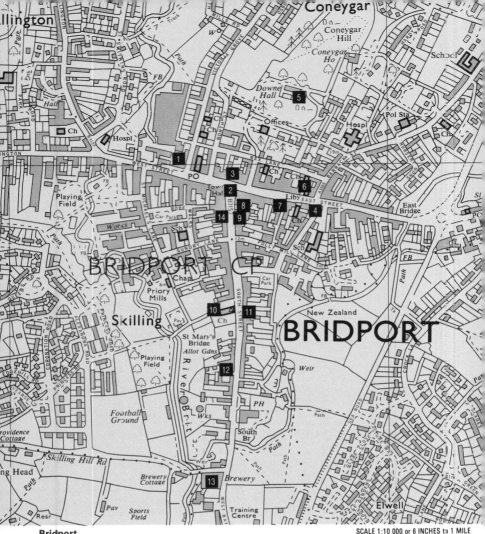

Bridport

SCALE 1:10 000 or 6 INCHES to 1 MILE

1 Bridport Gundry Company
2 Town Hall
3 Antique Shop
4 Bull Hotel
5 Downe Hall

6 Unitarian Chapel
7 No 34, East St.
8 Art Centre
9 Museum & Art Gallery
10 St Mary's Church

11 Almshouses & Friends
   Meeting House
12 Chantry House
13 The Old Brewery
14 Tourist Information Centre

The art gallery upstairs has a superb collection of dolls dating from the end of the last century. *The Church of St Mary (10)* lies on the west side of South Street, unusually far from the town centre. Essentially a Perpendicular building, traces of 13th century work can be found in the two transepts, one of which contains a fine late-13th century effigy of a cross-legged knight. *The Almshouses and Friends Meeting House (11)* across the road are a small group of 15th to 17th century buildings arranged around a tiny quadrangle entered via a modest arch. Continue walking south, passing some pretty 18th century cottages, until you reach *Chantry House (12)*, Bridport's oldest and most puzzling building. The last building of note in this part of the town is to be found on the junction of South Street and West Bay Road. Reputed to be

the only surviving thatched brewery in the country, *The Old Brewery (13)* of J.C and R.H Palmer was probably a former mill. The massive 18-foot diameter iron water-wheel weighs over 5 tons and remains in working order. Another relic of the Industrial Revolution, a vertical steam engine, is preserved within. *The Tourist Information Centre (14)* is at 32, South Street, opposite the Museum *(tel: Bridport 24901.)*

Broadwindsor (193) (ST 43-02) *7m N Bridport.* Delightful village sheltering into a deep bowl amid the dramatic uplands of west Dorset, with cottages and houses built on terraces at one level looking down at the chimneys of those below. Situated on the uppermost terrace is the church of St John

Baptist, sympathetically restored in 1868. Inside, note the different heights of the arcades: the south was built in 1180, the north in the early 1200s. In the early 15th century the vicar here was Thomas Fuller, a man of letters who wrote *The Holy War*, a history of the Crusades, and who was blessed with the rare and enviable ability to make his congregation roar with laughter during his sermons. When the Civil War broke out he was appointed chaplain to the army of Charles I. The beautiful seven-sided pulpit from which he preached is still here. A plaque on a cottage in the centre of the village states that Charles II slept here in 1651 after his escape from Worcester. In fact the King slept at the Castle Inn which formerly occupied the site of the cottage before it was burnt down in 1856. Amongst the visitors to the village in the late 18th century were the poet William Wordsworth and his sister Dorothy, who resided for a while at Racedown House, three miles to the west. Dorothy described Broadwindsor as 'the place dearest to my recollection upon the whole surface of the Island'. In order to fully appreciate the breathtaking scenery around the village walk south to Lewesdon Hill (NT). The arduous climb to the wooded summit, which is 892 feet above sea level, is well rewarded with good views over Marshwood Vale and the sea.

Brownsea Island (NT) (195) (SZ 02-87) *2m S Poole*. Covering an area of some 500 acres, Brownsea is the largest of the islands in the great land-locked harbour of Poole. Its name is derived from the latin words 'Brunci Insula', the Island of Bruno, Bruno having been the owner of Brownsea in the mid-11th century. In early medieval times the island passed into the possession of Cerne Abbey, whose monks built a small chapel on its deserted shores. After the Dissolution Henry VIII constructed a blockhouse here to guard the entrance to Poole Harbour. However, this was never exposed to military action, and had fallen into disrepair by the end of the 17th century. Not long afterwards the island was acquired by the notorious William 'Mad' Benson. He succeeded Sir Christopher Wren as

Quiet moorings off Brownsea Island.

Surveyor of Works in 1718, but after declaring (wrongly) that the House of Lords was in imminent danger of collapse was removed from office just one year later. Although this brought his architectural career to an abrupt end, it did not deter him from converting the ruined fort into a private residence. 'The Castle', as this became known, was further enlarged in the late-18th and 19th centuries, first by Sir Humphrey Sturt of More Crichel, and then by a certain Colonel Waugh, who bought the island in the mistaken belief that its china clay deposits would make him a a very wealthy man. He spent many thousands of pounds on building a village for the clay workers, a pier, a church, a school, and a public house, but it was then discovered that the clay was suitable for little else than the making of sewage pipes, and the unfortunate Waugh was ruined and fled to Spain. It is perhaps happier to recall that it was here in 1907, that General Baden-Powell held his first Boy Scout Camp, and similar camps have been held here ever since.

This unspoilt island, with its fine wood and heathland, sandy beaches, and interesting natural history, is well worth visiting. The landing pier is at the eastern end, near to the Castle (not open to the public) and the 'town', which includes a restaurant and several souvenir shops. Before setting out to explore the island it is well worth obtaining a copy of the National Trust's excellent leaflet describing its various features.

Brownsea Island

SCALE 1:25 000 or 2½ INCHES to 1 MILE

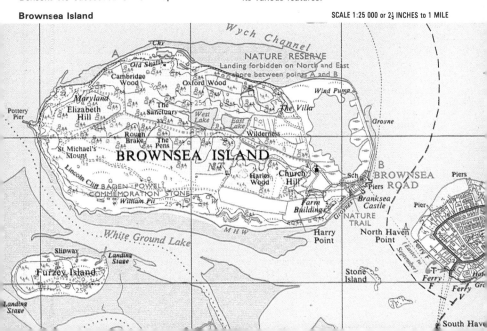

On the northern side of the island the Dorset Trust for Nature Conservation manages a 200-acre Nature Reserve, with a lagoon, two freshwater lakes, the second largest heronry in England, and a large colony of common terns. Access to this reserve is restricted to guided parties at fixed times. The southern half is an open reserve, with way-marked nature walks and picnic sites. A large number of semi-wild peacocks roam the grasslands by the church, and if exceptionally lucky the visitor may also see one of the shy red squirrels that live in the woodlands here. Colonel Waugh's interesting church contains several screens and some oak panelling which came from Richard III's Council Chamber at Crosby Hall in London. The island can be reached by passenger ferry either from Sand-banks or from Poole Quay. *(Tel: Canford Cliffs 707744.)*

Bryanston (194) (ST 87-06) *1m W Blandford Forum.* Hamlet at the edge of the parkland of Bryanston House, now home of the famous public school. The massive red and white mansion, built by Norman Shaw in the 1890's for the Second Viscount Portman, stands on the steep, wooded banks of the River Stour. It is reached by a mile-long driveway whose beginning is marked by a lofty archway, designed by James Wyatt in 1778. On the site of Wyatt's old house stand two churches, side by side. The old Georgian chapel is topped by a cupola and contains many memorial tablets to the Portman family. The second, much larger church of 1895-8 is of stone and possesses a fine tower.

Buckland Newton (194) (ST 69-05) *10m N Dorchester.* Lies almost hidden in a fold of the hills on the southern edge of the Blackmoor Vale, with a handsome Queen Anne house, Buckland Newton Place, and a number of 19th century buildings, now sufficiently mellowed to add to, rather than detract from, the flavour of this quiet village. The largely 15th century church has a 13th century (Early English) chancel, and was fortunate enough to be overlooked by the early and heavier-handed Victorian restorers. Beyond the vaulted two-storeyed porch, will be found an airy interior, with light flooding in through much clear glass. Do not miss the brass to Thomas Barnes of Dewlish Court, who died in 1624, and who was a distant ancestor of the Dorset poet, William Barnes.

Bulbarrow Hill (194) (ST 77-05) *8½m W Blandford Forum.* At 902 feet Bulbarrow is the highest of Dorset's central range of hills. From the summit there are glorious views across Blackmoor Vale over to the Quantocks and the Mendips. Walk half a mile west to Rawlsbury Camp, an Iron Age earthwork of quiet splendour, and admire the view over the vale to the right and the tumbling downs to the left. There is large parking-place here, making it an ideal base for walks. There are several good circular walks, one beginning and ending at Rawlsbury Camp the other starting at the barrow to the south of the radio mast and ending a quarter of a mile to the east at Delcombe Wood. (See also **Walk 8.**)

Burstock (193) (ST 42-03) *8½m NW Bridport.* Small village splendidly sited on the slopes of a narrow valley with views south-west to Pilsdon Pen★. Overlooking the few houses and cottages is

the church of St Andrew, a rather uninspiring building restored by the Victorians, but with an attractive tub-shaped Norman font. There are several delightful walks from here, that to Pilsdon Pen★ via Burstock Grange perhaps being the best.

Burton Bradstock (193) (SY 48-89) *3m SE Bridport.* A mile from the point where the River Bride passes through a gap in the coastal cliffs, lies this

Burton Bradstock — where the River Bride meets the sea.

large but exceptionally pretty village. Built along a labyrinth of narrow lanes and roads it is at its most lovely near the church. Here the stone walls of many of the thatched cottages are covered with roses and clematis. St Mary's church, entirely 15th century except for the unusual late-19th century south aisle, contains two aged desks both beautifully carved and a clock that originates from Christ's Hospital, London. In the 18th century The Drove Inn was used as a contraband distribution house by Dorset's most notorious smuggler, Isaac Gulliver. In one of the bars there is a table constructed from the hatch cover of the schooner *Flirt*, wrecked in the bay in 1897. A mile to the east the Dorset Coast Path★ passes Burton Mere (194) (SY 50-87), several lagoons populated by many different species of birds. There is a pleasant walk across Burton Cliffs down to the shingled mouth of the River Bride.

While in this area, do not miss a visit to the interesting 'Old Farming Collection' at Bredy Farm (194) (SY 50-89), under two miles to the east of the village.

Canford Magna (195) (SZ 03-98) *2m SE Wimborne Minster.* Riverside village just maintaining its separate identity from the sprawling suburban growth of nearby Merley★. Many of the existing thatched houses formed part of a Victorian model estate erected by the Welsh ironmaster Sir John Guest, who lived in the mansion to the north, now Canford School. It is Dorset's grandest Victorian house, and was constructed around a building that had belonged to many distinguished families including the Salisburys, Montagues, and Beauforts. The massive kitchen, with three open fireplaces, is the only surviving part of the 15th century manor house. In the mid-1800s Sir Charles Barry was instructed by Guest to make the house even larger, and he remodelled much of the work done on the house by Edward Blore in 1825-36. He also provided it with a gigantic entrance tower reminiscent of that he built for the Houses of Parliament. Standing close to the main entrance of the house is the village church, a most interesting, though not particularly beautiful building. It has a complex architectural history for it boasts work from the Anglo-Saxon, Norman, Tudor and Victorian periods. The widespread and excellent detail of the Norman work is especially noteworthy. Inside there are many Guest memorials including an impressive lifesize effigy of the First Lord Wimborne (1914). A short distance west of the church is a most unusual Victorian cast-iron bridge. Cross this to enjoy a splendid short walk along the north bank of the Stour.

Canford Pond (195) (SZ 04-99) beside the B3073 at Little Canford, has special 'disabled' coarse fishing facilities for users of wheelchairs *(for details tel: 0202 671144)*.

Cattistock (194) (SY 59-99) *9m NW Dorchester off A356*. 'Elbow streeted Cattistock' was the description the poet William Barnes gave to this place, and its 19th century houses still cluster around a very sharp hairpin bend. It is a pleasant place nestling in the upper valley of the River Frome, and dominated by the grand church, considered by Pevsner and Newman to be the best of Dorset's mid-to-late 19th century churches. It was rebuilt mostly by Sir George Gilbert Scott in 1857, but it was his son, George who was responsible for the most outstanding parts. In 1874 he pulled down the north tower and replaced it with an excellent two bay arcade. In the north-west corner he constructed a slim hundred-foot tower with long, recessed belfry windows. The bapistry, its walls painted in sombre purple, blue and dark red, was placed in the tower and separated from the nave by a stone screen. Do not miss the fantastic font cover, elaborately carved and all of 20 feet high.

Cerne Abbas (194) (ST 66-01) *7m N Dorchester*. Outstandingly beautiful stone, flint and brick village sheltering in the wide valley of the River Cerne and guarded by the massive Giant cut from the western slopes of Giant Hill. The origins of this great (180 feet high) nude hill figure are obscure though it is generally believed to be a Romano-British representation of the Roman Emperor Hercules, who claimed to be an incarnation of Hercules, a God associated with fertility, hence the aggressive male form. A more romantic origin is that it is the outline of a giant killed by the villagers because he persisted in eating their sheep. Above the giant is an earthwork known as the 'Trendle' or 'Frying Pan', which until not long ago, was the scene of Mayday celebrations including Maypole Dancing, a ceremony concerned with fertility worship. The Giant is best approached from a footpath beginning at the church.

A Benedictine abbey was established in the village in about AD 987 on the site of a 9th century monastery. The remains are to be found in the grounds of Abbey House, at the end of the street beyond the church. The lovely three-storeyed 15th century gateway, or porch, was built by Thomas Corton, the last abbot. The ornate oriel window shares many of the details found on the gatehouse at Forde Abbey ★. A much simpler oriel window is to be found at the smaller Guest House. The 14th century flint tithe barn in the south-west corner of

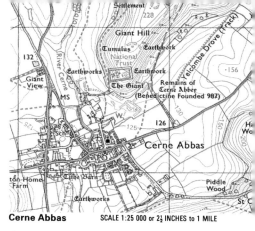

Cerne Abbas   SCALE 1:25 000 or 2½ INCHES to 1 MILE

the village has been partly converted into a dwelling.

Cerne Abbas was once a very important market and manufacturing town. There was a large leather industry here as well as brewing establishments which supplied quality ales to the London market in the 18th century. But it was bypassed by the railway and went into decline in the mid-19th century. Abbey Street is the most interesting part of the

The Cerne Abbas Giant.

village, and is dominated by the graceful 15th century tower of St Mary's church. The well-restored interior is wonderfully bright with light flooding in from the large Perpendicular east window, believed to have come from the abbey. The most important interior features are the 15th century stone rood screen, Jacobean pulpit with tester and 14th century wall paintings in the chancel. Opposite the church there is a beautiful row of timber-fronted cottages and a large Georgian residence with a fine shell porch. Here also is the Royal Oak Inn which incorporates stone salvaged from the ruins of the abbey. A legal document in the bar reveals that in 1771 the premises changed hands for a mere five shillings. Walk over Giant Hill into Minterne Parva (where it is possible to link with **Walk 6**) and then on to Minterne Magna ★.

Chalbury (195) (SU 01-06) *4m N Wimborne off B3078*. Tiny hamlet sited on a 330-foot-hill with good views over the gently rolling countryside of south-east Dorset to the hills of Purbeck. The small, well-kept and whitewashed 13th century church was re-fitted in the 18th century. Luckily it escaped Victorian restoration and retains its high-sided family box pews, three-decker pulpit, west gallery and clear glass.

Chaldon Herring (194) (SY 79-83) *10m SW Wareham*. Also known as East Chaldon, this very isolated place lies half-hidden among sweeping chalk downs a short distance from the sea. The name of the pretty thatched inn, 'The Sailors Return', was used by Edward Garnett in 1926 for the title of his well-known novel. The village boasts another literary connection, for the small red-bricked house called Beth Carr was one the home of the writer T.F.Powys. In his novel *Mr Weston's Good Wine* he renames the village 'Folly Down'. His brother, Llewellyn Powys also lived in a cottage on the downs close by. It is possible to walk south from here over to Durdle Door ★.

Charminster (194) (SY 68-92) *2m N Dorchester*. A large rambling village on the River Cerne, which joins the River Frome just to the south-west. The labyrinth of small streams and gullies between here and Dorchester has discouraged development that would possibly have joined the two. Dominating the skyline is the pinnacled 16th century tower of the church, the many stylized T's to be found outside and inside informing us that it was built by Sir Thomas Trenchard. The south chapel was the Trenchard chapel and it is likely that the two un-named 16th century marble monuments are Tren-chard tombs. The Trenchards were a wealthy sheep-farming family from Hampshire who obtained Wolfeton House (see below) through marriage in 1480. In 1506 the Archduke Philip of Austria and his Spanish wife came here after their ship had been wrecked in Weymouth Bay while en route to Spain. Speaking no Spanish, Sir Thomas Trenchard asked his friend John Russell to act as his interpreter. Russell was invited to accompany the Archduke to the court of Henry VII, where he made such an impression that he was eventually created 1st Earl of Bedford.

Regrettably the Tudor parts of Wolfeton House were savagely mutilated in the early 19th century and only the imposing twin-towered gatehouse and south-west corner of the original building remains. The items of particular interest inside are the fine stone staircase in the hall, the unusual stone doorway leading to the long gallery on the first floor and the four giant wooden Corinthian columns in the east drawing room. To the north is an early 17th century barn-like building considered to be the earliest surviving riding school in England *(tel: 0305 63500)*.

Charmouth (193) (SY 36-93) *2½m E Lyme Regis*. Jane Austen found this large seaside village a delightful place for 'sitting in unwearied contempla-tion' but now the peace is shattered by busy traffic winding its way up the steep main street. However, the place still retains an unmistakable Georgian flavour, with its coaching inns and many Regency stucco houses with neat bow-fronted windows. Though the Queen's Arms in the High Street appears Georgian it is actually two 16th century cottages joined together. The great beams, fine panelling and great stone fireplace clearly show the inn's Tudor ancestry. On one door frame there are

Charmouth, with Lyme Regis beyond — a view from Stonebarrow Hill.

carved the initials of Thomas Chard, the last abbot of Forde Abbey, and it is believed that when Charmouth belonged to the abbey this house was his headquarters. Another interesting inn is the George, an old coaching house with a little room over the porch from where intending travellers could look for the approaching coach. The Victorian church is not of great interest, but does contain a fine 15th century statuette of an abbot against a cross. In the churchyard there is a table tomb to James Warden, who was unfortunate enough to be shot through the heart while duelling with a neighbour.

The high dark cliffs overlooking the excellent beach have been popular with fossil-hunters since the end of the 17th century. A more recent collector of fossils, Mr Barney Hansford, has established a fascinating museum in the village, Barney's Fossil Museum. Do not miss a visit here. Also walk east along the cliff path to Stonebarrow Hill, and on to the National Trust's Golden Cap Estate, or west along the Spittles and into Lyme Regis.

Chedington (193) (ST 48-05) *11m N Bridport*. This consists of only a little church and a few substantial houses, and is superbly situated high in chalk hills near the source of the rivers Axe and Parret. From the undistinguished church there are sweeping views over Crewkerne out onto the Mendip Hills. On National Trust land a few hundred yards to the north there stands an impressive monument to the 43rd Division of the Dorchester Regiment, which distinguished itself in the bloody struggle for H II 112 during the Battle of Normandy in 1944. Just below the monument, the A356 passes through Winyarc's Gap, a famous cutting through which Charles I led his troops in 1644.

Chesil Beach (194) (SY 60-80, etc.) Sometimes described as 'the eighth wonder of the world', it is vast pebble bank stretches from Portland ★ to Abbotsbury ★ and encloses a brackish lagoon called the Fleet. The bank 'comes ashore' at Abbotsbury ★ and continues as a beach past West Bexington ★ to Burton Bradstock ★. Fifty to sixty feet above sea level at its highest point and never wider than two hundred yards, the bank came into existence some 80,000 years ago, at a time of low sea levels. As a result of tidal action, the pebbles get progressively larger and less rounded the further east one travels. So consistent is this graduation that it was said that fishermen or smugglers driven ashore in bad weather could locate their position by the size of the pebbles. Exposed to Atlantic storms

Chesil Beach from Abbotsbury, with the Isle of Portland in the far distance.

the beach has an appalling history of shipwreck, one of the worst disasters occurring on November 18th 1795, when three transport ships went down off Wyke Regis ★ with the loss of many lives. It is dangerous to swim from this shore because of the strong undertow and it is also extremely laborious to walk on, but perhaps because of this, there is a wonderful atmosphere of isolation upon Chesil Beach.

Chettle (195) (ST 95-13) *7m NE Blandford Forum off A354.* Peaceful, partly thatched village lying in a heavily wooded valley with little brooks flowing away to the south-east. Standing in its own small park is Chettle House, a glorious example of Baroque architecture designed by Thomas Archer, and built around 1710 by the Bastards of Blandford for George Chafin, who held the post of Ranger of Cranborne Chase. It is a handsome red-brick building with rounded corners and a fine balustraded parapet of Chilmark stone. In 1846 the house was bought by the Castleman family, and the two small stone castles on the parapet were added as a play on the name of the new owner. The sweeping double-flighted wooden staircase in the entrance hall is the most impressive interior feature. *(Tel: Tarrant Hinton 430.)*

The church of St Mary was heavily restored by the Castleman family in 1849, but restoration was carried out here in an unusually sympathetic manner, with much of the original character of the building being retained. There are several memorial tablets to the Chafin family, including one to Thomas Chafin, who commanded a troop of horse for the King at the Battle of Sedgemoor.

Chideock (193) (SY 42-92) *3m W Bridport.* Like Charmouth Chideock (pronounced 'Chiddick') has been spoilt by the A35 road which cuts through the middle of the village. Nevertheless it is still an attractive place of thatched cob and yellow sandstone cottages, being built upon the fertile slopes of the valley of the River Winniford, a mile before it enters the sea at Seatown (**Walk 2** starts from here). Chideock House Hotel was the headquarters of the local Parliamentary forces that fought in the 1645 campaign against the King's local supporters. During this campaign the 14th century castle that stood to the north of the village was destroyed, and now only traces of the moat remain. On a mound close by, a great wooden cross was erected to the memory of five Roman Catholic priests who were executed here for refusing to conform to the new religion. The 15th century church was much restored in 1884, but retains two fascinating items — a black marble effigy of a knight, said to be Sir John

Chideock, and a cross of mother-of-pearl thought to have come from Palestine. Next to the churchyard is a mausoleum built in the 1880s by Charles Weld. The Welds were the builders of the Roman Catholic chapel at East Lulworth ★ and succeeded the Arundells as Lords of the Manor in 1802, building Chideock Manor in 1810. A chapel added to the house in the 1870s has a most striking interior, with panelled roof and decorated arches. In the annexe there is a small museum. The two roads that lead to Seatown, Mill Lane and Duck Street, contain some very pretty houses, especially Swiss Cottage, which has a beautiful curving thatched roof and great brick chimneys, and Anvil Cottage, also displaying a lovely thatched roof.

Chilcombe (194) (SY 52-91) *4½m E Bridport off A35.* Minute hamlet set in glorious downlands, and consisting of an 18th century farmhouse, two cottages, and a charming church, which surely must be among the smallest in England. From a distance it appears to be a farm building for it stands literally in the farmyard, and is without tower or spire. The fabric is of 13th century origin but alterations were carried out in the 15th, 16th and 17th centuries. A path north leads to Chilcombe Fort, a small Iron Age earthwork situated on the summit of Chilcombe Hill.

Christchurch (195) (SZ 15-92). Surrounded on three sides by suburban and holiday developments, this small town has, by some miracle, preserved a delightful character all its own. It is situated between the Rivers Stour and Avon at the point where they join before entering the shallow waters of Christchurch Harbour. Most visitors will come here to see the magnificent priory and the ruins of the Norman castle, but it also has a reputation amongst anglers as one of the finest coarse fishing centres in the country.

In the late 9th century Twynham, 'the place between two rivers' as the town was then called, became one of Alfred the Great's fortified burghs, its position between the Stour and Avon making it easily defendable. It is likely that by this time it already had a small minster church, as well as other features common to many of the burghs, like a mill and town fields. Evidence suggest that during the reign of King Canute the town's defences were deliberately razed to the ground. However, its reputation as a religious centre grew apace, and by the time of Domesday there were 24 secular canons resident at the church. Towards the end of the 11th century the manor came into the possession of Ranulf Flambard, Bishop of Durham and friend of William Rufus, who had become the king's 'first minister'. Ranulf demolished the existing church and in its place erected a magnificent Norman church. In 1150 this became an Augustine priory, and new monastic buildings were erected to the north of the church. At the Dissolution these were pulled down, but fortunately the minster survived as the parish church.

According to at least one historian of the church *Christchurch Priory (1)* is one of finest churches below cathedral rank in England. It stands in beautiful grounds, almost at the apex of the piece of land which separates the Avon from the Stour, its high 15th century tower acting as landmark for miles around. All styles of architecture from the Norman to the Renaissance are represented in this

Christchurch Priory from the Harbour.

Perpendicular choir contains an excellent set of misericords (carvings under hinged choir stalls), including one from the early 13th century. Here also is a particularly colourful mid-14th century Jesse reredos which, although not as well carved as some, does retain some of its original figures. The visitor should also try to see the 'Miraculous Beam' situated high up in the south choir aisle. According to legend medieval carpenters cut this great roof beam so short it would not span the walls. However, the following day they discovered that it had miraculously lengthened and now fitted easily. So sure were they that its growth was the work of 'Christ the Carpenter' they renamed the building 'Christ's Church', hence the town's present name.

The remains of *Christchurch Castle (EH) (2)* lie a short distance north of the priory. It was built in the 13th century on an artificial mound originally raised by the Normans, but was derelict as early as 1540 and was by that time used for keeping cattle. It was, however, of some significance in the 17th century, and in the closing months of the Civil War it was captured by Parliamentary forces and like Corfe and Sherborne, was effectively demolished or 'slighted'. The ruins of the castle hall, or *Constable's House (EH) (3)*, can be seen in the gardens of the King's Arms Hotel. Considered one of the oldest houses in England, it is a wonderful example of Norman domestic architecture with beautiful round-headed windows and a fine circular chimney. Another old building is the lovely thatched *Old Court House (4)* in Castle Street. There is a wonderful view of the Priory and castle remains from *Christchurch Bridge (5)*, which is itself a fine

splendid building, still known locally as 'The Train' because of its great length (311 feet). The Norman features are particularly exciting, especially the fabulously decorated north-east turret of the north transept. Entry is through a massive 13th century north porch, reputed to be the largest in England. Note the long stone seats on both sides. The impressive nave measures 118 feet by 58 feet, and is flanked by massive Norman arches and pillars. Perhaps the most outstanding feature of the church is the Salisbury Chantry in the north choir aisle. Constructed from hardwearing Caen stone, it was built as a memorial for Margaret Pole, Countess of Salisbury, but was never used, as she was executed by King Henry VIII in 1541 and buried in the cemetery for traitors at the Tower of London. Another fine monument is the white marble memorial to the poet Shelley beneath the tower. The

Christchurch Harbour and Hengistbury Head

SCALE 1:25 000 or 2½ INCHES to 1 MILE

16   17   18

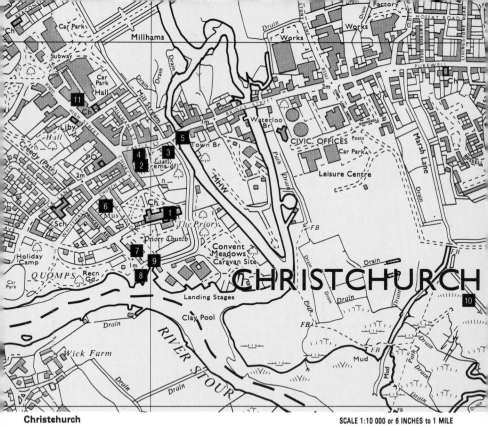

Christchurch

SCALE 1:10 000 or 6 INCHES to 1 MILE

1 Priory	5 Christchurch Bridge	9 Place Mill
2 Castle	6 Red House Museum	10 Stanpit Marsh Nature Reserve
3 Constable's House	7 Tricycle Museum	11 Tourist Information Centre
4 Old Court House	8 The Quay	

structure dating back to the 12th century.

Christchurch's **Red House Museum (6)** is in Quay Street, and like most good museums, the building in which it is housed is of historical interest. It was built in 1767 as a workhouse, accommodating 130 townspeople at a cost of 6 pence per head per week *(tel: Christchurch 482860)*. **The Tricycle Museum (7)** in the Priory Car Park is a fascinating little museum showing the development of the tricycle from the last century to the present day *(tel: Christchurch 3240)*. Not far from here is **The Quay (8)**, from where boats may be hired for pleasure or fishing trips. The town's historic **Place Mill (9)** stands besides a small bridge at the end of the quay. It dates from Tudor times, although there has been a mill here since before Domesday. Recently restored, it is open to the public, but in the summer months only. From here the visitor can walk along a charming footpath beside the mill stream to the old town bridge.

To the south east of the town is **Stanpit Marsh Nature Reserve (10)**, a marshy piece of land populated by many different sea and estuary birds. For information about this and other attractions in the town contact the **Tourist Information Centre (11)**, located in Saxon Square at the top end of the High Street *(tel: Christchurch 47180)*.

About 2 miles to the north-west, to the right of the road to Hurn, is St Catherine's Hill (SZ 14-95), a

pleasant piece of open heathland commanding fine views over the surrounding area. This may be explored by following the St Catherine's Hill Trail, which is described in an interesting guide leaflet available from the Tourist Information Centre.

Christchurch Harbour (195) (SZ 17-91) *To immediate S of Christchurch.* An impressive stretch of water between the confluence of the Rivers Stour and Avon, and the narrow channel into the open sea beside busy Mudeford Quay ★. It is bounded on the south by the sandy promontory of Hengistbury Head ★, and on the north by the Stanpit Marshes, where there is a Nature Reserve (see Christchurch ★). There is a little passenger ferry service running between Christchurch Quay and Mudeford Quay, calling in at the southern shore inland from Hengistbury Head.

Church Knowle (195) (SY 93-81) *5m S Wareham.* Overshadowed to the north by Knowle Hill, this unspoilt little village of grey Purbeck stone is splendidly sited on a hummock in the valley of the River Corfe. The plain stone-roofed church is mostly of the 13th century, but the tower and the north aisles are later additions. The most striking feature within is the threefold chancel arch, but also see the elaborate 16th century monument to Sir

39

John Clavell made almost 40 years before his death. Before they moved to Smedmore in the 1600s the Clavels lived at Barnestone, a late 13th century manor a half mile to the west. A path from the church leads to the summit of Knowle Hill, and then eastwards to Corfe Castle (see also **Walk 10**).

Clifton Maybank (194) (ST 57-13) *3½m SW Sherborne.* Here on the west bank of the River Yeo is part of a great house built by Sir John Horsey in the mid-16th century. The Horsey family acquired the manor here through marriage in the 14th century. They became owners of a vast estate, but by the early 17th century the family was bankrupt and Sir John Horsey had the misfortune to die in a debtors' prison. Only the tall south wing of the original house remains, but the centre of the main entrance may now be seen on the front of Montacute House in Somerset, and other fragments are to be found at Hinton St George and Over Compton.

Clouds Hill (NT) (194) (SY 82-90) *8m NW Wareham.* Isolated cottage in the heart of Moreton Heath where Lawrence of Arabia spent his final years. He bought it in 1925, when he was stationed at nearby Bovington Camp ★, but it was not until 1935 that he began to live in it permanently. Two months later he was tragically killed in a motor-cycle accident not far away (see also Moreton ★). The interior has been carefully preserved, and it has a somewhat oppressive quality, reflecting this man's very unusual character. The eating room looks particularly austere, with aluminium foil lining the walls to act as a heat insulator. There is an interesting collection of photographs illustrating his fascinating career from the time of his archaeological work in the Middle East, to his military exploits in the First World War. A commemorative tree was recently planted to mark the spot near Wool where he crashed. Lawrence enthusiasts should also visit Wareham museum, which contains an impressive collection of relevant items.

Compton Abbas (183) (ST 87-18) *3½m S Shaftesbury.* Until the Dissolution in 1539, the Abbey at Shaftesbury held this main road village; hence Abbas. It is attractively situated between the steep slopes of Melbury Hill and Fontmell Down, and overlooks the rich pastures of the Blackmoor Vale. At East Compton stands the tower of the original 14th century church, with the stump of an old preaching cross nearby. Three of the old tower bells hang in the new church, built in 1866-7, and possessing a fine vaulted chancel and some respectable modern stained glass. There are good walks from here onto Fontmell Down and Melbury Hill. It is also possible to watch small aircraft flying from Compton Abbas Airfield (183) (ST 88-18), on the downs about 1 mile east of village. Refreshments are available close to a public viewing area and pleasure flights are available throughout the year *(tel: 0797 811767).*

Compton Acres Gardens (195) (SZ 05-89) *2m SW Bournemouth.* Here, on the pine covered slopes of a sandy chine overlooking Poole Harbour, are a series of magnificent and unique gardens. Laid out by T.W. Simpson in 1919 and restored in the 1950s by the architect J.S. Beard, these lovely gardens

At Compton Acres Gardens.

comprise nine separate arrangements, each totally different from the other. Perhaps the most delightful is the Japanese garden, reputed to be the only complete garden of its type in Europe, but see also the Woodland and Sub-tropical Glen, with its palms, mimosas, eucalyptus, bamboos and chain of small lakes. *(Tel: Canford Cliffs 708036.)*

Corfe Castle (NT) (195) (SY 96-81) *4m SE Wareham.* The many picturesque grey stone houses and cottages of this outstandingly popular Purbeck village nestle beneath one of the most dramatic castle ruins in the country. Splendidly sited on a steep sided, conical hill which dominates the narrow cleft carved in the Purbeck hills by the little River Corfe, the castle has a long and often violent history. Although the present structure dates from the time of William the Conqueror, it was the site of a Saxon lodge where the young King Edward the Martyr was murdered on the orders of his stepmother Elfrida in 978. In the early 13th century the Norman castle was greatly extended and improved by King John, who used it as a royal prison. Here he imprisoned and starved to death 22 French knights who had supported his nephew's claim to the throne. Further modifications were made to the fortress in the reign of Edward I. Corfe passed out of the hands of the Crown in the 16th century, when Queen Elizabeth I granted it to one of her court favourites, Lord Chancellor, Sir Christopher Hatton. Just eight years before the outbreak of the Civil War the castle was purchased by Sir John Bankes, Attorney-General to Charles I. During that great conflict it was held for the King by Lady Bankes and was twice besieged, first in 1643 and again in 1645. The tiny garrison was eventually forced to capitulate in February of 1646, after one of the defenders had turned traitor and opened the castle gates to the Parliamentary forces. The following month Parliament ordered that Corfe be 'slighted'. However, although Cromwell's experienced engineers ruined the castle they were unable to obliterate it completely, so that even today the key features of the building, like the outer wall, mural towers and the massive 70-foot Norman keep, are easily recognisable. Under the will of the late N.J.R. Bankes Corfe Castle was given to the National Trust, together with Kingston Lacy ★, Badbury Rings ★, and the many acres that made up his great estate. *(Tel: Corfe Castle 480442.)*

From the castle ruins, the village of Corfe Castle spreads southwards, along a little cul-de-sac and the busy A351. In the Middle Ages it was the centre of the Purbeck stone and marble industry, and, on Shrove Tuesday, the Society of the Purbeck Stone Cutters and Marblers meet here to preserve their ancient rights. In view of its association with the Purbeck stone industry it is not surprising to find that nearly all the houses here are constructed of this grey, rather sombre material. The Market Square is dominated by the Greyhound Hotel, which was built in 1733, with a quaint porch over the street supported by Tuscan columns. Standing on the south side of the Square behind the Town House, once the residence of the Mayor and now the National Westminster Bank, is Corfe's handsome church. This large Perpendicular-style building was almost completely rebuilt in the mid-19th century, but the splendid 15th century tower with its fine gargoyles has happily survived. Below the church in West Street is the Town Hall, an odd red brick structure now housing Corfe's small museum. The scale model of the village is well worth visiting for it gives a good impression of what the castle looked before Cromwell's men did their best to destroy it. Walking possibilities from here are almost limitless, but we particularly recommend the walk east along the Purbeck ridge to Nine Barrow Down. (See also our **Walk 10** which heads westwards along the same ridge.)

Corfe Mullen (195) (SY 98-97) *2m W Wimborne Minster.* This has grown to its present size as a suburb of Poole and Bournemouth. Fortunately the attractive old village near the River Stour remains detached from the unsightly residential area to its south. The 'Mullen' part of the name is probably a corruption of the French word 'moulin', a mill, for such a building has existed here since at least Norman times.

Set in meadowland almost opposite, and adjacent to the B3074 road is the church of St Herbert, a modest little building with a robust Norman tower of red-brown stone, and a fine plastered barrel-roof with brightly painted carved bosses. The Norman font has lost its cover but there are the remains of the iron fastenings to which it was locked to prevent witches stealing the Holy Water. An altar tomb in the churchyard commemorates Lord of the Manor, Thomas Phelpis (1663), who willed that 'ten poor people of the parish should receive four pennyworth of bread and cheese every Sunday'.

Corscombe (194) (ST 51-05) *17m NW Dorchester.* Peaceful village strung out across the wooded slopes and hollows of the glorious country between Yeovil and Beaminster, with a Perpendicular church rebuilt in the 15th and 19th centuries, and an immaculately thatched inn called the Fox. Court Farm to the north-east is a lovely moated building that dates from the 13th century, when it was a grange of Sherborne Abbey ★. In the 1700s it was the home of the great democrat, Thomas Hollis, who allegedly named one of his woods Stuarts Coppice because he enjoyed beheading it.

Cranborne (195) (SU 05-13) *11m N Wimborne Minster.* Set astride the River Crane at the edge of the rolling chalk uplands of Cranborne Chase ★, this tranquil little north Dorset village was once one of the most important places in the county, with its own court, manor house, priory and market. The Benedictine Priory, to which Tewkesbury was subordinate, was founded in AD 980. However, in about 1102 most of the monks moved from here to the rebuilt abbey at the far-off Gloucestershire

town, and the priory gradually declined until there were only two monks left at the time of the Dissolution. Nothing survives of the priory but the size of the church is evidence of its original importance. It is a most impressive building with a fine Norman north doorway, a nave entirely of the 13th century and a mighty 15th century tower. Though marred by the dull Victorian chancel there is still much to see and admire within. Note especially the 14th century wall paintings depicting 'The Seven Deadly Sins' and 'The Seven Acts of Mercy', the many interesting monuments, and the fine 15th century oak pulpit.

The other notable building here is Cranborne Manor, a 13th century Royal hunting lodge greatly expanded in the 1400s by the Earls of Gloucester and then again in the 17th century by Robert Cecil, Earl of Salisbury. The house, which is still in the hands of the Cecils, is not open to the public, but the garden is open at certain times *(tel: Cranborne 248).* This is considered one of the finest in England, with its Jacobean mount garden, river garden, and old kitchen garden. There is also a good Garden Centre which is open daily. From the 13th to the late 17th century, Cranborne was the administrative centre of Chase Law (see Cranborne Chase, below).

Cranborne Chase (184, 195) 150,000 acres of open chalk grassland spread out over the counties of Dorset, Hampshire and Wiltshire, and bordered by the valleys of the Stour and Avon. Its many woods and small coppices are reminders of the great forest that once covered this whole region.

The Chase was a royal hunting ground until the early 17th century, when King James I granted the hunting rights to Robert Cecil, Earl of Salisbury. After being held briefly by Lord Shaftesbury they came into the possession of the Pitt-Rivers family of nearby Rushmore. Introduced to preserve the many deer that roamed the woodlands, the Chase Law gave wide, and seemingly unfair powers to the Lord of the Chase. For example he could legally prevent a landowner from uprooting the vegetation that grew on his land. In the 18th century farmers increasingly objected to these ancient laws, which prevented them from introducing modern farming techniques. They also complained that the Chase Law in fact fostered an atmosphere of lawlessness, and it was certainly true that the Chase was by that time popular with both poachers and smugglers, the latter finding it an ideal place to hide their contraband after bringing it inland from the coast. To try to put an end to the smuggling, the customs men enlisted the help of the army, but despite this the violence increased, and it was only in 1830 that the notorious Chase Law was finally abolished, and order slowly brought to the area.

Although the axe and plough may have altered

Quiet woodland on Cranborne Chase.

the physical appearance of the Chase they have not destroyed its sense of strange isolation, and the high country along the Dorset-Wiltshire border is especially beautiful. Here footpaths lead through gloriously wooded bottoms onto chalk hills, which provide superb views across the whole of the Chase.

Creech (195) (SY 91-83) *4m S Wareham*. Here in a delightful hollow beneath the densely wooded northern slope of Ridgeway Hill is Creech Grange (SY 91-82), a fine Elizabethan stone manor house extensively remodelled in the 18th and 19th centuries. Since 1686 it has belonged to the Bond family who gave their name to fashionable Bond Street in London. Nearby is a mid-19th century neo-Norman church, which includes a fine Norman chancel arch from Holme Priory. At the summit of nearby Ridgeway Hill (SY 91-81) stands Grange Arch, an 18th century folly built by Thomas Bond, and sometimes still referred to as 'Bond's Folly'. The arch and the acre of ground in which it stands were donated to the National Trust in 1942. (See also **Walk 10**.)

Dewlish (194) (SY 77-98) *7m NE Dorchester*. Prettily sited in the narrow valley of the Devil's Brook and with high chalkland country above it to the north and west, Dewlish village has several attractive stone houses and a flint and stone church heavily restored in 1852. To the south-west is Dewlish House, an early 18th century hipped-roofed building of pleasing simplicity. Here lived several generations of the Michel family including Sir John Michel, a distinguished soldier who fought in India, China and the Crimea and rose to the rank of Field-Marshal, and who is remembered by a massive and rather cumbersome monument in the church.

Dorchester (194) (SY 68-90). A busy but delightful market and county town built on the slopes of a spur between the Rivers Frome and Winterborne. It is the oldest town in Dorset, with a history stretching back to Roman times. The discovery of some of their military equipment suggests that there could have been a small Roman garrison here around the time when the Second Legion Augusta was engaged in subjugating southern Britain. Around AD 70 the vanquished tribe of the Durotriges were forcibly moved from the great earthworks of Maiden Castle ★ to the site of the present town where they established the civilian settlement of Durnovaria. Sadly very little remains of this once thriving Roman town. The wall which surrounded it was demolished in the Middle Ages, although a tiny fragment survives in West Walks Road. The line it

The Dorset Military Museum, Dorchester.

took is marked today by beautiful avenues of trees planted in the early 18th century and known as The Walks. In 1937 the foundations and mosaic floor of a substantial 4th century **Roman Town House (1**, were uncovered behind the County Hall, and this feature is normally open daily without charge. Situated to the south of the town, just off the A354, are **Maumbury Rings (2)**, a Neolithic henge monument redesigned by the Romans for use as an amphitheatre. In 1642 Parliamentary troops converted the arena into a fortified gun emplacement to guard the road to Weymouth. In the 18th century it was used for public executions. One of the most horrific occurred in 1705, when the 19-year-old murderess, Mary Channing, was strangled and then burnt in front of a crowd of 12,000. Several Roman cemeteries are known to exist in the vicinity, but the only one to have been extensively investigated lies at **Poundbury Camp (3)**, an Iron Age earthwork situated to the north-west of the town. From its north-west-corner may be seen an embankment running north-westwards, up the Frome Valley. This is the most evident remains of a long Roman aqueduct, which brought water to the city, probably from as far away as the hamlet of Notton (194) (SY 60-95), where it would have been fed from the River Frome.

Following the collapse of the Roman Empire, Dorchester's history, like that of Dark Age Britain as a whole, is uncertain, although the survival of the name 'Durnovaria' as 'Dornwaraceaster' in Saxon times indicates that a settlement of some kind must have persisted. In the 10th century it is likely that Edward the Elder fortified the town, incorporating it into the chain of defensive burghs built by Alfred the Great to protect Wessex against Viking and Danish attack. Despite this it is thought that Dorchester was plundered and burnt by the Danes, possibly by their king, Sweyn, in 1003.

In the Middle Ages it became a significant market town and also an important centre for the production of wool and beer. Few buildings survive from this period, for like many other Dorset towns Dorchester was devastated by a series of fires the most serious occurring in 1613, when 300 houses and 2 churches were burnt to the ground. The only church to escape these conflagrations was the **Church of St Peter (4)**, standing at the very centre of the town. It is an imposing battlemented structure, mainly 15th century, but with a late 12th century doorway reset inside the south porch. Under this porch is the tomb of the Reverend John White, a famous Puritan who founded the colony of Massachusetts in 1624. The Hardye Chapel within is named after Thomas Hardye, founder of the town's Grammar School in 1599. Thomas Hardy the author is also remembered here. His signed plan of the church reminds us that he first worked as an apprentice architect to John Hicks of Dorchester, and we may suppose that he helped in the restoration work of 1856. A fine bronze statue of the Dorset poet William Barnes stands before the south wall of the high pinnacled tower.

The town's other two churches, All Saints in East Street and Holy Trinity in High West Street, are both 19th century rebuilds, and are not of exceptional interest. However the visitor should try to see **St George's Church (5)**, situated in the suburb of Fordington. It is mostly Victorian and Edwardian Gothic, although the fine tower and part of the south aisle and porch are of 15th century origin. Above the south doorway is an exceptional Norman

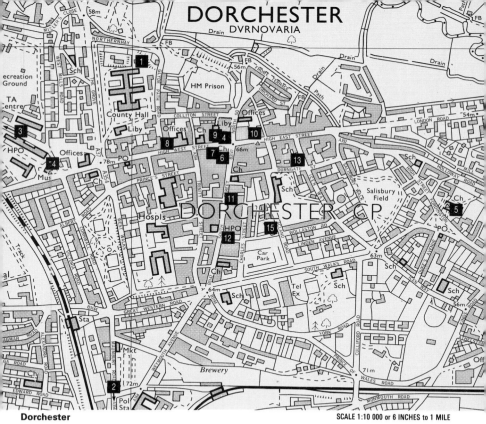

DORCHESTER
DVRNOVARIA

Dorchester

SCALE 1:10 000 or 6 INCHES to 1 MILE

1 Roman Town House
2 Maumbury Rings (off map to south)
3 Poundbury Camp (off map to north-west)
4 St Peter's Church
5 St George's Church
6 Antelope Hotel
7 Judge Jeffreys' Lodgings
8 Old Shire Hall
9 County Museum
10 King's Arms
11 Henchard's House
12 Napier Almshouses
13 Dinosaur Museum
14 Dorset Military Museum
15 Tourist Information Centre

tympanum showing St George slaying the Turks at the Battle of Antioch. The most exceptional item within is a unique Roman memorial stone of the first century, but note also the Elizabethan stone pulpit and the late 15th century font.

At the outbreak of the Civil war Dorchester declared for Parliament, and although over £15,000 was spent on elaborate defences, the town promptly fell to Royalist troops with hardly a shot being fired. Several years later it was recaptured by Lord Essex for Parliament. A bloodier episode in Dorchester's history occurred 41 years later, in 1685, when the infamous Judge Jeffreys tried the local followers of the ill-fated Monmouth Rebellion. The so-called 'Bloody Assize' was held in the great oak room of the **Antelope Hotel (6)** in South Street, and for the duration of his short visit to the town the Judge stayed in the 17th century half-timbered house now appropriately called *Judge Jeffreys' Lodgings (7)*. At the beginning of the trial Jeffreys informed the accused that they must '... be on their best behaviour and not waste the court's time by pleading their innocence.' The rebels appear to have heeded this advice, for all but 30 of the 312 on trial pleaded guilty. In all the judge condemned 74 Dorset men to death, including 29 of the 30 who entered pleas of 'not guilty'. Another

famous trial took place in the Crown Court Room of the **Old Shire Hall (8)** in 1834. Here the six Tolpuddle Martyrs were found guilty of conspiring to form a Trades Union (see Tolpuddle ★). The court was bought by the Trades Union Congress in 1955 and is preserved as a memorial to the Martyrs. *(Tel: Dorchester 65211)*

Dorchester's history is well-documented in **The County Museum (9)**, adjacent to St Peter's. This is one of the most outstanding town museums in the country, and the visitor is strongly advised to allow sufficient time to see its many treasures. The archaeological exhibition on the first floor is outstanding, but the glory of the museum is the 'Thomas Hardy and Other Dorset Worthies Collection' in the magnificent Main Hall. The principal item is the reconstruction of Thomas Hardy's study from Max Gate, his house outside Dorchester. It contains the largest collection in the world of his manuscripts, books and poems. *(Tel: Dorchester 62735.)*

No other place in Dorset is more closely associated with Hardy than Dorchester. He attended school here until his 16th birthday, when he was articled to one of his father's employers, the architect John Hicks. It is interesting to note that Hicks's office in South Street was next door to the

43

school kept by that other great literary figure of Dorset, the poet William Barnes. In 1874 Hardy and his wife, Emma Gifford, moved to Sturminster Newton, but in 1883 they returned to Dorchester to supervise the building of his house at Max Gate (not open to the public). Here he died on the 11th January, 1926. The splendid bronze figure of Hardy by Eric Kennington, at the 'Top o'Town' was unveiled in 1931. In his Wessex novels Dorchester is renamed 'Casterbridge', and as we might expect from its title figures prominently in *The Mayor of Casterbridge*. Readers of this book will recognise many of the landmarks that served as models for Hardy's fictitious creations. In East Street is *The King's Arms (10)*, where Thomas Henchard, the Mayor of Casterbridge, was first encountered. Ahead is the lofty tower of the 'grizzled' church of St Peter. The Antelope Hotel opposite is where the ill-fated Lucetta first met Henchard. *'Henchard's House' (11)*, a handsome Georgian building faced with 'dull red and grey old brick', now housing Barclay's Bank, is located further down South Street. The almshouses referred to in the novel are probably the *Napier Almshouses (12)*, erected by Sir Robert Napier in 1616 but much altered in the 19th century. More commonly known as 'Napper's Mite', these now provide a shopping and leisure area.

The *Dinosaur Museum (13)* in Icen Way is the only museum in Britain devoted to the animals which roamed our earth 65 million years ago *(tel: Dorchester 69880)*. Housed in the monumental Victorian gatehouse of the former Dorchester barracks is the *Dorset Military Museum (14)*, which records the long and proud history of the Dorset Regiment (the Devonshire and Dorset Regiment since 1958) *(tel: Dorchester 64066)*. The *Tourist information Centre (15)* is situated just off Acland Road. *(Tel: Dorchester 67992.)*

Dorset Coast Footpath (193, 194, 195) This waymarked footpath is the the shortest of the four sections of the South-West Peninsula Coast Path, which itself stretches from Dorset around to Minehead in Somerset. The Dorset section runs for 72 miles, from Poole Harbour in the east to Lyme Regis in the west, and passes over some of the south country's most dramatic and varied coastal scenery. Indeed the whole of the path, except for the disappointing urban area around Weymouth, is in the Dorset 'Area of Outstanding Natural Beauty'. To avoid Weymouth, walkers should use the far more interesting inland route between Osmington Mills ★ and West Bexington ★ (see Landranger Sheet 194).

Please remember that all Dorset cliffs are dangerous from above and below and keep away from caves and quarry faces.

Durdle Door (194) (SY 80-80) *10m SW Wareham.* Massive rock archway situated on the western side of the Durdle promontory. Geologically the promontory consists of near vertical Portland and Purbeck rock strata, joined to the mainland by a narrow neck of Wealden clay. The sea will eventually breach the softer Wealden clays and transform the promontory into an island. There are beautiful shingle beaches on either side of the headland, but swimmers should not venture too far out, as there are strong tidal currents here. This may be reached by taking the Dorset Coast Path from Lulworth

Durdle Door.

Cove ★, but the nearest access is from the car park beyond the large caravan site to the immediate north-east of Durdle Door itself. (See map on Page 54).

Durlston Country Park (195) (SZ 03-77) *1m S Swanage.* This 261-acre Country Park encloses an area of unspoilt coastland at the south-eastern tip of the Isle of Purbeck. It includes 19th-century Durlston Castle (now a restaurant) and the Great Globe, a massive structure of Portland stone erected in 1887. An Information Centre provides details of three separate waymarked walks, and leaflets are available on the history of the Park and its wildlife, which include many species of sea birds and butterfly. Cut into the cliffs are the Tilly Whim Caves, former quarries much used by smugglers in the 18th century. Because of their unsafe condition these vast rock caverns are sadly no longer open to the public. (See map on Page 76).

East Chelborough (194) (ST 55-05) *15m NW Dorchester.* The church of this diminutive place stands in secluded woodland over a mile away, and is reached via a narrow twisting lane leading to Lewcombe Manor. It was built in the 16th century and refashioned in the early 18th century, and must be one of the smallest churches in England. Motte and bailey earthworks on Castle Hill to the south suggest that a castle once crowned the summit, but nothing is known of its history.

East Lulworth (194) (SY 86-82) *5m SW Wareham.* Prettily sited with downs before and woods behind, less than a mile inland from the coast, this village is dominated by a castle which although convincingly castle-like, was always used as a country residence and not a fortress. Built by the third Viscount Bindon at the beginning of the 17th century, it is a tall, square battlemented block with substantial round towers at each corner. In 1641 it was sold to Humphrey Weld and remained in the possession of his descendants until it was made uninhabitable by a fire in 1929. Because it is still in an unsafe condition, there is no public access, but it can be viewed from a distance. In the landscaped gardens are two churches; the Parish Church and the Catholic chapel of the Weld family. Though the church of St Andrew has a handsome 15th century pyramidal tower, it is the Catholic chapel which is the more interesting, for it was the first to be built in

England after the Reformation. King George III allowed the Weld family to construct the chapel on condition it did not resemble a church, hence its unusual style; a 'Pantheon in miniature', as the novelist Fanny Burney once called it. Inside, white Purbeck columns support galleries in three of the four apses and a great central dome is painted as a sky with clouds.

When the park around the castle was extended, part of the old village was demolished and replaced by thatched estate cottages, grouped loosely and informally a short distance away. Monastery Farm to the south incorporates buildings put up by Thomas Weld in 1795 for Trappist monks escaping from the French Revolution. Drive east, subject to the opening arrangements for the road through the Lulworth Ranges (see Tyneham ★), to the car park and picnic site at the summit of Povington Hill (SY 88-81). Then, again subject to restrictions, walk south-westwards until you reach Flowers Barrow Fort (SY 86-80), an Iron Age earthwork probably constructed by Belgic invaders who had landed earlier at Lulworth Cove.

East Stour (183) (ST 79-22) *4½m W Shaftesbury*. As the name suggests this scattered village lies to the east of the River Stour along the main Shaftesbury to Sherborne road. Church Farm stands on the site of an old manor house in which the novelist Henry Fielding lived with his first wife, a young lady from Salisbury. He inherited the house from his mother in the 1730s, and he spent three very happy years here before his profligate habits forced him to move penniless to London, where he soon embarked upon his career as a writer. Adjoining the farm is the church, rebuilt in neo-Norman style in 1842, with an interesting Norman font, salvaged from the earlier building.

Edmondsham (195) (SU 06-11) *11m NE Wimborne Minster*. Secluded hamlet situated in a lush wooded hollow at the head of a small valley, and with a most unusual Elizabethan house with Georgian wings. Though now rendered this wonderfully tall and compact house was built of brick. The house and large garden are open only on Bank Holidays and Easter Sundays, but the garden is open more frequently *(tel: Cranborne 207)*.

Eggardon Camp (194) (SY 54-94) *10m W Dorchester*. A fine Iron Age earthwork spectacularly sited upon a high windswept ridge of the Dorset uplands. There are commanding views in all directions but the outlook is especially magnificent to the south-west towards the sea by Golden Cap ★, and to the north-west towards the hills around Beaminster. Note the impressive south-eastern entrance and the many small depressions within; the remains of pits probably used for storage. There is a useful car park and picnic site at Shatcombe Lane, not far to the east (see also **Tour 2**). (See map on Page 66).

Evershot (194) (ST 57-04) *14m NW Dorchester*. This is perched attractively on the slopes of a well-wooded spur, and at 700 feet above sea-level, is the second highest village in Dorset. It is a compact but surprisingly large village possessing shops, a bakery, hotel, school and doctors' surgery. The raised walkway, the street-lighting, and the bow windows of the grey-stone houses are 19th century additions, probably constructed at about the same time as the opening of a new railway station at Holywell, a mile to the east. The church is of the 15th and 19th centuries, and has a tower with a strange stair turret culminating in a small stone spire. Within there is a very fine brass portrait of William Grey, rector here in the early 16th century. Nearby is the Acorn Inn, renamed the Sow and Acorn in Hardy's novel *Tess of the d'Urbervilles*. Melbury Gate at the other end of the village leads to Melbury House ★, for many generations home of the Strangways, one of Dorset's most illustrious families. Sitting atop the gate piers are statues of two extremely docile and friendly-looking lions. The village lies at the centre of a network of paths making it an extremely good base for walking. If possible walk north to Melbury Osmond ★, passing through the attractive grounds of Melbury House (see **Walk 3**).

Eype (193) (SY 44-91) *2m SW Bridport*. Lies on the eastern slopes of a steep coombe a few hundred yards from where a tiny stream mysteriously disappears into beach shingle at Eype's Mouth. The Victorian church stands on high ground overlooking the hamlet, but is not of great interest. The car park at Eype's Mouth allows for the exploration of the surrounding area on foot, and there are good walks along the cliff tops and onto bracken-covered Eype Down to the north-west. Almost the entire stretch of coastline from here to Charmouth is owned by the National Trust, including the two highest cliffs in southern England, Golden Cap ★ and Thorncombe Beacon.

Farnham (184) (ST 95-15) *8m NE Blandford Forum*. One of the most attractive of the Cranborne Chase villages, with many picturesque, white-washed thatched cottages lining its long main street. On a hillside stands the greensand and flint church, 12th century in origin but extensively remodelled in 1886. Close to the church entrance is a charming well, sheltered by a thatched lychgate. The Museum Hotel recalls the famous museum established here by the eminent 19th century archaeologist General Pitt-Rivers. Housed in a building to the south of the village it contained a great variety of prehistoric and medieval exhibits including articles excavated from the Romano-British settlement at nearby Woodcutts. The museum has been closed for some years, but many of its former contents may be seen at either the Salisbury Museum or the Pitt-Rivers Museum at Oxford.

Fiddleford (194) (ST 80-13) *7m NE Blandford Forum*. Lying on a quiet spur road off the main A357 this scattered hamlet has a splendid mill house and an old disused mill exquisitely situated besides the meandering River Stour. Fiddleford Mill is part of a medieval hall, built in the late 14th century for William Latimer, sheriff of Somerset and Dorset in 1374 and 1380, and altered in the 16th century. The interior, recently restored by English Heritage and open to the public, is considered to be one of the finest of its type in the county; the elaborate open timber roofs are particularly spectacular. An inscription dated 1566 on the Mill House is an exhortation to the miller. A footpath from the mill complex passes along a catwalk above the giant iron machinery used to control the flow of water from the mill pond into the Stour. It then leads through delightful meadowland to Sturminster Newton ★ — in the summer months, a walk not to be missed.

Fifehead Magdalen (183) (ST 78-21) *6m W Shaftesbury off A30.* Prosperous place on the slopes of a tree-covered hill overlooking the Stour Valley. The church of St Mary Magdalen is of 14th century origin except for the north chapel which was added in the mid-18th century, and which contains a splendid wall monument to Sir Richard Newman and his family. Walk south from here across the River Stour to Marnhull.

Fifehead Neville (194) (ST 76-10) *8½m NW Blandford Forum.* Small hamlet in watery country of the Blackmoor Vale. The churchyard of All Saints Church is dominated by giant yew trees and a massive 18th century table tomb, or mausoleum, to the Brune family. Inside the church a memorial to Robert Reyves (1658) tells us that he was 'a sincere lover of the royal family, for which he suffered much in the time of rebellious persecution' (the Civil War). Where the road fords the River Divelish also stands a lovely old stone pack-horse bridge, its wooden handrails painted white.

Fleet (194) (SY 63-80) *3m NW Weymouth.* Surrounded by trees this minute place is delightfully situated on low ground to the east of Chesil Beach ★. The elegant church, built in 1829 at the expense of the vicar, John Gould, has a beautifully decorated chancel ceiling. See also the excellent monument to John Gould, this vicar's son. East Fleet to the south was once much larger but during an awesome storm in 1824 the sea breached Chesil Bank and swept away many of the thatched cottages and all but the chancel of the old church. On the south wall of this tiny ivy-covered building is a brass plaque commemorating the writer John Meade Faulkner, for this place is much associated with his famous smuggling novel *Moonfleet*. The Mohun family, who play an important role in the book, are remembered by two fine brass plaques in the chancel and beneath the church is the family vault which really does have a secret passage, though we can only speculate on its possible use by smugglers, as it was so in *Moonfleet*. Walk north-west to the Moonfleet Hotel, parts of which date back to the early 17th century, and which was reputedly built by the Mohuns.

Folke (194) (ST 65-13) *3m SE Sherborne.* Small hamlet in quiet country between the A352 and A3030, with several lovely old stone houses dating from the 17th century. St Lawrence's Church was rebuilt in 1628 and is a rare and interesting example of Jacobean Gothic. Many of the interior fittings are contemporary, including two oak screens, oak bench ends and communion rail.

Fontmell Magna (183) (ST 86-16) *8m N Blandford Forum.* Referred to as 'Funtmell' in the oldest surviving West Saxon Charter, this large village lies on the lower road between Blandford and Shaftesbury, beneath a steep chalk ridge bordering Cranborne Chase. Fontmell Brook flows clear and strong through here and once provided power not only for three mills, but also for a brewery and a foundry. A thriving pottery now exists in the old brewery

Summer grazing on Fontmell Down.

building *(tel: Fontmell Magna 811597).* The striking feature of the large Victorian church is the parapet of solid quatrefoils running right round the roof. A yellow stone in the graveyard reminds us of Lt. Philip Salkheld, posthumously awarded the Victoria Cross for bravery shown while leading the group of men who blew up the Kashmir Gate in the siege of Delhi in 1857. Walk east through Longcombe Bottom onto Fontmell Down (ST 88-18), part of a 280-acre stretch of glorious chalk downland owned by the National Trust, and famous for its flora and butterflies and its wonderful views out over the Blackmoor Vale.

Forde Abbey (193) (ST 35-05) *11m N Lyme Regis.* Exquisite battlemented and towered house of golden Ham Hill stone standing in picturesque grounds on the Dorset side of the River Axe. This Cistercian Abbey was founded in the 12th century with an abbot and eleven monks. At the Dissolution in 1539 the church and the southern half of the cloisters were destroyed, but the remaining abbey buildings were spared, and in 1649 they were bought by Edmund Prideaux, Attorney General to Oliver Cromwell, who converted them into a private residence. Prideaux's son, another Edmund, was imprisoned in the Tower of London for entertaining the Duke of Monmouth here during his first and perfectly legal visit to England in 1680. Between 1815 and 1818 the house was rented by the great philosopher, Jeremy Bentham.

The house is mainly of the 16th and 17th century but the chapel, originally the chapter house, was built in the mid-12th century. The abbot at this time was Earl Baldwin of Exeter, who succeeded Thomas à Becket as Archbishop of Canterbury and died while on crusade with Richard the Lionheart. The sumptuous Great Hall and magnificently detailed gatehouse were constructed in the early-16th century by the last Abbot, Thomas Chard. In the mid-17th century Prideaux remodelled the existing buildings and created a large saloon. Here may be seen some fine Mortlake Tapestries, based on the cartoons drawn by Raphael for Pope Leo X, and depicting the Acts of the Apostles. Note also the superb woodwork and plasterwork in the dining-room and drawing-room. All this rich grandeur lies in a garden of outstanding quality. *(Tel: South Chard 20231.)*

Frampton (194) (SY 62-95) *5m NW Dorchester.* Unspoilt main road village with a late 17th century church which has a remarkable, perhaps unique, west tower, complete with two tiers of eight Tuscan columns, which act as corner buttresses. Inside this exceptionally wide church are many handsome memorials to the Browne family, the finest of which remembers Robert Browne, builder of the bizarre tower. He also built Frampton Court, the residence of the Browne family until the mid-19th century, when it passed through marriage to Thomas Sheridan, son of the playwright. His sister, Caroline Norton, became friendly with the Dorset dialect

Cottage near the church, at Frampton.

poet, William Barnes, and through her association with London's high society, helped to spread his fame. Regrettably the house was demolished in 1935. The village houses, many of which are thatched, stand on the north side of the road, those on the south side having been demolished and replaced by a belt of trees by the Lord of the Manor in 1840.

Frome St Quintin (194) (ST 59-02) *13m NW Dorchester*. Here on the eastern slopes of the upper Frome valley are a few houses and a church which suffered a disastrous restoration in 1879. Across the valley is Chantmarle House, an attractive early 17th century stone building constructed in the Tudor style by Sir John Strode of Parnham ★. In the 1920s St John Hornby printed many excellent books here at his Ashendene Press. The house is now a Police Training College, but may be visited by appointment. *(Tel: Evershot 391.)* There is a good walk north from here to Evershot ★.

Gillingham (183) (ST 80-26) *4m NW Shaftesbury*. Lying in quiet and undramatic country beside the River Stour, Gillingham is a sprawling, rather featureless town, with only a few buildings of architectural merit. In medieval times the town was surrounded by a large Royal Forest, and on the eastern outskirts, at King's Court, there are the earthwork remains of a royal hunting lodge.

In the 18th century Gillingham became a minor centre for the throwing and manufacture of silk, and there are several houses surviving from this prosperous period. However it is sad to record that the town's finest 18th century building, the three-storey stone silk mill in the centre of town, was recently gutted by fire. Items connected with the town's silk industry can be seen in the excellent little museum in Church Walk *(tel: Gillingham 2173)*. The church, surprisingly large for such a town, has a 14th century chancel, but otherwise is 19th and 20th century. The interior is not of outstanding interest, having been swept of all medieval ornamentation by the Victorian restorers. However it retains some 15th century bench-ends with carvings of poppy heads, a few 18th century box pews and several pleasant monuments.

Glanvilles Wootton (194) (ST 67-08) *15m N Dorchester*. Well spread-out village lying at the southern edge of the Blackmoor Vale. Its church was badly restored by the Victorians, although the outstanding mid-14th century south chapel was spared. Note the many pieces of medieval painted glass in its south windows, the 14th century effigy of a civilian and several interesting wall monuments. Walk south-east below Dungeon hill, topped by a small unexcavated earthwork.

Godmanstone (194) (SY 66-97) *5m N Dorchester*. Attractive village nestling in the narrow valley of the River Cerne astride the A352. Its most interesting building is the Smith's Arms Inn, a delightful 17th century single-storey thatched building which claims to be the smallest tavern in the country; its one tiny bar measures just twenty foot by ten. It received its licence in 1665 from King Charles II, who stopped here to have his horse reshod while out hunting. The blacksmith was unable to comply with the King's request for a drink because he did not possess a licence, whereupon the king immediately granted him one. The largely 15th century church has a fine Norman chancel arch, and several charming mid-19th century wall monuments. If possible try to walk north to Cerne Abbas, up the east side of the Cerne Valley.

Golden Cap (NT) (193) (SY 40-92) *4m E Lyme Regis*. At 626 feet above sea level this dramatic cliff is the highest point along the entire south coast. Its unmistakable flat summit is covered by a layer of golden sandstone, which contrasts sharply with its sombre grey cliff-face. The views from the top are exhilarating, especially from the western end of the plateau which overlooks the lovely St. Gabriel's Valley. Here one can also peer down at the sloping and often jagged cliff-face. Owing to sea erosion it is estimated that these cliffs are retreating inland at the rate of about three feet a year.

Golden Cap is the centre of a complex of National Trust properties, which in total covers some 2,000 acres of farmland, woodland, cliff, undercliff and gorse-covered common, extending along seven miles of coast between Lyme Regis and Eype's Mouth. The many signposted footpaths crossing the area make it ideal walking country. The best car park is at Stonebarrow Hill (SY 38-93), which is reached by a minor road running eastwards from Charmouth ★.

Gussage All Saints (195) (SU 00-10) *9½m NE Blandford Forum*. A rambling place situated in a shallow chalk valley in the heart of Cranborne Chase ★. Standing boldly on the valley slope at the western end of the village is All Saints Church, a large well-proportioned building which, apart from its Victorian chancel, dates from the 14th century. The most outstanding feature within is an ornately carved 14th century Easter Sepulchre, which was used to house the Blessed Sacrament from Good Friday to Easter Sunday. It is one of only two such recesses to survive in Dorset; the other can be seen in Tarrant Hinton ★ church.

Gussage St Andrew (195) (ST 97-14) *7m NE Blandford Forum.* Diminutive hamlet lying just off the main A354, at the head of the Gussage valley. Behind the large farmhouse is the church of St Andrew, a beautifully simple flint building of the 12th and 13th centuries, which was originally the chapel of a nunnery founded by the Abbess of Shaftesbury. Remains of late 13th century wall paintings depict such scenes as 'The Betrayal of Christ', 'The Crucifixion' and 'The Suicide of Judas'. Note also the 12th century font and the plain Jacobean pulpit.

Gussage St Michael (195) (ST 98-11) *8m NE Blandford Forum.* Situated in a well-wooded part of the Gussage valley this village has a church which displays a curious mixture of styles; the tower is Norman, the arcades Early English, the aisles Perpendicular and the chancel Victorian. Among the interior fittings are a late-Norman font and a fine Jacobean oak tower-ladder.

A path north leads onto Gussage Hill, where there are the earthwork remains of a Celtic farmstead. These are bisected by the two parallel banks of the Dorset Cursus, the longest known Neolithic cursus in Britain (see also Pentridge ★). The course of Ackling Dyke ★ runs just to the east, and it is possible to walk north along it to the Bronze Age barrow complex on Oakley Down (see also Pentridge ★).

Halstock (194) (ST 53-08) *7m SW Sherborne.* Set in quiet country on the western edge of the Blackmoor Vale, this scattered village has a 15th century church which was rebuilt to the designs of A.W. Pugin in 1845-6. The sign of the Quiet Woman Inn, showing a woman with her head under her arm, recalls the ancient story of St Juthware, a local girl who was beheaded by her jealous stepbrother. Lifting up her severed head, Juthware walked to the church, where she placed it on the altar before collapsing. In about 1080 her remains were transferred from the church to the cathedral at Sherborne ★.

Hambledon Hill (194) (ST 84-12) *5m NW Blandford Forum.* Is there a more impressively sited Iron Age hill settlement in southern England? Its massive triple ramparts, 40 to 50 feet high in places, were carved from the soil of a noble chalk hill rising 623 feet, and commanding sweeping views over the Stour Valley. It seems likely that this fort was not besieged by the Romans, but that the occupants surrendered peacefully after seeing how easily the 2nd Augusta Legion captured Hod Hill ★, the settlement just to the south-east. Many centuries later during the Civil War, the hill was the scene of a skirmish between 50 Cromwellian troops and 2,000 peasants known as the Clubmen. These men supported neither the King nor Parliament, but demanded that both sides should stop plundering their land. However the ill-armed locals were no match for the professional dragoons, and 12 were killed, 300 taken prisoner and the rest put to flight. Contrary to popular belief there is regrettably no firm evidence to suggest that General James Wolfe trained his troops on the hill for the assault on Quebec in 1759.

To the south-east of the ramparts are the barely visible remains of a Neolithic causeway camp.

There are steep paths up the hill from Child Okeford and Iwerne Courtney ★, and it is also possible to walk south to Little Hanford, passing through one of the largest yew woods in Europe.

Hammoon (194) (ST 81-14) *2m E Sturminster Newton.* This quiet hamlet lies in meadowland besides the River Stour, and once belonged to the manor of William de Mohun, who fought alongside William the Conqueror at the battle of Hastings. The church is mostly 13th century, although the bell turret is an unusual Victorian addition. The fine 15th century stone reredos was uncovered in a London scrap-yard in 1946. See also the attractively panelled timber roof and the oak pulpit of 1635. Overlooking the church is Hammoon Manor, a beautiful low thatched house dating from the early 16th century, with a striking classical porch added in the 1600s.

Hardy Monument (NT) (194) (SY 61-87) *6m W Dorchester.* Erected in 1844 to commemorate Nelson's friend, Admiral Sir Thomas Hardy, this 70-foot high, octagonal tower stands on the summit of Blackdown Hill, and is a prominent landmark from many points in central Dorset. It has been likened to 'a factory chimney with a crinoline', 'a chess pawn' and 'a pepper mill', but we prefer Sir Frederick Treves's description of it as bearing 'a strange resemblance to a telephone receiver placed on end' — he was writing in the early 20th century, when telephones were of the 'candlestick' variety. The views from here are magnificent, especially towards the coast. Our **Walk 5** starts from the car park here and there is also a good walk south over the bracken-covered hill to Portesham ★, early home of Admiral Hardy.

Hazelbury Bryan (194) (ST 74-08) *11m W Blandford Forum.* A scattered parish standing on small hills standing in the Blackmoor Vale, with an interesting church lying on a hillside well to the south-west. Its 15th century stone tower is one of the finest in the Vale, and within are some splendid old roofs with moulded beams. The 12th century font with its attractive late 17th century cover is also worthy of note, as are the 18th century canopied pulpit and the fragments of ancient glass in the north windows. This church was beautifully restored in 1935 by that most sensitive of architects, Sir Charles Nicholson.

Hengistbury Head (195) (SZ 17-90) *2½m S Christchurch.* A long headland of shingle situated on the south side of Christchurch Harbour. The high sandy promontory commands superb views of the Isle of Wight, as well as Christchurch and Bournemouth Bays. In the Iron Age the headland was fortified, and a double rampart and ditch dating from this period can be seen at the western end. The discovery of pre-Roman coins and pottery of continental origin suggest that there was a busy trading port here in the centuries preceding the Roman occupation. The water-filled pits behind the head are the remains of 18th century ironstone quarries, the ironstone being used in the construction of naval ships at Buckler's Hard in Hampshire. A quaint little miniature passenger railway runs from the car park near the Double Dykes to the Head, but many visitors may prefer to walk here.

Hengistbury Head.

Hermitage (194) (ST 64-07) *7m S Sherborne.* Described as a 'Rip Van Winkle village' by Sir Frederick Treves, this sleepy little settlement lies on sloping ground at the foot of High Stoy, a magnificently wooded hill over 800 feet above sea level. The Augustinian hermitage from which it takes its name, was abandoned as long ago as 1460. Standing at the end of a lane is St Mary's church, of 17th century appearance but in fact built at the turn of the 19th century. There is a charming bellcote with stone ball on top, but the interior has been badly refurbished and is not of great interest to visitors.

Highcliffe (195) (SZ 20-93) *3m E Christchurch.* A pleasant residential area not far from the Hampshire border. There is a good beach here with car park and cafeteria. This is backed by cliffs on whose western boundary are the remains of 19th century Highcliffe Castle. The castle grounds, including the Steamer Point Woodland, with its wealth of wildlife and a picnic area, are open to the public and provide pleasant walks and fine views out over the sea to the Isle of Wight and the Purbeck Hills.

Higher Bockhampton (Hardy's Cottage) (NT) (194) (SY 72-92) *2m E Dorchester.* 'It faces west, and round the back and sides high beeches, bending, hang a veil of boughs, and sweep against the roof.' So wrote Thomas Hardy of the picturesque thatched cottage where he was born and spent his early years. It stands at the very end of a leafy lane, almost enveloped by the dark gloom of Puddletown Forest ★. How such a position must have inspired the imaginative Hardy!

The simple two-storey cottage was built by Hardy's great-grandfather in 1800. It is similar in style to other cottages of the period, though there is a narrow opening in the porch said to have been inserted to allow Hardy's grandfather, who appears to have indulged in a spot of brandy-smuggling from time to time, to keep a watch for excisemen. The downstairs accommodation comprises three living rooms and a small office from which Hardy's father conducted his building business. Upstairs are the three bedrooms, all with low-beamed ceilings. Hardy was born in the middle bedroom on the night of the 2nd June 1840, and it was here, at a desk by the window, that he was later to write *Under the Greenwood Tree* and *Far from the Madding Crowd*. The grim granite memorial stone behind the cottage was erected by American admirers in 1932.

The best way to reach the cottage is along the lovely woodland path from the nearby car park. This path is one of a number of Nature Trails passing through Puddletown Forest ★. There is also a picnic area here. *(Tel: Dorchester 62366.)* (See map on Page 66).

Hilfield (194) (ST 63-05) *13m NW Dorchester.* Minute place looking northwards out over the Blackmoor Vale, and backed by the steep wooded slopes of Telegraph Hill. Standing on open ground away from its few houses is the attractive little church of St Nicholas, 15th century in origin but much renewed in 1848. The splendid set of bench-ends, depicting scenes from the New Testament, are said to have come from Cerne Abbey, although they are of continental design. Their date poses a problem. Are they medieval or could they have been carved by a skilled 19th century copyist? Walk south to the picnic site and viewpoint on Gore Hill.

Hilton Church.

Hilton (194) (ST 78-03) *7m SW Blandford Forum.* Superbly situated between two high spurs of Bulbarrow Hill ★ this beautiful, partly thatched village clusters round the high tower of its unexpectedly grand 15th century church. Though disastrously restored by the Victorians it still contains three treasures, all brought from nearby Milton Abbey after its dissolution: a splendid fan-vaulted south porch, a range of grand Perpendicular windows in the north aisle, and hanging in the tower, an interesting series of medieval panels with paintings of the Apostles. There is a good walk north onto Bulbarrow Hill ★.

Hinton St Mary (183) (ST 78-16) *10½m NW Blandford Forum.* This compact main road village is situated on high ground between the River Stour and one of its tributaries, Chivrick's Brook, and looks south towards Sturminster Newton ★. The church was rebuilt in 1846, although, as was so often the case, the medieval tower was allowed to remain. It contains a 12th century font, an attractive 18th century pulpit, and a good 17th century monument to Thomas Freke, builder of the adjoining manor house. The lovely tithe barn, converted into a private theatre in 1929, was formerly part of a nunnery that stood on the manor site. In 1963 a large Roman mosaic pavement dating from the late-4th century was discovered beside the village forge.

Hod Hill (NT) (194) (ST 85-10) *3½m NW Blandford Forum.* Here is yet another hill settlement, this one on the summit of a glorious chalk hill with extensive views over the River Stour and its verdant hinterland. It is the largest of the Dorset Iron Age settlements, covering an area of 54 acres, and with its companion Hambledon Hill, protected the important Stour Valley.

Despite its seemingly impregnable position, this fort was one of the first to fall to the 2nd Augusta Legion, probably from concentrated ballista fire and not a direct assault. After its capture the Romans immediately began to construct a fort of their own in the north-west corner. It covered an area of 11 acres and provided accommodation for both infantry and cavalry (approximately 700 men and 250 horses). Evidence suggests that the Roman period of occupation was almost certainly confined to the first few years of the Roman conquest, from around AD43 to AD51. None of the Roman buildings remain but the defensive earthworks with their two entrances are clearly visible.

Holt (195) (SU 02-03) *3m N Wimborne Minster.* Small village with a modest mid-19th century brick-built church, and a Craft Centre in a converted dairy farm, which also incorporates a Brass Rubbing Centre. Restaurant picnic area and children's play area *(tel: 0202 887211).* Less than two miles to the east there is a pleasant forest walk (195) (SU 04-03) which starts just to the south of Higher Row (see also **Tour 7**).

Holwell (194) (ST 70-11) *6m SE Sherborne.* Here, at the end of an isolated cul-de-sac in pastoral country of the Blackmoor Vale, is a church, an 18th century vicarage, and a pleasant group of thatched stone cottages. The brown-stoned church is a pleasing example of local 15th century design. Note the rectangular stair projection of the west tower and the horrific gargoyles on the battlemented aisles. The interior is marred by cemented walls, but see the handsome panelled roofs and the attractively carved capitals of the arcade columns. A path from the church leads north to Bishops Caundle.

Horton (195) (SU 03-07) *5m N Wimborne Minster.* The first building the visitor sees when approaching this compact Cranborne Chase village is Horton Tower, rising 120 feet above Horton Hill to the south. It was built in 1762 by Humphrey Sturt as a look-out for deer. Now a ruin, Richard Hale's description of it as resembling 'a Russian Vostock rocket, albeit ivy clad, ready on its launch pad' is very appropriate. In the village itself the church of St Wolfrida demands closer inspection. It is on the site of an old monastery and although much rebuilt in 1722, incorporates parts of the old priory church. Externally are the strange-looking pyramidal tower which catches the eye, while the most striking features within are the two exceptional 14th century effigies of Sir Giles de Braose and his wife. See also the monument to Henry Hastings, who died in 1650, aged 99. He was by all accounts a wonderfully eccentric character, who hunted both deer and the ladies with equal enthusiasm until well into his eighties.

Horton Heath (195) (SU 06-06) *6m NE Wimborne Minster.* It was here that the Duke of Monmouth was captured after the defeat of his rebel army at Sedgemoor in 1685. He was found dressed as a farm-hand cowering in a ditch beside an ash tree by a militia man, Henry Perkin, who had been alerted to his whereabouts by an old woman named Amy Farrant. Monmouth's disguise as a shepherd might have been more convincing had he not been carrying The Order of the Garter, cosmetic recipes, a purse, and an expensive watch. He was taken before the magistrate of Poole and then sent to the Tower, where he was beheaded on 15th July 1685. Unfortunately for the Duke his executioner Jack Ketch, was not particularly proficient at beheadings, being more used to the rope than the axe. His first swing missed the Duke's head altogether, and it was only after four further blows that his grisly task was finally accomplished.

The ash tree beneath which the Duke was found, died long ago, but in its place stands another ash, perhaps a 100 years old, and still known as 'Monmouth's Ash'.

Ibberton (194) (ST 78-07) *9m W Blandford Forum.* Perched upon the lower slopes of Ibberton Hill, the thatched and tiled houses of this peaceful little village look out across the pastoral country of the Blackmoor Vale. The church of St Eustace, one of only three in England to be dedicated to the canonized Roman general, Eustachius, stands in a striking position above the village. Saved from ruin at the beginning of this century, the walls of this mainly 15th century building still lean outwards. The pleasant interior contains fragments of pretty 15th century stained glass. A footpath near the church leads to the summit of Ibberton Hill, from which there are magnificent views of northern Dorset and southern Somerset. It is also possible to walk eastwards to Turnworth ★, passing the remains of two ancient cross-dykes.

Isle of Portland *(See Portland, Isle of.)*

Isle of Purbeck *(See Purbeck, Isle of.)*

Iwerne Courtney or Shroton (194) (ST 85-12) *5½m N Blandford Forum.* Attractive village situated besides the River Iwerne on a spur road which loops off from the main A350. In the Domesday Book it was known as Shroton ('Sheriffs town'), and even today the locals prefer to call it by this name. The famous Shroton Fair, the last of which was held just before the outbreak of the First World War, attracted folk from all over north Dorset, and rivalled that held at Woodbury Hill near Bere Regis. The Perpendicular church was much enlarged and altered by Sir Thomas Freke in 1610, and there is a grandiose monument to him in the chapel. Note also the unusual terracotta reredos. In 1645 the church was converted into a temporary prison to hold some of the Clubmen, rebels who had been defeated by Cromwellian troops on nearby Hambledon Hill ★. Adjacent to the church is a substantial and very impressive 18th century thatched barn, while to the south is Ranston house, a much reduced 18th century building designed by the Bastard brothers of Blandford for Thomas Reyves. It is not open to the public.

A lane from the village leads north-westwards to Shroton Lines, the name recalling the fact that a large military tented camp was established here in 1754. The presence of Lieutenant-Colonel James Wolfe at this camp no doubt explains the unsubstantiated legend that Wolfe trained his troops on

Hambledon Hill ★ in preparation for the assault on Quebec's Heights of Abraham.

Iwerne Minster (194) (ST 86-14) *6½ m N Blandford Forum.* A sizeable village partly astride the main Blandford to Shaftesbury road. It has expanded greatly in the last few decades, but it still possesses a trim, well-ordered atmosphere, especially in the back lanes round St Mary's church. Although heavily restored in 1870 and again in 1880, St Mary's is a most interesting building, displaying work from the late-Norman period to the Renaissance. The 14th century tower is topped by one of the few medieval stone spires in the county, though it was much shortened during the 1870 restoration — the removed stones being used to repair the roads! The Norman north arcade is particularly impressive, as is the South chapel, built in 1880 by J.L. Pearson, the architect best known for the creation of Truro Cathedral. See also the memorial tablets to the Wolverton family, who lived at the large Victorian mansion designed by Alfred Waterhouse in the 1870s. This is now Clayesmore School, but it is possible to catch a glimpse of it from the footpath which runs through the grounds.

Jordan Hill (EH) (194) (SY 69-82) *2m NE Weymouth.* On this hill overlooking Weymouth Bay are the rectangular foundations of a small Roman building, dating from about the 4th century. Archaeologists believe it was a temple, for a cemetery was discovered just to the north and north-east. The best approach to the site is by a footpath from the A353 road.

Kimmeridge (195) (SY 91-79) *5m S Wareham.* Here is a tiny church and a few small stone-walled thatched cottages set against a splendid backdrop of steep hills from which there are magnificent views of Kimmeridge Bay and the immediate coastline. The village contains no buildings of note; the Norman church was badly restored by the Victorians, and it is best to head for the fascinating bay. This belongs to the estate of Smedmore House (see below), and a small toll has to be paid to gain access, although this also secures a parking place. The cliffs around the bay contain a type of rock known as Kimmeridge Clay, within which are thin seams of oil shale, of which the most famous is Blackstone. This was mined by the Romans to

Tower, above Kimmeridge Bay.

make ornaments and jewellery. The shale deposits were also used as a source of fuel known as 'Kimmeridge Coal', but 19th century schemes to exploit this commercially proved impractical; one project to export the fuel to Paris foundered because Parisians could not stand its pungent fumes. Of greater success has been the extraction of crude oil, which was discovered beneath the cliffs in 1959, and which is still pumped out by a 'nodding donkey' sited above the bay. The ruined Clavell's Tower on Hen Cliff was built in the early 1800's by the Reverend John Richards who adopted the name of Clavell when he inherited Smedmore House in 1817. In the late 19th century this tower was used as a look-out for the lifeboat station which was established here. Because of the black shale and its many seaweed-covered ledges, Kimmeridge Bay is not ideally suited for bathing. However, for those who like exploring, it is one of the most interesting places on the Dorset coast. It is also extremely popular with skin-divers, fossil hunters and sail-board enthusiasts.

Smedmore, splendidly situated in open country to the south-east of the village, is a 17th and 18th century manor house, with an interesting interior and a charming walled garden. It is still lived in by the family who built it. *(Tel: Corfe Castle 480717.)*

The Dorset Coast Path passes along the cliff tops above the bay, and it is possible to walk along it for a considerable distance in both directions. Particularly recommended is the walk eastwards from Clavell's Tower to Chapman's Pool.

Kingston (195) (SY 95-79) *5½m SE Wareham.* Situated high on a Purbeck ridge, with outstanding views of Corfe Castle to the north, this unpretentious, mainly 19th century stone village, is dominated by the high tower of St James's church. Built

Kimmeridge, Kimmeridge Bay and Smedmore House   SCALE 1:25 000 or 2½ INCHES to 1 MILE

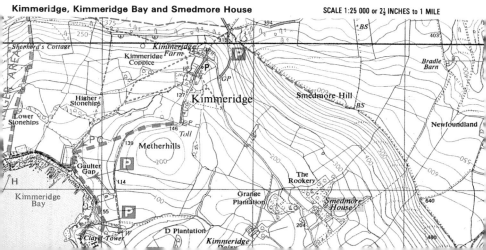

between 1873 and 1880 at a cost of £70,000, this impressive edifice was donated to the village by the Third Earl of Eldon, owner of nearby Encombe House. The architect was G.E. Street, perhaps best known for his work on London's Law Courts, who considered it 'quite my jolliest church'. The noble interior, with clustered black Purbeck marble pillars, stone-vaulted roofs and great west rose window is seen to best effect on a bright day. Note also the pulpit and high screen, both fashioned from wrought-iron, a material much beloved by Street. The village boasts another 19th century church, simpler in style though by no means small. Leave your car in the car park by the church and follow the rough track that leads to Chapman's Pool. A footpath from this track leads onto Kingston Down where there are well-preserved 'Celtic' fields covering about 150 acres.

Kingston Lacy (NT) (195) (ST 97-01) *1½m NW Wimborne Minster.* This splendid 17th century country house was bequeathed to the National Trust in 1981, along with a vast estate of 16,000 acres, which included Badbury Rings ★ and Corfe Castle ★. Almost in a state of ruin, the house was extensively restored, and was opened to the public in the spring of 1986. It was built in 1663-5 for Sir Ralph Bankes as a replacement for Corfe Castle, which had been slighted by Parliamentary troops during the Civil War. The designer was Sir Roger Pratt, and although extensively remodelled by Sir Charles Barry in the 1830's, is the most important surviving work of this distinguished 17th century architect. Barry's external alterations, which included refacing the house with Caen stone, lowering the front to turn the basement into the ground floor, and building huge chimneystacks at

the four corners, did not dramatically change the outside appearance of Pratt's original house.

Inside, however, Barry remodelled everything in Italianate style, in order to provide what was considered to be a suitable setting for the extensive collection of European works of art acquired by W.J. Bankes. Despite the relatively small area available, Barry managed to create a remarkably spacious and grand interior. Note especially the majestic hall with its sumptuous staircase of Carrara marble. In niches on the half-landing are life-size statues of Charles I, Sir John Bankes, and Lady Bankes, all by Baron Marochetti. The state rooms on the first floor are also extremely opulent and contain paintings by Raphael, Titian, Tintoretto, Rubens, Van Dyke, Velasquez, Murillo and Giorgione. The beautiful park is stocked with many lovely specimen trees, as well as a herd of fine Red Devon cattle. There is also an Egyptian obelisk, removed from the Island of Philea and placed here in 1827. *(Tel: Wimborne Minster 88342).*

Kingston Maurward (194) (SY 71-91) *2m E Dorchester off A35.* Tiny hamlet on rising ground close to the River Frome. Standing on an eminence in magnificently wooded grounds is Kingston Maurward House, the 'Knapwater House' of Thomas Hardy's novel *Desperate Remedies*. This stately mansion was built in 1720 for George Pitt, cousin of William Pitt the Elder. Originally constructed of red brick, it was recased in Portland ashlar after George III, in giving his opinion of the house, was heard to utter, 'only brick, Mr Pitt, only brick!'. Nearby is the Old Manor House, built in about 1591, and recently saved from dereliction. Both buildings are now part of the Dorset College of Agriculture, and are closed to visitors. However, the attractive gardens are

Kingston Lacy and Badbury Rings

SCALE 1:25 000 or 2½ INCHES to 1 MILE

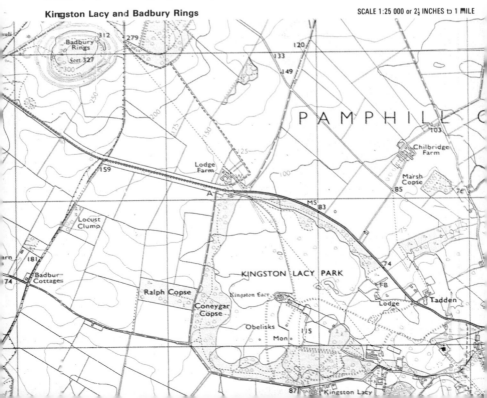

open on certain days of the year. *(For information telephone the Dorchester Tourist Information Office on Dorchester 67992.)*

Kington Magna (183) (ST 76-23) *7½m W Shaftesbury off A30*. Prettily sited on the steep western slopes of Stour Hill, this small village has a church with one of the best views in Dorset. It stands almost at the top of the hill, and looks out across the lush green pastures of the Blackmoor Vale. The church has a squat 15th century tower, but the rest is a 19th century rebuild, and is not of great interest to the visitor.

Knowlton (EH) (195) (SU 02-10) *7m N Wimborne Minster*. Just off the B3078 road, in the open downland country of Cranborne Chase ★, are three prehistoric henge monuments known as the Knowlton Circles (EH). Two of these circular enclosures have been badly damaged by ploughing, but the middle one is clearly discernible, and consists of a rampart over 100 metres across, with an internal ditch designed not so much to prevent invaders from entering, but if local legend is to be believed, to stop evil spirits from escaping outside. There are many other henge monuments in England, but none contain, as this one does, the ruins of a church. This little building dates from the 12th century, but it is likely that the site was used for Christian worship long before this time. Why was a church placed in the middle of this pagan monument? One theory suggests that it was built to exorcise the malignant spirits of the old gods. This objective does not appear to have been achieved for long, for in the 14th century most of the villagers almost

Knowlton Church and earthworks.

certainly perished in the Black Death, and with no community to serve, the church eventually fell into disrepair.

Langton Herring (194) (SY 61-82) *4m NW Weymouth off B3157*. Attractive stone-built village straggling down a well-wooded hill above the Fleet (see Chesil Beach ★). The picturesque Elm Tree Inn contains an old ship's mast (now a beam in the public bar), from which a dishonest fisherman was hung in 1780. The simple church was over-restored in the 19th century, but is worth visiting to see the Jacobean pulpit and altar rails. There is a pleasant walk south to the shores of the Fleet.

Langton Long Blandford (195) (ST 89-05) *½m E Blandford Forum*. Tiny hamlet hidden among trees on the northern bank of the River Stour, with a relatively large mid-Victorian church. It contains some interesting memorials, the oldest being a splendid triple brass to John Whitewood who died in 1457. Many of the others are of the Farquharson's, an ancient Scottish family who came to the village in the 18th century.

Langton Matravers (195) (SY 99-78) *1½m W Swanage*. This widespread village lies less than a mile from the sea, and consists of many charming stone and thatch cottages, once the homes of workers who laboured in the Purbeck quarries. The Coach House Museum is devoted to the Purbeck stone and marble industries, illustrating their growth from Roman times to the present day *(tel: Swanage 423168)*. Nearby is St George's church, rebuilt in 1876 and looking decidedly strange with its clerestory roof rising above its tower. There is a particularly fine walk south to Dancing Ledge, so named because at high-tide waves appear to dance as they crash over the limestone ledges (see **Walk 11**).

Leigh (194) (ST 61-08) *6m S Sherborne*. A large village which sprawls along a network of narrow lanes in gently undulating Blackmoor Vale country. The brownstone church has a sturdy Perpendicular tower, but the rest is largely the result of Victorian rebuilding. There are however some plain 16th century bench-ends. The fragmentary remains of the famous Leigh Miz-Maze can be seen in a field near here. It can be reached by one of the many footpaths which criss-cross the village.

Leweston (194) (ST 63-12) *3m S Sherborne*. Here on the top of a well-wooded hill in the Blackmoor Vale are a few houses, a late-18th century manor house, and an attractive Jacobean chapel, all looking across to the village of Leigh ★. The chapel escaped the over-enthusiasm of Victorian restorers and retains its original fixtures and fittings, including a good set of carved benches and a splendid two-decker pulpit.

Littlebredy (194) (SY 58-89) *7m W Dorchester*. Exceptionally picturesque place, beautifully situated in the deep green valley of the River Bride, between Warren Hill and Whatcombe Down, the latter being covered by a great number of ancient tumuli. These form part of the Poor Lot Barrow Cemetery, a magnificent group of 44 Bronze Age barrows. The village consists of some delightful thatched cottages, a Victorian church with a distinguished spire, and a few farm buildings adapted from an old Jacobean structure. Bridehead House, mainly 19th century and not particularly attractive, lies in a glorious landscaped park beside a large man-made lake. Walk south-eastwards to the Valley of the Stones, a remarkable glacial valley littered with hundreds of stones known as sarsens, with the remains of a 'Celtic' field system on its slopes. It is also possible to walk southwards up onto the downs overlooking Abbotsbury, to the delightfully named Grey Mare and her Colts, a chambered long barrow (SY 58-87).

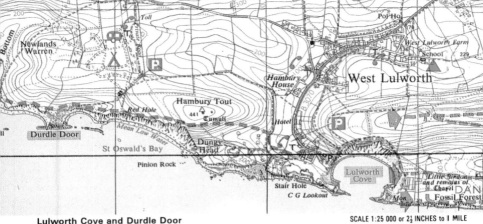

Lulworth Cove and Durdle Door

SCALE 1:25 000 or 2½ INCHES to 1 MILE

Loders (193,194) (SY 49-94) *2m E Bridport*. This small settlement of attractive yellow stoned cottages lies at the bottom of the close-sided valley of the River Asker, between Boarsbarrow Hill and Waddon Hill. In the 12th century the Monastery of St Mary de Montebourg in Normandy founded a Benedictine Priory here, and it is said that its Norman monks introduced cider-making into West Dorset. The priory was dissolved in 1411. The interesting church, unspoilt, despite extensive restoration, contains work from the 12th to the 15th century. Of especial interest is the two-storey battlemented porch with turret staircase. Features to note inside include a late 14th century tomb recess, known as an Easter Sepulchre; a 17th century wall painting; and a pulpit entered by a rood-loft staircase.

Long Bredy (194) (SY 56-90) *7m W Dorchester off A35*. Perched at the top of the main street of this long thin village is the church of St Peter's, 15th century in character but much restored in 1863. From the churchyard it is possible to spy Kingston Russell House, a distinctive rectangular mansion dating from the mid-17th century, with a classical west front added in the 1730s. Admiral Thomas Hardy, Nelson's 'Captain Hardy', was born in the house in 1769, and the noted historian J.L. Motley, author of the *The Rise of the Dutch Republic*, died here almost a hundred years later.

Lower Blandford St Mary (195) (ST 89-05) *(See Blandford St Mary ★)*

Lulworth Cove.

Lulworth Cove (194) (SY 82-79) *9m SW Wareham*. A much-visited, but exceptionally beautiful oyster-shaped cove, formed by the sea breaching through a weak joint of the hard Portland limestone cliffs and eroding away the softer rocks behind. Immediately to the west of it a new cove is in the process of formation at Stair Hole. Eventually it will join up with Lulworth Cove, and the promontory on the west side of its present entrance will become an island. Note how the rock strata have been violently contorted by immense movements in the earth's crust millions of years ago.

Today the cove is a delightful haven for yachts and other pleasure craft, but in the 18th and 19th centuries many of the boats anchoring here would have been involved in the lucrative smuggling trade. The caves in the cliffs above Mupe Rocks were probably used by the smugglers to store their contraband.

The cliff scenery in this area is quite spectacular, and it is strongly recommended that the visitor walk westwards along the Dorset Coast Path to Durdle Door ★. When the Army firing ranges are open (see Tyneham ★) the walk east to Mupe Bay should also be attempted. This walk passes Lulworth's famous Fossil Forest, which contains the petrified remains of tree stumps.

Lydlinch (194) (ST 74-13) *8m E Sherborne*. A small hamlet partially astride the Blandford to Sherborne road, and built on the slopes of a small hill, close to the confluence of the Rivers Caundle and Lydden. The 15th century tower of St Thomas à Becket holds a fine peal of five bells, remembered in a poem by William Barnes, which runs thus:

> *For Lydlinch bells are good for sound*
> *And liked by all the neighbours round.*

As a small boy Barnes lived just across the River Lydden at Bagber, well within earshot of the bells. It is possible to walk north to Stalbridge ★, passing Thornhill House, the 18th century home of the famous Dorset painter, Sir James Thornhill, who will always be remembered for his magnificent painted ceilings, especially that of the Royal Naval College, Greenwich. Also visible from the path is a tall thin obelisk, erected by Thornhill in 1727 to commemorate the accession of George II.

Lyme Regis (193) (SY 34-92). Sleepy seaside town beautifully situated on the western edge of Dorset, in a narrow valley carved out by the tiny River Lim. Today the town owes its living to the holiday trade, but it was once an important south coast port and a centre of woollen manufacture. The earliest settlement dates from about 774, when Cynewulf, King of the West Saxons, granted land here for the extraction of salt by boiling sea water. In 1279 Edward I made the town a borough and Regis was added to its name after that date. *The Cobb (1)* was probably here at this time. This great curving stone wall was constructed to make an artificial harbour for trading ships and to protect the town from the great storms that rolled in from the southwest. The Cobb not only made the town an important port but also earned the townsfolk renown as builders of such primitive jetties. In the 16th century they repaired the piers of Hastings and St Peter Port. In 1685 the Duke of Monmouth landed at the Cobb to begin his ill-fated attempt to remove King James II from the throne. *The Pilot Boat Inn (2)* occupies the site of an earlier inn where the Duke of Monmouth declared himself king, and *Monmouth House (3)* was where he spent his first night in England. After the revolt was crushed twelve Lyme men were hanged at the spot on the beach where the Duke came ashore, as a reward for their revolutionary fervour.

In the 16th and 17th centuries the town prospered, its ships carrying merchandise to places as far as Guinea and the West Indies. *The Tudor House Hotel* in Church Street is the only surviving building from this great period in Lyme's history. In the late 1600s, as larger ships were built which were unable to use the small harbour, the town's prosperity declined. Like Weymouth its decline was reversed in the 18th century by the sudden passion for sea-bathing. Two of the first people to come here for the sea air were the Earl of Chatham and his sickly son, the future Prime Minister, William Pitt the Younger. Its isolated position made it popular with those seeking a secluded resort, and it became especially fashionable with the middle classes recuperating from a too-hectic Bath Season. Many distinguished visitors came here. The writer Henry Fielding based the character of Sophie in *Tom Jones*, on Sarah Andrews, a lady from the town with whom he tried to elope. His insulting denunciation of her guardian can be seen in the museum. Lord Tennyson came to Lyme in 1874 to visit the novelist F.T. Palgrave, who lived in a house above the town. The American artist James Whistler spent eight weeks here in 1895, and had a studio above what is now the *Olde Tobacco Shop (4)*. However, the writer most associated with Lyme is Jane Austen. She stayed here with her family in 1803 and 1804. At the western end of Marine Parade is *'Jane's Garden' (5)*, marking the site of the house where she stayed and where she began writing *Persuasion*. In the novel Miss Austen uses the Cobb as the spot where the impetuous Louisa Musgrove has her famous fall. The Cobb also features prominently in *The French Lieutenant's Woman*, the novel by John Fowles, who lives in Lyme Regis.

Hemmed in by the hills the town has not been overdeveloped and it has retained the character of a

1 The Cobb
2 Pilot Boat Inn
3 Monmouth House
4 Olde Tobacco Shop
5 Jane's Garden

6 Guildhall & Tourist Information Centre
7 Museum & Art Gallery
8 Broad Ledge
9 St Michael's Church

10 Peek Memorial Chapel
11 Congregational Chapel
12 Belmont House
13 Umbrella Cottage
14 Ware Cliffs

Lyme Regis

SCALE 1:10 000 or 6 INCHES to 1 MILE

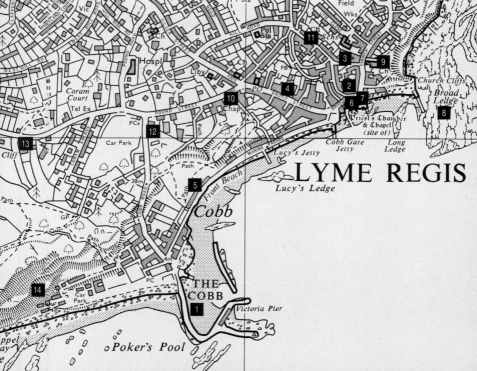

late Georgian resort. The centre lies a few hundred yards to the east of the Cobb, where the River Lim enters the sea. Grouped here are the 19th century **Guildhall (6)** and a Dutch-styled 20th century building with Victorian tower, which is **The Museum and Art Gallery (7)**. Inside there is a fine display of fossils, including one of an Ichthyosaraurus. See also the gruesome boarding spike on which the defeated rebels of the Monmouth uprising were displayed. **The Tourist Information Centre (6)** is in the Guildhall (tel: Lyme Regis 2138). Before moving up Church Street look at the massive **Sea Wall** behind the museum, built to prevent sea erosion. It is likely that medieval Lyme reached some further way into the sea, for records show that **Broad Ledge (8)**, now only visible at low tide, was once crowded with houses.

Standing proudly on a cliff-top on the east side of Church Street is **The Church of St Michael (9)**. It is not a very attractive church but has an interesting architectural history, for it is two churches in one, the earlier Norman church having been incorporated in the present early 16th century building. The main items of interest within are a fine Flemish tapestry representing the marriage of Henry VII to Elizabeth of York, and a memorial window to Mary Anning, the famous fossil collector of the early 19th century. Two other religious buildings worthy of note are the **Peek Memorial Chapel (10)** with splendid red and gold mosaic of Christ in Majesty above the altar, and the handsome Georgian-fronted **Congregational Chapel (11)** in Coombe Street. **Broad Street** is mainly Georgian and ascends into Pound Street, at the end of which stands **Belmont House (12)**, a most curious late 18th century dwelling elaborately decorated in Coade stone. It belonged to Mrs Eleanor Coade who gave her name to this artificial material which was widely used in many private and public buildings, including the Brighton Pavilion and St George's Chapel, Windsor. **Umbrella Cottage (13)**, with its quaint conically-shaped thatched roof, was originally a toll house. A footpath from this part of town leads to the beautifully wooded **Ware Cliffs (14)**, and beyond, more adventurously, to the Landslip, scene of several massive cliff subsidences (the greatest of which took place on Christmas Day, 1839), and now covered by dense undergrowth. Another footpath from the centre of the town follows the course of the River Lim to Uplyme, and passes some of the old stone mills which were once powered by this fast-flowing river.

Lytchett Minster (195) (SY 95-92) 4m NW Poole. Thomas Hardy rechristened this scattered collection of cottages and houses 'Flychett'. It used to lie on the main road but mercifully the traffic is now bypassed around its southern edge. It has two inns, the Bakers Arms, an attractive 18th century thatched building, and the unusually named St Peter's Finger. This was formerly known as St Peter ad Vincula (St Peter in Chains), and it was here that the tenants of the village paid their dues to the Lord of the Manor, normally on the Commemoration Day of St Peter. The church has a 15th century tower, but the rest was unfortunately rebuilt in the 19th century, and is not of great interest to the visitor.

Maiden Castle (EH) (194) (SY 66-88) 1½m SW Dorchester. 'It may be likened to an enormous, many limbed organism of an antediluvian time, lying lifeless, and covered with a thin green cloth, which hides its substance, while revealing its contour.' Thus wrote Thomas Hardy of this, one of the largest and most impressive hill-forts in Europe. Its gigantic earth ramparts, measuring over 60 feet in height, curve around the slopes of a low hill, enclosing an area of no less than 47 acres. Extensive excavations by Sir (then Dr) Mortimer Wheeler in the 1930s revealed that the fort was constructed between 350 BC and 75 BC, and superseded a Neolithic camp. It is likely that improvements in the complex defences were being made right up to the arrival of the Romans in Britain in AD 43. Wheeler has suggested that by this time the fort had a population of around four to five thousand people. The battle-hardened troops of the 2nd Augusta Legion swiftly subjugated the fort, though not before a short but bloody battle involving the death of scores of tribesmen, many of whom were buried

Maiden Castle ... one of Europe's most impressive hill-forts.

Maiden Castle

SCALE 1:25 000 or 2½ INCHES to 1 MILE

in a war cemetery discovered near the eastern gate. The fort continued to be occupied for several decades after the Roman invasion, until the inhabitants moved to the new Roman town at Dorchester. Towards the end of the 4th century a small pagan temple was built within the fort, together with a two-roomed house. Their foundations can be seen close to the eastern entrance. Many of the objects uncovered during the excavations are on display at the Dorchester County Museum. There is a good car park north-east of the western entrance.

Mapperton (194) (SY 50-99) *5m NE Bridport.* This diminutive place should not be confused with the hamlet of the same name at Almer in east Dorset. Standing cheek-by-jowl in a delightful green hollow of the high hills of west Dorset is an exquisite yellow-stoned manor house and a tiny church. The oldest part of the house is the projecting north wing, which was built around the mid-16th century for Robert Morgan. The rest was erected just over a 100 years later by Robert Brodrepp, whose family came into possession of the manor in 1618. Its delightful interior contains much 17th and 18th century panelling and some striking Tudor plaster ceilings, as well as several massive Jacobean overmantles. The modest early 18th century stone chapel forms the south wing of the house. Inside there are many pieces of continental stained glass of the 16th, 17th and 18th centuries. See also the fine mid-18th century monument by Peter Scheemakers of Richard Brodrepp and his daughter. The glorious terraced gardens extend down a deep glen to the east of the house. *(Tel: Beaminster 441.)*

In 1660 the village of Mapperton was almost wiped out by the bubonic plague. The survivors gathered and placed posies of herbs to protect them from the sickness, under the 'Posy Tree', an old oak tree half a mile to the west of the village

---

Mappowder (194) (ST 73-06) *12m NE Dorchester.* This is situated at the southern edge of the Blackmoor Vale, within sight of Bulbarrow Hill ★. The mainly 15th century brownstone church was well restored by the Victorians, and has a splendidly light and airy interior. There is an interesting miniature 14th century effigy of a crusader, probably indicating a heart burial, and several memorials to the Coker family. Mappowder Court, the ancient seat of the Coker's, is but a fragment of a large mansion demolished in the mid-18th century. There is a pleasant walk south-east to Melcombe Bingham ★.

Marnhull (183) (ST 77-18) *6m SW Shaftesbury.* A more diffuse village than Marnhull would be hard to find. It consists of a multitude of ancient and modern houses scattered along an interconnecting network of small roads on an escarpment above the River Stour. The church is one of the loveliest in the Blackmoor Vale, and has a splendidly upright 15th century stone tower with pinnacles and fine canopied niches. The interior was partially restored in the 19th century, but the visitor should not miss the fine 15th century altar tomb with alabaster effigies, nor the similarly dated panelled wagon-roof to the nave. Note also the single Norman pier in the north arcade, the medieval wall paintings beneath the tower, and the amusing inscription to John Warren which begins:

Here under this stone
Lie Ruth and old John
Who smoked all his life
And so did his wife
And now there's no doubt
But their pipes are both out.

Close to the church is Senior's Farm, a much altered early-16th century stone house which was possibly built as a grange of Glastonbury Abbey. Another notable building here is Nash Court, the rebuilt residence of Henry VIII's sixth and last wife, Catherine Parr.

In Thomas Hardy's novel, *Tess of the d'Urbervilles,* Marnhull is renamed Marlott, Tess's home village. She is reputed to have been born at 'Tess's Cottage' on its outskirts, but the cottage is in private hands, and the privacy of the owners should be respected. Hardy's delightfully named 'Pure Drop Inn' is believed to have been modelled on the attractive Crown Inn.

Marshwood (193) (SY 38-99) *6m NE Lyme Regis.* This scattered parish is magnificently sited on an open hill above the vale to which it gives its name, and has a church that was built as late as 1884. The view from the churchyard, out across the whole valley, is breathtaking. Traces of Marshwood Castle are visible at Lodge House Farm. The word 'castle' is misleading, for it was really a fortified manor house built in the 13th century for the de Manderville family. By using a combination of footpaths it is possible to walk to Lambert's Castle, a large Iron Age settlement constructed on the flat summit of Lambert's Hill. The site is owned by the National Trust, and there is a car park on the B3165 to the west of the village (SY 36-98), and information boards indicating what birds and flora are to be found here.

Martinstown (194) (SY 64-88) *2½m W Dorchester.* Its old name of Winterborne St Martin indicates that this was another settlement in the South Winterborne valley. It is a long village with several small bridges crossing its stream. The church has a pleasant 15th century tower, but its interior was heavily restored in the latter half of the 19th century. There are a staggering 118 round barrows in the parish, more than in any other parish in Dorset.

Melbury Abbas (183) (ST 88-20) *1½m SE Shaftesbury.* A small village hidden in a leafy depression beneath the imposing mass of Melbury Hill. The church stands on an elevated site above the road, but is an uninteresting example of Victorian rebuilding. Melbury Abbas Mill, one of several mills in the parish, has been restored to full working order, and is open to the public *(tel: Shaftesbury 2163).*

Melbury Bubb (194) (ST 59-06) *14m NW Dorchester.* Compact little village quietly situated at the end of a no-through-road, below high and wooded Bubb Down Hill. Of the church built over 500 years ago only the pleasant tower remains. The rest was remodelled in 1875 by R.H. Shout, who retained some of the old material, including some excellent pieces of 15th century stained glass. The extraordinary beaker-shaped font, with intricate carvings of wild animals intertwined, is reckoned to be pre-Conquest, and could possibly be the shaft of a Saxon cross later hollowed out by the Normans.

Melbury Osmond (194) (ST 57-07) *14m NW Dorchester off A37.* Glorious village of picture-postcard thatched houses set upon the steep slopes of an idyllic green valley not far from the Somerset border. It was in St Osmond's church that Thomas Hardy's future mother, Jemima Hand, married Thomas Hardy Senior on December 22 1839. At that time the church must have had a pleasant Georgian appearance, but it was thoroughly 're-Gothicised' in a restoration in 1888. Now its only really noteworthy feature is a strange 10th or 11th century stone carving of what appears to be a deformed frog entangled in foliage, although some suggest that it represents 'Abraham's ram caught in the thicket'. That part of the village beyond the delightful water-splash is known as 'Town's End'. Here the road stops at a northern entrance to Melbury House, but a right of way enables visitors to walk through the park to Evershot★ (see also **Walk 3**).

Melbury Sampford (194) (ST 57-06) *14m NW Dorchester.* Not the most beautiful house in Dorset, but certainly one of the most interesting, Melbury House is a massive and rambling mansion on high ground to the west of the Blackmoor Vale. It was built for Sir Giles Strangways in the 16th century, but was considerably modified and altered by succeeding generations of the Strangways family, notably in the 17th and 19th centuries. However, the most interesting and dominating feature of the house is still the fine Tudor hexagonal tower. It has large windows, suggesting that it was intended as some form of look-out tower, perhaps for viewing deer-hunting in the surrounding park.

Beside the massive house the church appears deceptively small. It is mostly of the mid-15th century, and contains a vast number of monuments to the Brownings and Strangways. Note especially the two 15th century canopied tombs with alabaster effigies of two knights in armour. They both originally commemorated members of the Browning family, but one was appropriated by Sir Giles Strangways, who died in 1547. Although the house is not open to visitors there is a public footpath through the magnificent 600 acre park (see **Walk 3**).

Melcombe Bingham (194) (SY 76-02) *11 SW Blandford Forum.* Prettily sited in a green dell on the southern side of the chalk downs, Melcombe Bingham, or Bingham's Melcombe, takes its name from the former owners of the manor, the illustrious Bingham family. Their former ancestral home is one of the most exquisite medieval manor houses in the county. It is described as 'rambling round three sides of a court' with 'hardly one straight line, one right angle, or one dead level in the whole'. The house is not open to the public, but visitors can see parts of it from the church next door. The latter is mainly of the 14th and 15th centuries, and has a dumpy stone tower. Within are many fragments of medieval glass, and a simple Georgian font. (See **Walk 8**.)

Melplash (193) (SY 48-98) *3½ m N Bridport.* Small main road village with westerly views out over the narrow valley of the River Brit. The well-known Melplash Agricultural Show, now held at Bridport, originated from a challenge between two men to

see which of their sons was the more accomplished farmer. The church, built by Benjamin Ferrey in 1846, is a fine example of Victorian neo-Norman architecture. A footpath northwards skirts around Melplash Court, an attractive honey-coloured Tudor manor house.

Merley (195) (SZ 02-98) *1m S Wimborne Minster.* The tropical bird gardens at Merley House are an oasis of beauty in this densely populated area of eastern Dorset. They lie hidden behind a high wall, and provide a delightful setting for many exotic species of birds, including lorikeets, Amazonian parrots and Australian rosellas. There is also a large collection of penguins, beautiful water-gardens containing fabulous koi carp, a children's pets corner, and a play area. *(Tel: Wimborne Minster 883790.)*

Milborne St Andrew (194) (SY 80-97) *7½ m SW Blandford Forum.* Unimpressive village in a valley, partially astride the busy A354, with a large 'milk factory' on the hillside above. The church of St Andrew has an excellent Norman south doorway, and a fine canopied table tomb to John Morton, nephew of Cardinal Morton, who was born in the village in the 15th century. South of the village is Weatherby Castle, an Iron Age settlement covered with trees. At the centre, but shrouded by the trees, is an unusual brick obelisk erected in 1761.

Milton Abbas (194) (ST 80-01) *7m SW Blandford Forum.* The exceptionally picturesque village of Milton Abbas is a glorious example of 18th century estate planning, with a long curving street dropping down towards an artificial lake, and woods rising on each side. Lying back from the road, behind wide grass verges, are two rows of delightful, near identical, white-walled thatched cottages. Chestnut trees used to stand between each pair of houses, but these grew so tall that they had to be cut down in 1953, and be replaced by smaller ash trees. At the centre of the village is the red sandstone church of St James, built by James Wyatt in 1786, though badly disfigured by Victorian 'restorers' in 1888. The late 16th century brick almshouses opposite the church originally stood in the old village. They were dismantled and re-erected here in 1779.

The old town of Milton, or Middleton (the middle town of Dorset), lay in the valley south of Milton Abbey★. In medieval times there was a sizeable settlement of 100 buildings here, including a grammar school, a brewery, several inns and a vicarage. In 1752 the Milton estate, which comprised the town, the abbey buildings, and 8,000 acres of land, was purchased by Joseph Damer, a rich local man. Damer, who became Lord Milton in 1753, felt that the town would ruin the outlook from the new mansion he planned to erect beside the abbey, and thus set about planning its destruction. From 1760 to 1780 he acquired, by fair means or foul, the leases of most of the properties in the town. Some of the tenants were quite happy to leave, but most were not. Mr Harrison, the town lawyer, secure with a lease of three lives on his property, proved particularly resistant to all attempts to make him vacate his home. In a final act of desperation his Lordship had the sluice gate of the Abbot's pond opened and flooded the obstinate lawyer out. By 1771 the project for the demolition of the town was sufficiently advanced for Lord Milton to initiate plans for the construction of his palatial house. Nonetheless it was not until 1784 that the last of the town's buildings, the school, was finally demolished. The new village, built according to plans by Capability Brown and Sir William Chambers, arose between 1773 and 1780. For a fascinating account of Milton Abbas, read Richeldis Wansbrough's *The Tale of Milton Abbas*.

There is an interesting Farm Museum at Park Farm (ST 80-02), about a quarter of a mile north of the village. Displayed here are a large collection of agricultural, brewery and rural bygones from the surrounding area. *(Tel: Milton Abbas 880216.)*

Milton Abbey (194) (ST 79-02) *7m SW Blandford Forum*. A mighty abbey and a large mansion stand side by side in an exceptionally beautiful natural amphitheatre of wooded hills. The Norman church which replaced the Saxon building established here in the 10th century by King Athelstan, was itself destroyed by fire in 1309. Rebuilding began almost at once after this disaster, but for some reason, perhaps because of the Black Death or the Dissolution, the nave was never built. The massive bricked-up arch on the west front is evidence of this omission. After the Dissolution the abbey estate was bought by Sir John Tregonwell, ancestor of Lewis Tregonwell, founder of Bournemouth ★. In 1752 the monastic buildings were sold to Joseph Damer, who had them all destroyed apart from the Abbot's Hall, this later building being incorporated into the great house designed by Sir William Chambers in 1771.

Had the abbey been completed it would have been a gargantuan structure. As it is, it measures 136 feet in length, and consists of choir, crossing tower and transepts. It belongs mostly to the 14th century, but the north transept and crossing tower were rebuilt in the early 16th century. Entry to the abbey is by the inadequately sized west porch, erected in 1865 by Gilbert Scott. The cavernous interior is beautifully light and airy, but is somewhat lacking in atmosphere owing to heavy-handed restoration by James Wyatt in 1789. One of the few surviving medieval items in the church is the splendid 15th century oak Hanging Tabernacle on the north chancel wall. This nine-foot-high structure was designed to cover the Pyx. The huge three-tiered stone reredos, originally highly coloured, is an impressive, though hardly imaginative piece. In the north transept is an excellent monument erected by Lord Milton, later the Earl of Dorchester, to his wife Caroline, who died in 1775. It shows the Earl gazing into the face of his lifeless wife, and was carved by Agostino Carlini. The wonderfully colourful Jesse window in the south transept was designed by Pugin in 1849.

Though a massive piece of masonry, Lord Milton's house is neither impressive nor very beautiful. It is built in a most unconvincing Gothick style, and its colour, a pinkish grey, contrasts sharply with the golden hues of the adjoining abbey. Even the creator of the house, William Chambers, dismissed it as 'this vast ugly house in Dorset'. Inside Chambers, and later James Wyatt, worked in the Classical style, and it looks much the better for it. However, the finest interior feature is the extraordinary complex late 15th century timber roof of the old Abbot's Hall. The house is now a boys' public school, but the Abbot's Hall and

several of the state rooms are open to the public in the Easter and Summer school holidays.

High up on the wooded hill above the abbey is St Catherine's Chapel, a small flint-built structure dating from the Norman period. In medieval times unmarried women would come here and pray that they never became old maids.

Minterne Magna (194) (ST 65-04) *5½m N Dorchester*. Minterne Magna, the 'Great Hintock' of Thomas Hardy's novels, lies astride the A352, in a deep wooded valley between Little Minterne Hill and East Hill. Concealed behind high trees is Minterne House, a wonderfully elaborate country mansion built at the turn of the century by Leonard Stokes, one of the most interesting of the Arts and Crafts architects. The seat of the present Lord Digby, the property has been held by his family since 1768, when it was purchased from the widow of General Charles Churchill, brother of the Duke of Marlborough. The house is not open to the public, but the beautiful gardens, containing at least 350 species of rhododendrons, can be visited from April to October. *(Tel: Cerne Abbas 370.)*

The thin tower of the small 15th century church backs onto the busy main road, and visitors should beware of traffic as they enter through the tower door. The interior is rather overwhelmed by memorials to the Churchills, Napiers and Digbys. The largest, an immense monument of reredos type, commemorates Sir Robert Napier, who died in 1615. Minterne Parva is a minute hamlet just over a mile to the south-east of Magna.

There is an excellent circular walk from Minterne Magna, running up Little Minterne Hill, along to Clinger Farm, and finally returning to the village by way of Dogbury Hill (see also **Walk 6**).

Moor Crichel (195) (ST 99-08) *8m N Wimborne Minster*. Like Milton Abbas, this village was 'removed' in the 18th century to improve the setting of a large country house. In this instance the destructive landowner was Humphrey Sturt, Member of Parliament and builder of that 'megalomaniac folly', Horton Tower (see Horton ★). He found the modest house built by his uncle, Sir William Napier, far too insignificant, and on inheriting it in 1765, immediately set about transforming it into something resembling a palace. The architect of Crichel House is unknown, but it is possible that Thomas Archer was responsible for much of the work. James Wyatt, who was working at Milton Abbas and Bryanston in the 1770s, probably completed it, and may have designed the magnificent drawing and dining rooms in the east front. The latter has been described by Sacheverell Sitewell as one of the loveliest 18th century rooms, not only in England, but in the whole of Europe. The house is not open to the public.

Morcombelake (193) (SY 39-94) *5m W Bridport*. A scattered settlement in exceptionally hilly country, with fine views westwards, out over the delightful Marshwood Vale. It was here that the famous Dorset Knob biscuit was first produced about 150 years ago by a local farmer's wife. Today these delectable chunky round biscuits, which must be baked three times, are manufactured in a small pink-washed bakery on the south side of the A35. The bakery is open to visitors, and there is a shop selling its produce. Overlooking the main road is the tiny black-beamed and cream-washed church of 1841.

Walk southwards to Golden Cap ★, passing the remains of St Gabriel's Chapel. At one time a chapel of Whitchurch Canonicorum, this small 14th century church fell into ruin at the end of the 19th century.

Morden (195) (SY 91-95) *5m N Wareham off A35.* Though uncomfortably close to the sprawling mass of Bournemouth and Poole, this village is surprisingly peaceful and unspoilt, with many delightful 18th century thatched cottages. It lies in gently undulating country west of Lytchett Heath, and has a church rebuilt in the latter half of the 19th century. The interior is noteworthy for the striking 16th century monument to Thomas Earle, who lived at Charborough House about a mile to the north.

Moreton (194) (SY 80-89) *7m E Dorchester.* Unassuming village lying in pastoral country beside the River Frome, with an exceptional Georgian Gothick church, built by James Frampton in 1776. In the mid-19th century it was tastefully enlarged by adding a north aisle, and improvements were made to the 'very plain, bald and poor interior'. During the Second World War the church was badly damaged when a German bomb fell in the churchyard close to the north wall. However, restoration work was so skilfully done that it is now hard to distinguish the new from the old, that is apart from the remarkable windows, which have been filled with delicately engraved glass. These are the work of Laurence Whistler, perhaps the most brilliant of 20th century glass engravers. Note also the delightful mid-18th century mural tablet.

In the cemetery across the road is the grave of Lawrence of Arabia, its simple headstone carved by his friend, Eric Kennington. It is possible to walk north from here to Lawrence's modest cottage at Clouds Hill ★, first crossing the attractive little footbridge over the Frome (see **Walk 9**).

Mudeford (195) (SZ 18-92) *1m SE Christchurch.* Much enlarged in recent years, Mudeford is a quiet holiday resort situated on the south-eastern shore of Christchurch Harbour ★, between the little River Mude and the sea. It has a good sandy beach, but is best known for its lively quay overlooking the entrance to Christchurch Harbour. George II and Lewis Tregonwell both stayed here, but went away and founded resorts further along the Dorset coast (Weymouth and Bournemouth respectively). In the 18th and 19th centuries the area was popular with smugglers, and the Haven House Inn at the end of the quay was a favoured haunt of these 'gentlemen of the night'.

A passenger ferry runs from the quay to the sand spit that juts northwards from Hengistbury Head ★.

Netherbury (193) (SY 46-99) *5m N Bridport off A3066.* Pleasant settlement of yellow stone cottages in the narrow valley of the River Brit, which is here crossed by a picturesque 17th century three-arch bridge. On a hillside above the village is the church of St Mary, an attractive building of 14th century origin. The interior was sensitively restored by the Victorians, and possesses a fine Jacobean pulpit and a 15th century alabaster effigy of a knight in armour. This is believed to be James More, who was killed in a skirmish near here during the Wars of the Roses. If possible walk north to Parnham House ★.

Nether Cerne (194) (SY 66-98) *5m N Dorchester.* Just a church and a few houses sheltering in the Cerne valley below the central Dorset Downs. Though the church is no longer used it is kept in immaculate condition by the Redundant Churches Fund. Its interesting Norman font has been described as being shaped like half a Charente melon. Walk east onto East Hill from which there are good views of the Cerne valley, and return to Nether Cerne by dropping down to Godmanstone ★, and returning along a path by the river.

Nether Compton (183) (ST 59-17) *3m W Sherborne off A30.* Delightful village set in a wooded depression close to the Somerset border, with a collection of picturesque stone cottages grouped around a small green. The small Perpendicular church stands on the south side of this green, and contains a handsome 15th century stone screen.

North Poorton (194) (SY 51-98) *5m NE Bridport.* Minute hamlet remotely situated at the head of a deep indentation of the high West Dorset hills. The small church, with its elaborate stone pulpit, was built in 1861 by John Hicks, the Dorchester architect to whom Thomas Hardy was once apprenticed. Nearby are the fragmentary remains of the medieval church.

Okeford Fitzpaine (194) (ST 80-10) *6½m NW Blandford Forum.* Attractively sited on the green lower slopes of high Okeford Hill, this large village of pleasant brick, flint and stone dwellings has been sadly disfigured by a large poultry-processing plant and a concrete-making works. It takes its name from the 'ancient and knightly family of the Fitzpaines', descendants of the Paine's. Robertson of Paine fought with Simon de Montfort against King Henry III at the Battle of Lewes in 1264. The defeated king was placed in the care of Paine, who took the opportunity to 'borrow' the royal seal and use it on a document excusing him from paying taxes on his estate! Apart from the early 15th century tower, the parish church was almost entirely rebuilt in 1866. The interior is dark and plain, but does contain a well-restored, carved and painted stone pulpit. We also enjoyed the inscription on one of the church bells:

I often have been beate and banged
My friends rejoice to see me hanged
And when my friends do chance to die
then I for them will loudly crie.

From the churchyard there is a good view of the thatched and tiled roofs of the houses, and there is a pleasant picnic site near the summit of Okeford Hill (ST 81-09), with superb views northwards out over the Blackmoor Vale, and eastwards to the great mass of Hambledon Hill ★ (ST 84-12).

Osmington (194) (SY 72-83) *3m NE Weymouth.* Pretty village straggling down the valley of the little Jordan River, with many beautiful stone and thatched buildings, including a delightful thatched polygonal-shaped bus shelter. The church has a

The Osmington White Horse ... 'a hill figure with obscure origins'.

15th century tower, but the rest was refashioned by Benjamin Ferrey in 1846. However, do not overlook the 17th century Warham monument in the chancel, considered by many to be the most crudely lettered in the county. The three inscriptions are surprisingly irreverent, especially the last, which is in Latin. Translated it reads: 'I have entered harbour, Goodbye Hope and goodbye Fortune; I am through with you. Now play with someone else'. The ruined manor house beside the church was probably the ancestral home of the Warham family, one of whom, William, became Archbishop of Canterbury in the late 15th century.

High on the hillside above the village is the Osmington White Horse, a large chalk figure cut from the turf of the downs. Covering nearly an acre, it is the only 'white horse' hill-figure in Britain to carry a rider. Its history is rather obscure, but it was cut around the beginning of the 19th century, according to one theory, to commemorate George III's first visit to Weymouth. An alternative theory suggests that it was the work of engineers stationed in Weymouth at the time of the Napoleonic Wars. In his novel *The Trumpet Major*, Thomas Hardy ascribes it to a commemoration of the Battle of Trafalgar.

The quaint little seaside hamlet of Osmington Mills consists of an inn, a hotel and a few houses, all set on the banks of a small stream close to its entry to the sea. It was to Osmington that the famous landscape painter John Constable came on his honeymoon in 1816, to stay with friends at the vicarage. His well-known painting of Weymouth Bay now hangs in the National Gallery, and he also painted several views of Osmington Bay. The Smugglers Inn, a partly thatched building dating back to the 13th century, was the headquarters of the notorious smuggler Pierre Latour, known as French Peter.

Over Compton (183) (ST 59-16) *2½m W Sherborne off A30.* Small village on wooded ground above the valley of the Trent Brook. Compton House, a picturesque early 19th century Tudor-style mansion, is now the home of Worldwide Butterflies. Here visitors can see many different species of butterfly flying naturally amongst the exotic settings of the Palm House, the Tropical Jungle and the Butterfly House. Here also is the famous Lullingstone Silk Farm which provided silk for the wedding dresses of both Princess Diana and the Duchess of York. *(Tel: Sherborne 74608.)*

The Victorianised church stands in the beautiful grounds of Compton House. It has a fine three-tiered Jacobean pulpit, and in the north chapel many interesting monuments to the Goodden family. Of these the most outstanding is the full length portrait-sculpture of Robert Goodden, who died in 1828. The artist of this superbly animated piece is unknown, but the Royal Commission on Historical Monuments attributes it to either John Flaxman or John Bacon the younger.

Owermoigne (194) (SY 76-85) *6m SE Dorchester.* Compact village astride a little lane off the A352. There are some charming thatched cottages beside the church, but elsewhere it is marred by modern development. The church itself was poorly restored in 1883, and is of little interest to visitors. Moigne Court to the north of the village, dates back to the 13th century, and is one of the oldest fortified manor houses in Dorset (open by written appointment only).

Parnham House (193) (SY 47-00) *1m S Beaminster off A3066.* This beautiful house, the home of the John Makepeace School for Craftsmen in Wood, lies in the wooded valley of the River Brit, among the rolling hills of west Dorset. Built by Robert Strode in the mid-16th century, it was extensively altered in the 18th century and then again in 1810, when John Nash completely redesigned the south front and added battlements and pinnacles. During the Second World War it was requisitioned by the War Office, and was used as a military hospital, the headquarters of the 16th Infantry Division of the US army, and finally a prisoner-of-war camp. After the war it gradually fell into a state of disrepair, and its future was uncertain until it was purchased by the well-known furniture designer, John Makepeace, in 1976. He and his wife, Jennie, immediately set about restoring the house and the finely landscaped gardens.

Unlike most other country houses open to the public, Parnham is not a museum. It contains no ancient furnishings, no Old Masters, no family heirlooms. Rather it is a working house, whose fine old rooms are used to display the magnificent pieces of contemporary furniture made in the adjoining workshops. In the Strode Room there is a splendid four-poster bed made by the craftsmen from a single yew tree. Many of the items on display may be purchased here, but these are the antiques of the future and are therefore unlikely to be cheap. The house is set amongst beautiful gardens, both formal and informal, and there are several attractive walks along the banks of the River Brit. *(Tel: Beaminster 862204.)*

Pentridge (184) (SU 03-17) *9½m NE Blandford Forum off A354.* Secluded hamlet tucked away at the end of a little lane beneath Pentridge Hill. There must have been a settlement since ancient times, for it bears a Celtic name — the hill of the boars. Its church, with short tower and broach spire, is dedicated to the 8th century Celtic saint, Rumbold, but was much renewed in the mid-19th century. Inside a memorial on the south wall of the nave informs us that Robert Browning, 'the first known forefather of Robert Browning the poet' died in this parish on 25th November 1746.

Pentridge lies in an area of Cranborne Chase ★ rich in ancient monuments. To the north is Bokerley Ditch ★, an impressive Romano-British earth rampart thrown up to protect the tribesmen of Dorset from the invasions of the Anglo-Saxons (see **Walk**

Summertime below Pilsdon Pen.

12). The largest (if barely visible) prehistoric monuments in Britain, the Dorset Cursus, passes to the west, while to the south-west is the Oakley Down barrow group, one of the finest Bronze Age cemeteries in England, comprising over 20 barrows, including several excellent examples of bell-barrows. Here also is Ackling Dyke★, the best preserved stretch of the Roman road running from Old Sarum to Badbury Rings★.

Piddlehinton (194) (SY 71-97) *5m N Dorchester.* A pleasant little village situated in the narrow valley of the River Piddle. Our prim Victorian ancestors decided to change the name of this clear chalk stream to Puddle, and Piddlehinton became Puddlehinton. It was not until the 1950s that the ancient name was restored, and even today some old folk of the village still refer to it as Puddlehinton. The handsome 15th century tower of the church is contemporary with the rest of the fabric. The contents include several fine brasses, one of which commemorates William Golding, who died in 1562.

Piddletrenthide (194) (SY 70-99) *6m N Dorchester.* Straggling along the valley floor of the Piddle, beneath the beech woods of East Hill, Piddletrenthide — 'the Piddle village of thirty hides' — has several attractive inns, a pleasing 18th century manor house, and a handsome church built of stones of varying hues from buff to grey. Its exceptional Perpendicular tower is adorned with an amazing number of hideous gargoyles, and a fine gilded weathercock. The Latin inscription over the west door of the tower is of interest, as it includes the date, 1487, in Arabic numerals, and not Roman numerals as was usual at that time. The interior was over restored in 1852, but there is a good 12th century doorway in the south porch. In the churchyard are two rounded tombstones of the Dumberfield family, ancestors to Hardy's d'Urbervilles. Also buried here is Ralph Wightman, broadcaster and author of several excellent books on Dorset.

Pilsdon (193) (ST 41-99) *5½m NW Bridport.* Minute hamlet nestling beneath the height of Pilsdon Pen★, on the northern edge of the Marshwood Vale, close to the source of the River Char. The church, a largely 19th century building with a stone bellcote and tiny stone spire, is sited next to Pilsdon Manor. During the Civil War this attractive Tudor house belonged to Sir Hugh Wyndham, a staunch supporter of the Royalist cause. When King Charles II was in Dorset attempting to secure a passage across to France, Sir Hugh was suspected of sheltering the Royal fugitive. Not only was his home ransacked, but all the women of the house were thoroughly searched because the king was believed to be dressed as a woman. It is said that one poor female servant was accused of being the king in disguise!

Pilsdon Pen (193) (ST 41-01) *6m NW Bridport.* At 908 feet above sea level Pilsdon Pen is the highest point in Dorset. From its bare summit there are spectacular views south, out over the Marshwood Vale to the English Channel, and westwards to the distant outline of Dartmoor. A short path opposite the lay-by on the B3164 leads to its top, which is ringed by a small Iron Age earthwork.

Pimperne (195) (ST 90-09) *1½m NE Blandford Forum.* A large and unexceptional village in a hollow of the North Dorset downlands. The large church was rebuilt by Lord Portman of Bryanston in 1873, but incorporates some fine Norman work, notably the south doorway and the arch of the north chapel. The font is also Norman, and has a delightful stone cover of 1861. The arms of Henry VIII in a niche under the doorway of the old vicarage remind us that the manor of Pimperne was granted in succession to his last two wives, Catherine Howard and Katherine Parr.

A mile to the north-east is the Pimperne Long Barrow (ST 91-10), a Neolithic burial chamber 350 feet long and about 9 feet high, and undoubtedly one of the finest long barrows in the country. It is reached from the A354 by a footpath which can be followed beyond this to Tarrant Gunville★.

Plush (194) (ST 71-02) *7m NE Dorchester off B3143.* Attractive hamlet of thatched cottages sited at the head of a secluded valley amid the glorious uplands of central Dorset. Its small church was built by Benjamin Ferrey in 1848, but apart from the fine hammerbeam roof of the nave, is not of great interest to visitors. The charming Brace of Pheasants Inn was converted from a smithy and a pair of farm cottages built in the 16th century of thatch, brick and flint. Above the main entrance is its unique sign, a brace of stuffed pheasants in a glass case. A thriving orchid nursery behind the inn breeds rare orchids for both the export and the domestic market. (See also **Walk 7**.)

Poole (195) (SZ 01-91). Situated on a peninsula on the north side of Poole Harbour this thriving town has always depended on trade for its wealth. It became an important south coast port in the late-13th century when it replaced Wareham as the primary anchorage in this area. Until 1248 the town lay in the demesne of Canford but in that year Longspee of Canford, in need of money for a proposed crusade to the Holy Land, allowed the citizens to purchase a charter for a small fee. In 1433 Poole became a staple port and in 1568 Elizabeth I made it a county in its own right, a status it retained until the 19th century. During the 15th and 16th centuries the town gained much of its wealth from privateers, who found the many inlets of the harbour ideally suited as hiding places for their vessels after returning from forays in the Channel. One of the most successful of these buccaneers was Harry Page, known to the French as 'Arripay'. The most important building to survive from this period is *'The Old Town House' (1)* or Scaplen's Court, in Sarum Street. Considered one of the finest 15th century town houses on the south coast, this stone and brick building has been Poole's first Guildhall, an inn and the 18th century residence of

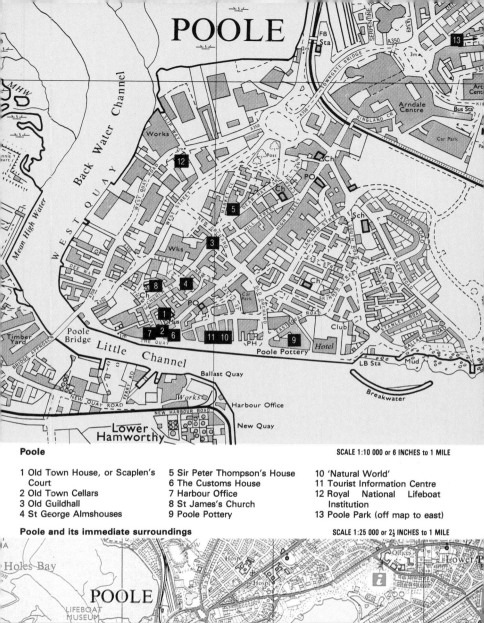

POOLE

Poole

SCALE 1:10 000 or 6 INCHES to 1 MILE

1 Old Town House, or Scaplen's Court
2 Old Town Cellars
3 Old Guildhall
4 St George Almshouses
5 Sir Peter Thompson's House
6 The Customs House
7 Harbour Office
8 St James's Church
9 Poole Pottery
10 'Natural World'
11 Tourist Information Centre
12 Royal National Lifeboat Institution
13 Poole Park (off map to east)

Poole and its immediate surroundings

SCALE 1:25 000 or 2½ INCHES to 1 MILE

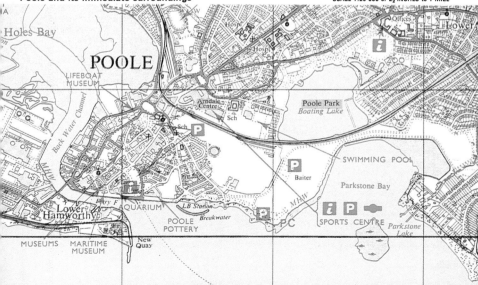

John Scaplen, the town's Sheriff. Saved from ruination earlier this century it now houses a fine museum showing the history and development of Poole. Among its most important possessions is a large Bronze Age dug-out canoe dredged from the harbour. *The Old Town Cellars (2)* in Paradise Street is another medieval structure, and in the 15th century this was used to store wool. It has been converted into a splendid museum exhibiting items connected with the town's seafaring history. Throughout the Civil War Poole was held by the Parliamentarians and in 1643 was used as a base for the siege of Corfe Castle. After the Restoration Charles II punished the town by ordering the destruction of its defences, but a portion of the town wall and an old postern gate dating from the reign of Richard III survives in St Clement's Lane.

In the 17th and 18th centuries the town became the centre for the Newfoundland fishing trade. Many new buildings were constructed in these prosperous times, including the *Old Guildhall (3)* in Market Street. This elegant building, with its pair of curving stairs, was built in 1761 in typical Georgian style. Today it is a museum portraying Poole's civic and social history. Further down Market Street are *St George Almshouses (4)*, 15th century in origin but much altered in the 19th century. *Sir Peter Thompson's House (5)* in Dear Hay Lane is a fine 18th century house designed by Thomas Bastard of Blandford Forum. Two other handsome Georgian houses, Beech Hurst and Poole House, can be seen in the High Street and Thames Street respectively. *The Customs House (6)* in West Quay Road was built around 1788, but was reconstructed after a fire in 1813 rather after the design of the Old Guildhall. A tablet near here states that at the outbreak of the 1830 Revolution in France the exiled monarch, Charles X, landed at Poole. Standing almost opposite to the Customs House is the *Harbour Office (7)* of 1822, a plain colonnaded building with a relief portrait of the mayor of 1727 on its east wall. The *Church of St James (8)* is an imposing ashlar faced edifice erected in 1820 to replace a medieval church demolished a year earlier. The arcade pillars are made from the trunks of giant Newfoundland pine.

After the collapse of the Newfoundland trade in the 1820s the port was used to transport pottery clay found in the district to the factories in the north. In 1873 two local craftsmen established a pottery factory on the quay, but it was not until the 1920s, when the outstanding Staffordshire pottery designer John Adams joined the company, that *Poole Pottery (9)* acquired its real fame. Guided tours of the recently modernised factory are available and there is also a museum dedicated to the pottery's history and a large showroom displaying the entire range of Poole pottery *(tel: Poole 672866)*.

Today the central section of the quay is a leisure area where visitors may come and observe the shipping activities of this bustling port. Many of the old warehouses lining the waterfront have been converted into tourist attractions, one of which houses an exhibition of Dorset village crafts, and an aquarium and serpentarium known as *'Natural World' (10) (tel: Poole 686712)*. On the second floor is a model museum with one of the largest model railways in the country. An interesting way to travel to Bournemouth from here is by boat; the *Poole Belle* and *Bournemouth Belle* make regular sailings from the quay to Bournemouth Pier. For informa-

tion about this and other sailings in Poole Harbour, including trips to beautiful Brownsea Island ★ and fishing trips, visit the *Tourist Information Centre (11)* on the quay *(tel: Poole 673322)*. Poole is also proud to be the headquarters of the *Royal National Lifeboat Institution (12)*, and a museum in their building in West Quay Road illustrates the history of the service *(tel: Poole 675151, extension 3550)*.

With its vast indoor shopping complex/sports centre, arts centre and other modern buildings, northern Poole stands in complete contrast to the picturesque historical precinct at the southern end of the High Street. To the east of the town centre is *Poole Park (13)*, a lovely recreational area with tennis courts, miniature golf course, large boating lake, miniature railway, and tea room. There is also a small Children's Zoo here *(tel: Parkstone 745296)*.

Poole Harbour (195) (SZ 00-88 etc.) *To immediate S of Poole*. One of the largest natural harbours in the world, this great stretch of water contains several islands, including the National Trust's Brownsea Island ★ and Furzey Island, the latter now in the hands of the oil drillers. It has been described, with some justice, as a leisure seekers' paradise, with boat trips, watersports, harbourside walks and beaches. Apart from boat trips from Poole across to Brownsea Island and Sandbanks, it is also possible to go up the River Frome to Wareham Quay. Quieter explorations of the southern shores may be made from Arne ★ or from the car parks to the north of Studland ★. See also Poole ★, and Sandbanks ★.

Portesham (194) (SY 60-85) *6m NW Weymouth*. This pretty village shelters in a small coombe immediately below Portesham Hill, which is itself overshadowed by the windswept summit of Blackdown Hill. The north nave wall of St Peter's Church contains 12th century work, but the rest of the fabric is mainly of the 15th century. Although the interior was restored in the 19th century it is worth visiting to see the Norman font, the Jacobean pulpit, and the medieval screen. Portesham Manor, an attractive little 17th century house, was once the home of Admiral Thomas Hardy, and it was from here that he left to become the captain's servant on board HMS 'Helena' at the age of 12.

North of Portesham, between Portesham Hill and White Hill, will be found a small Bronze Age stone circle of nine upright stones. Half a mile to the east is another prehistoric monument, the Hell Stone. This incorrectly reconstructed group of nine stones was once the inner burial chamber of a Neolithic long barrow. There is an excellent walk north from Portesham to the Hardy Monument ★ on Blackdown Hill, to link with our **Walk 5**.

Portland, Isle of (194) (SY 68-73 etc.) *2m S Weymouth*. In his novel *The Well Beloved*, Thomas Hardy renames Portland 'The Isle of Slingers', in ancient times the islanders being accomplished users of the sling, and describes it as 'the Gibraltar of Wessex', 'stretching out like the head of a bird into the English Channel'. About four and half miles long by two miles wide, it is not a true island but a vast slab of grey rock linked to the mainland by a long, thin isthmus. However, such is its unique character that it fully deserves its title, much more so than that Dorset's other quasi-island, the Isle of

Purbeck.

From the northern end, where the rocky heights of the Verne rise to almost 500 feet, the ground gradually slopes south until, at the Bill of Portland, the cliffs are barely 20 feet above the sea. The powerful current called the Portland Race runs off this treacherous headland. The pretty red and white lighthouse, the third to have been built here since 1720, can be visited at certain times. From its lofty summit it is possible to see the massive outcrop known as the Pulpit Rock, with the old lighthouse close by which has been converted into a bird observatory. The Isle's only significantly wooded area is on the slopes above the ruined Rufus Castle (SY 69-71) at Church Ope Cove.

Like the Isle of Purbeck, Portland is also famous for its stone, which is easy to carve but exceptionally durable. Although it has been quarried here since the Middle Ages, it was not worked extensively until the 17th century, when the architect Inigo Jones used it in the construction of the splendid Banqueting House in Whitehall. At the end of the 17th century St Paul's Cathedral was faced with Portland Stone by Christopher Wren, and in recent times it was used in the United Nations Building in New York.

There is no town of Portland, but rather a series of settlements, the largest of which, Fortuneswell (SY 68-73), spreads up the north-western slopes of the Isle. From the hill above Fortuneswell there is a panoramic view of Weymouth, Chesil Beach and Portland Naval Base, which has here one of the largest and safest harbours in the world. This is enclosed on its eastern side by an elaborate system of breakwaters constructed by prison convicts between 1849 and 1902, the prisoners being housed in what is now an institution for young offenders. Adjacent to the Royal Navy Helicopter Base is Portland Castle (EH) (SY 68-74), the best preserved of a chain of coastal fortifications erected by King Henry VIII in the mid-16th century. In the Civil War it changed hands several times, before eventually yielding to Parliament in 1646. It is now in the care of English Heritage, and is open to the public in the summer. Older than Portland Castle, indeed the oldest building on the Isle, is Rufus Castle or Bow and Arrow Castle (SY 69-71). Although the existing ruins date from the late 15th century, records indicate that there has been a castle on this site since the 12th century. Close by is Pennsylvania Castle, a castellated mansion built at the turn of the 19th century for John Penn, a Governor of Portland and grandson of the founder of Pennsylvania. Beside the main entrance is Portland's excellent museum. This is partly housed in Avice's Cottage, a quaint mid-17th century building which features in Hardy's novel The Well Beloved. Displays tell the story of the island, with special emphasis on the stone industry and the prison service (tel: Portland 821804,.

St George's church in Easton is perhaps the finest church on the island. Superbly positioned on a barren windswept site, it is an impressive, though slightly bizarre Georgian building. Its odd appearance is due mainly to the half dome over the central crossing. The interior has retained most of its contemporary fittings, including box pews and galleries. Note the exceptional number of finely carved tombstones in the churchyard. Another church worthy of a visit is St Peter's in The Grove (SY 69-72). Designed by Major-General Edmund Du Cane of the Royal Engineers, this big, bold edifice

was constructed by convict labour in 1872, the beautiful mosaic paving in the chancel apparently being laid by the infamous 19th century murderess Constance Kent.

Powerstock (194) (SY 51-96) *4m NE Bridport*. Its delightful stone and thatch cottages ramble aimlessly up a steep hillside above a stream, in the high country of West Dorset. Perched on a knoll overlooking the rest of the village, is the grey stone church, drastically restored in 1859, but retaining an exceptionally ornate Norman chancel arch and a fine 15th century south doorway with an interesting sculpture of a man holding a staff and book and a woman with a young child.

Powerstock ... one of Dorset's most attractive villages.

On a hill south-east of the village are the motte and bailey earthworks of a Norman Castle. In the early 13th century King John had this converted into a hunting lodge, paying the Sheriff of Devon £129 for the work undertaken. It is possible to walk south and then east to the great Iron Age hill-fort on Eggardon Hill ★, and there is also a little-used road heading in the same direction (see **Tour 2**).

Poxwell (194) (SY 74-84) *5m NE Weymouth*. Main road hamlet situated between two hills, a mile and half from the coast. Poxwell Manor, the 'Oxwell Hall' of Hardy's novel The Trumpet Major, is a 17th century building of Portland stone, with a fancy mellow-brick and stone-tiled gatehouse of the same period.

Poyntington (183) (ST 65-20) *2½m N Sherborne*. Pleasant village set in the valley of the infant River Yeo, with a church belonging structurally to the 15th century, but much restored by over-enthusiastic Victorians. However it contains several ancient relics, including a beaker-shaped Norman font and a much-mutilated 14th century alabaster effigy of a knight in armour. Adjacent to the church is the handsome Court House where the infamous Judge Jeffreys is reputed to have held one of his 'bloody assizes' following the supression of the Monmouth Rebellion.

Preston (194) (SY 70-83) *2m NE Weymouth*. Its attractive old thatched cottages have been overwhelmed by many modern houses, and its 15th

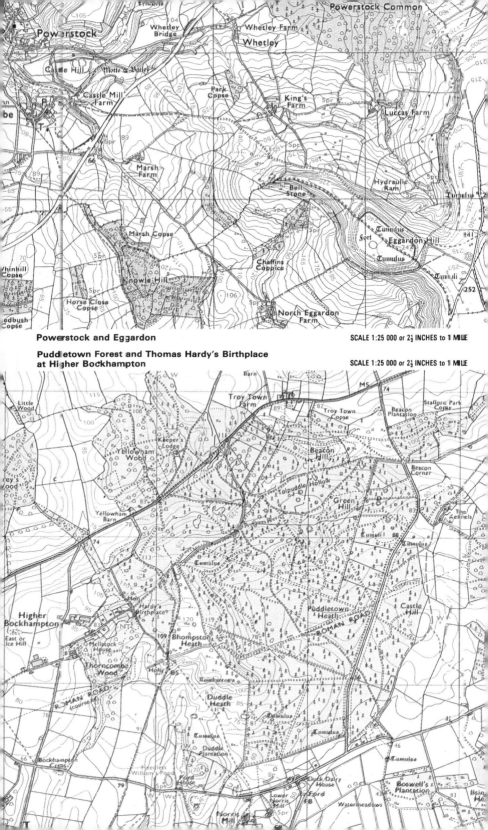

Powerstock and Eggardon
SCALE 1:25 000 or 2½ INCHES to 1 MILE

Puddletown Forest and Thomas Hardy's Birthplace at Higher Bockhampton
SCALE 1:25 000 or 2½ INCHES to 1 MILE

century church by the static caravans of holiday-makers The interior of the latter was heavily restored by the Victorians, but retains an unusual 17th century sculptured figure of an unnamed vicar, who died in 1614.

Puddletown (194) (SY 75-94) *5m NE Dorchester.* Hardy's 'Weatherby' suffers from being situated on an important road junction, but fortunately its most picturesque part, the old square, is set well back from the busy highway with a delightful row of whitewashed thatched cottages close by. The fine, mainly 15th century church almost entirely escaped Victorian restoration, and retains a great number of interesting features including a panelled nave roof, a magnificent three-decker pulpit, a fine Norman font, and a series of bold and detailed 16th and 17th century inscriptions upon the walls. The Athelhampton Chantry, the burial place of the Martyns, who used to reside at Athelhampton Hall ★, contains six magnificent alabaster effigies dating from the 13th to 15th centuries, two excellent medieval brasses, and a large 17th century wall monument to the Brune family.

South-west of here there is a fine 2¼ mile waymarked walk through the conifer plantations of Puddletown Forest. This begins and ends at 'Rhododendron Mile', the open road through the forest, lined with 20-foot-high rhododendron bushes, which are brilliant with colour in late spring.

Pulham (194) (ST 70-08) *7m SE Sherborne.* Sloping settlement with views east over the Lydden valley towards Hazelbury Bryan. Its interesting little Perpendicular church lies at the end of a leafy track, and is worth visiting to see the exquisitely carved medieval corbels and the Purbeck marble Norman font. A small room above the porch was used by priests visiting from Milton Abbey ★. The splendid Old Rectory close by was built in the 18th century, and is a fascinating mixture of Classical and Gothick styles.

Puncknowle (194) (SY 53-88) *6m SE Bridport off B3157.* Pronounced 'Punnel', this delightful village lies in a peaceful little valley, less than a mile from the sea. The church was extensively restored in the 19th century, but retains much Norman work, including a simple tower arch. The two fonts are also Norman, the one with rope work having been removed from West Bexington ★ church after it was destroyed during a French raid in the mid-15th century. Beside the church is a beautiful 17th century manor house with stone mullioned windows, and across the tree-shaded street lies the picturesque stone and thatch Crown Inn. A later tenant of the manor house was Colonel Henry Shrapnel, who invented and gave his name to the devastating fragmentation bomb which was first used during the Crimean War.

Purbeck, Isle of (194) (195) *To S of Wareham.* This so-called Isle is bounded by the sea on its south and east, and the River Frome to its north. Its western boundary is not so clearly defined, but is said to be formed by the Luckford Lake (194) (SY 87-84 etc.), a small stream which rises near East Lulworth and joins the Frome at West Holme. As most schoolboy geologists soon learn, the Isle is made up of six very different rock formations, aligned from north to south. These widely varying formations account for the Isle's amazing variety of coastal and country scenery. The oldest of these rocks is the Kimmeridge Clay, best seen at Kimmeridge ★. Laid down some 140 million years ago, it contains several thin layers of bituminous shale which is generally known as Kimmeridge Coal. The higher ground immediately to the north and east of Kimmeridge consists of Portland and Purbeck limestone. A great freshwater lagoon covered the Isle when the Purbeck limestone was deposited, and it contains numerous fossils of prehistoric animals. Indeed, according to one expert, 'no region in the British isles, perhaps, yields such abundant and continuous tracks of fossil footprints'. Sets of these footprints, as well as fossils of fish and small rodents can be seen in Dorchester Museum ★.

The Purbeck stone is thinly bedded and particularly easy to work, so that many of the villages on the Isle are built of this excellent material. Within the Purbeck Beds lies a thin seam of the famous Purbeck Marble, a fine limestone largely made up of thousands of minute fossilised snail shells, which when polished, has a bluish-grey appearance. Purbeck Marble was first quarried by the Romans, who originally used it for inscribed slabs on the outside of public buildings. However, they soon learned that when exposed to the weather it rapidly deteriorated, and henceforth confined its use to interior work. In the 13th and 14th century it was used in many of the great English cathedrals, including both Salisbury and Exeter. Corfe Castle became the centre of the English marble industry, and strict regulations ensured that only 'islanders' could work in the quarries; for example 'islanders' could only marry outsiders with the permission of the Constable of Corfe (see also Corfe Castle ★). This material is still worked today, but on nothing like the previous scale. For a local example of its use, visit the splendid 19th century church at Kingston ★.

Between the Purbeck Beds and the Purbeck Hills there is a broad valley, which has been carved out of the softer clays and sands of the Wealden Beds. Beyond this valley lies the chalk ridge forming the Purbeck Hills, which stretch from Old Harry Rocks (195) (SZ 05-82) to Lulworth ★, the only gap being at Corfe Castle ★. The sandy heathland on the northern side of the hills lies on the Bagshot Beds, which contains the ball-clay used to make some of the finest 19th century china, including Wedgwood's incredible 1000-piece service, made for Empress Catherine of Russia. A tramway used to take the clay from pits near Corfe Castle to Goathorn Pier (195) (SZ 01-86) in Poole Harbour. One of the old clay pits is the Blue Pool ★, famous for its clear water and beautiful surroundings. Interestingly the ground beneath the Purbecks now yields another valuable product, oil (see Kimmeridge ★ and Wytch Farm ★), but inevitably its extraction in this delightful area continues to be the subject of great controversy.

The Isle of Purbeck possesses some of Britain's finest coastal scenery, and this may be explored by using the Dorset Coast Path ★, which runs all the way between South Haven Point, Studland (195) (SZ 03-86) and Kimmeridge Bay (195) (SY 90-78). To explore the Isle, make use of the Ordnance Survey's 1: 25 000 Outdoor Leisure Map 'Purbeck'. See also our **Walks 10** and **11**.

Purse Caundle (183) (ST 69-17) *4½ m E Sherborne off A30.* Small village situated in low, wooded country less than a mile from the Somerset border, with an appealing church of 14th century origin. The interior was over-restored by those forceful Victorians, but look out for the three medieval brasses in the chantry chapel and the pieces of medieval glass in some of the windows. Purse Caundle's pretty manor house dates from the 15th century, and though it has been enlarged and altered there have been few changes since the reign of James I. The most impressive rooms within are the Great Hall and the Great Chamber. *(Tel: Milborne Port 250400.)*

Radipole (194) (SY 66-81) *1m NE Weymouth off A354.* The old village clusters round a little bridge over the River Wey and consists of an ancient church, a 17th century manor house and several attractive stone and thatched buildings.

Just south of the village is Radipole Lake, a vast freshwater lake which is now a bird sanctuary. Among the many different species which breed here are the rare bearded tit and Cetti's warbler. There is also a large colony of swans, and an excellent information centre run by the R.S.P.B..

Rampisham (194) (ST 56-02) *10m NW Dorchester.* Lying in a narrow green valley beneath the northern slopes of Rampisham Hill, this well spread-out village has a pretty thatched Post Office and a charming creeper-covered inn called the Tiger's Head. The church was rebuilt in the 19th century, and contains little of interest except a 16th century brass to Thomas Dygenys and his wife. In the churchyard is the large base of an early 16th century cross. It is elaborately carved with figures representing the stoning of St Stephen and the assorted martyrdoms of Thomas à Becket, St Edmund and St Peter.

Ringstead (194) (SY 75-81) *6m E Weymouth.* Several modern seaside bungalows mingle with one or two ancient cottages above a shingle beach. The long-vanished medieval village of Ringstead was said to have been burnt by the French in 1420, although it is more likely that it was depopulated by the plague. One of the cottages contains the chancel arch of the old church.

The Burning Cliff above Ringstead Bay is so called because the bituminous shale within the cliff has been known to ignite. A path up the immense chalky cliff-face of White Nothe was used by smugglers, and is mentioned in J.Meade Faulkner's adventure story *Moonfleet.* The Burning Cliff and White Nothe form part of the Southdown Farm Estate, owned by the National Trust. Access to the estate is by foot only, and visitors must leave their cars in the park situated on the crest of the down.

St Aldhelm's (or St Alban's) Head (195) (SY 96-75) *5m SW Swanage.* St Aldhelm's chapel stands on the grassy windswept summit of this 350-foot-high headland, the most southerly point in the Isle of Purbeck. It is a remarkable little Norman structure, square in plan with a single immense central pier supporting a stone-vaulted roof in the dark interior. The small turret at the apex of the low pyramidal roof probably supported a fire cresset, or brazier, to warn sailors of the treacherous rocks below.

There are magnificent views of the interesting and often spectacular Dorset coastline from this dramatic headland. Walk east to Winspit Bottom, where there are extensive remains of abandoned stone quarries, or walk north and then west to Chapman's Pool (195) (SY 95-76).

Sandbanks (195) (SZ 04-87) *4m SW Bournemouth.* Long thin promontory forming the northern entrance to Poole Harbour. Owing to modern development most of the 'sand banks' have disappeared, but a few still exist, especially or the seaward side, where there is a wide, flat expanse of sand. This superb beach ensures that Sandbanks is crowded with holidaymakers all summer long. A chain ferry at the tip of the peninsula allows both motorists and foot passengers to cross over to the Isle of Purbeck ★, and a passenger ferry to Brownsea Island ★ also operates from here.

Sandford Orcas (183) (ST 62-20) *3m N Sherborne.* This attractive stone village lies in a peaceful dale among little hills on the Somerset border. For many generations it was held by the Oresculiz family, and it was from them that the village took the second half of its name. However, the present manor house, a delightfully unspoilt building of Ham Hill stone, was built by Edward Knoyle in the early 16th century. The decorative details on the gatehouse are remarkably similar to those found on the parlour wing of Athelhampton, suggesting that they were possibly both built by the same stonemason. The mullioned windows of the Hall contain some fine pieces of 16th century armorial glass and there is also much Jacobean woodwork. See also the ornately carved overmantle, brought from the Joiners Hall, Salisbury. *(Tel: Corton Denham 206.)*

Alongside the manor house is the 15th century church, also of Ham Hill stone, with an interesting 13th century font and several good memorials to the Knoyle family.

Seatown (193) (SY 42-91) *3½m SW Bridport off A35.* This is sited in a narrow gap in the cliffs overlooking a shingle beach, and consists of a picturesque 18th century inn and a few cottages. The splendid cliff coastline between Eype and Charmouth is within the National Trust's Golden Cap Estate ★, and it is possible to walk the 6 miles between these two points, with Seatown approximately midway. The car park here is also the start of our **Walk 2.**

Shaftesbury (183) (ST 86-22). Dorset's only hill town, Shaftesbury is a busy little place built upon a

Gold Hill, Shaftesbury.

700-foot greensand spur commanding majestic views across the eastern part of the Blackmoor Vale. A town of great antiquity it once boasted a castle, three mints, an immense abbey, twelve churches, four market crosses and even several hospitals. Sadly, little remains to remind us of its glorious past, and if the visitor comes here expecting to find a miniature Winchester or York he will, as Thomas Hardy wrote, be thrown 'into a pensive melancholy'.

Known to the Saxons as Sceaftesbyrig — 'a fortified settlement at the end of a promontory' — the town is possibly the site of the older Celtic town Caer Palladore, though this theory has not been substantiated. Towards the end of the 9th century King Alfred founded the Benedictine *Abbey (1)* for his daughter, Aethelgive. The abbey's power and wealth grew immensely when the remains of the boy King Edward the Martyr were reinterred here in 979. Miraculous occurrences supposedly took place at the king's tomb, pilgrims flocked to the shrine, and the town prospered accordingly. Athelstan authorised two mints here and in the 11th century Edward the Confessor licensed a third. The Normans enlarged the abbey further, and such was its power in the 15th century that it was said that had the Abbess been able to marry the Abbot of Glastonbury their heir would have owned more land than the king. Such an exalted position ensured that it was most ruthlessly destroyed at the Dissolution. Totally demolished, it was not until

1861 that the foundations were uncovered. They were excavated and the visitor is now able to easily trace out the plan and the most important features of the vast church. In the place where the high altar stood there is now a market cross, moved to the abbey site from *Angel Square (2)*. A small museum contains Norman stone relics as well as a few Saxon fragments and some floor tiles. In 1931 the tomb and bones of Edward the Martyr were discovered but were sadly removed to a bank in Worthing. It is hoped that they may yet be returned to their established resting place.

The abbey site lies besides *Park Walk (3)*, a promenade donated to the citizens of the town by a local man hoping to gain political favour. Deplorably, the lovely 18th century beech avenue was cut down in the 1950s, but it is still an attractive place to walk and admire the wonderful views out over the Blackmoor Vale. Below is the village of *St James (4)*, with pretty stone cottages and an attractive group of houses ranged around a courtyard with an old pump in the centre. From the esplanade walk east through a gap between two shops, into the northern end of the High Street. Immediately to the north is *King Alfred's Kitchen*, the town's only surviving timber-framed building; while a little further beyond is the *Grosvenor Hotel (5)*, an old coaching inn noted for its intricately carved Chevy Chase sideboard.

The Earl of Grosvenor was responsible for the building of the early 19th century crenellated *Town*

1 Abbey
2 Angel Square
3 Park Walk
4 St James (village)
5 Grosvenor Hotel

6 Town Hall
7 Tout Hill
8 Gold Hill
9 Town Museum
10 Bimport St.

11 Holy Trinity Church
12 Ox House
13 Castle Hill
14 Tourist Information Centre

Shaftesbury

SCALE 1:10 000 or 6 INCHES to 1 MILE

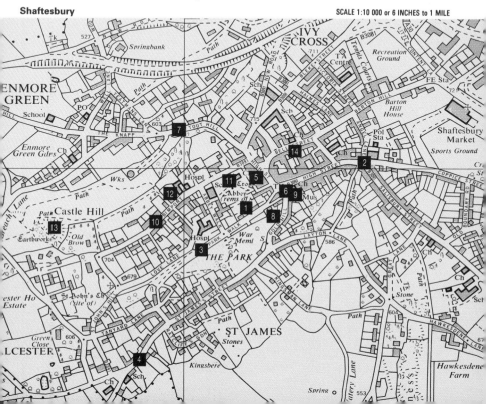

Hall (6) which stands at the top of Gold Hill. Contained within is the Byzant, a unique late medieval implement used in an annual water festival held at the foot of *Tout Hill (7)* in Enmore Green. The festival was a time to celebrate and give thanks to the Lord of the Manor for allowing Shaftesbury's citizens to obtain their water supply from wells located here. Obtaining water was always a problem for the town; it was said that Shaftesbury had more beer than water; and it was not until the 1830s that water was pumped and piped up to it. Next to the Town Hall is the *Church of St Peter*, its Perpendicular tower precariously placed on the edge of the upper end of Gold Hill. Saved from ruin in the 1970s this church is mainly 15th century with some 16th and 17th century alterations. The best feature inside is the well-carved late 15th century vaulting in the disused west porch. For a long time the church crypt was used as a beer cellar by the neighbouring inn, hence the saying 'The spirit above is the spirit Divine, the spirit below is the spirit of wine'.

Gold Hill (8) is undoubtedly the most spectacular and evocative place in Shaftesbury. The fame of this steep cobbled street, with a massive buttressed 14th or 15th century wall on one side and a delightful row of stepped cottages on the other, was further enhanced by the Hovis television advertisment that featured a small boy struggling to push his delivery bicycle up the hill. It also featured prominently in the film of Hardy's *Far from the Madding Crowd*. At the top is a modest building formerly used to accommodate both travelling men and vagrants. It is now the *Town Museum (9)* and among its many fascinating items are a lock of Queen Victoria's hair, a number of old cinema projectors and magic lanterns, and a dried cat from a cottage roof, where it was once used to scare away mice and rats.

Bimport Street (10) was the main street of the Saxon town. At the eastern end is *Holy Trinity Church (11)*, a large early Victorian Church built on the site of a chapel once associated with the abbey. Beyond is *Ox House (12)* which is renamed 'Old Groves Place' in Hardy's *Jude the Obscure*. Walk to *Castle Hill (13)* at the western end of Bimport Street for excellent views to the Mendip and Quantock Hills. *The Tourist Information Centre (14)* is at the County Library in Bell Street which runs parallel to the High Street *(tel: Shaftesbury 2256)*

Shapwick (195) (ST 93-01) *4m NW Wimborne Minster.* Peaceful, partly thatched village set in pastoral country besides the meandering River Stour. The 12th to 15th century church, with its attractively chequered stone and flint tower, is beautifully sited on a willow-bordered river bank close to the point where the Roman road from Badbury Rings to Dorchester must have passed through a ford. The interior has undergone Victorian restoration, but still retains several interesting features including a Norman tower arch and two medieval brasses.

A poem displayed inside the Anchor Inn tells the amusing story of the 'Shapwick monster'. The monster was in fact nothing more than a giant crab which had fallen off the back of a travelling fishmonger's cart, but to the ignorant villagers, who had never seen such an animal, it probably appeared to be a most frightening creature.

Sherborne (183) (ST 63-16) Perhaps the most beautiful of all the Dorset towns, this ancient place lies on the green northern slopes of the Yeo Valley not far from the Somerset border. No other town in the county can boast so many medieval buildings, ranging in size and grandeur from the magnificent abbey to the small conduit in Cheap Street. The surest way to see all these architectural treasures is to make a detailed exploration on foot of not only the main streets but also the many hidden lanes and alleyways.

The best starting point is *The Abbey (1)*, which is situated in the very heart of the town, and described by the Royal Commission on Historical Monuments as 'the most important architectural monument in the county'. In common with much of Sherborne this majestic building is constructed of warm, golden coloured Ham Hill stone. Its history dates back to AD 705, when King Ine of Wessex established a new diocese here. The first bishop, St Aldhelm, built a cathedral church, to which was attached a body of secular canons. The diocese was moved to Old Sarum in 1075, but the Benedictine monastery, established in 998, continued until the Dissolution. During the Middle Ages a flourishing town grew up around the monastery, and in the 14th century the townsfolk built themselves a separate parish church, Allhallows, at the west end of the abbey. In 1437 a serious dispute arose between the parishioners and the monks over the latter's decision to move the abbey font, still used to baptize the town's children, to a less convenient site. In retaliation the citizens set up their own font in Allhallows. Despite intervention by the Bishop the dispute intensified, until a rather rash parish priest shot a flaming arrow into the abbey roof, setting the building ablaze. Evidence of the great fire can be seen in the reddened stonework or the pillars west of the tower. After the Dissolution the abbey passed to Sir John Horsey, who sold it to the town for 320 pounds. No longer required, Allhallows was demolished about 1541. Remnants of it can be found at the west end of the abbey.

Visually the present abbey is largely 15th century, but it incorporates much of the Norman church, built by Bishop Roger of Caen about 1120. Traces of the older Saxon cathedral can also be found on the north-west side. The outstanding feature of the resplendent interior is the incredible 15th century stone fan-vaulted roof of the nave and choir. A coin-operated spotlight enables the visitor to illuminate the whole choir roof. The Victorian choir stalls retain an interesting series of 15th century misericords, one showing a woman beating a man. In the choir aisles are the remains of three Abbots' tombs, the oldest belonging to Abbot Clement, who died in 1160. The south transept has a fine Te Deum window designed by A.W. Pugin, and a vast

Sherborne New Castle.

monument to John Digby, third Earl of Bristol. East of the north transept is the Wykham Chapel, containing the splendid 16th century canopied tomb of Sir John Horsey. Note the similarly styled tomb of John Leweston (1584) in St Katherine's Chapel. Some 15th century glass is incorporated in the windows of this chapel. After the Dissolution the Lady Chapel was converted into a residence for the masters of Sherborne School, and it was not until 1921 that it was once again reincorporated into the abbey. The fine modern glass reredos was engraved in 1967-8 by Lawrence Whistler. The peal of eight bells in the tower is reckoned to be the heaviest in the world, and includes the famous two and a quarter ton 'Great Tom' tenor bell, donated to the abbey by Cardinal Wolsey in the 16th century.

The surviving monastic buildings lying immediately to the north of the abbey now form part of the premises of *Sherborne School (2)*. This was endowed as a grammar school by Edward VI in 1550, although an educational establishment had existed here since 705. South-west of the church, at the corner of Half Moon Street, are the *Almshouses of St John the Baptist and St John the Evangelist (3)* . Built in 1437-42, for 'twelve poor men and four poor women', it is still used for its original purpose. The remarkably well-preserved south wing is pleasantly complemented by the Victorian extension running to the north. The

chapel contains an exceptional triptych, painted in the 15th century by a unknown artist, probably German or Flemish. Also see the rare 15th century glass in the south window.

From the almshouses walk east along Half Moon Street, passing a row of humble Tudor tenements, built as a series of shops with a church meeting room above. At the end of this street proceed north into Cheap Street. On the left is the hexagonal *Conduit House (4)*, dating from the 16th century. It was originally situated in the abbey cloisters, and was used as the monks lavatorium. Pass through the 15th century archway behind here to the *Abbey Gate House (5)*, now Sherborne Museum. Return back into Cheap Street and walk north. At the junction with Abbey Road is *Abbeylands (6)*, an excellent example of a 16th century half-timbered house. Turn left into Abbey Road to see 18th century *Abbey House (7)*, and then turn right into Hospital Lane, where stands *Abbey Grange (8)*, formerly part of the tithe barn of the abbey. Hospital Lane leads to an area called The Green. Here are several interesting buildings, including The Julian and the George Inn, both 16th century, and Greenhill House, a fine 17th century dwelling. Sherborne's finest house stands in Newlands. This large building, now *Lord Digby's School (9)*, was constructed in 1720 to the designs of Benjamin Bastard, brother of the Blandford Bastards. These

1 Abbey	6 Abbeylands	11 The Old Castle (off map to east)
2 Sherborne School	7 Abbey House	
3 Almshouses	8 Abbey Grange	12 The New Castle (off map to east)
4 Conduit House	9 Lord Digby's School	
5 Abbey Gate House	10 Tourist Information Centre	

Sherborne   SCALE 1:10 000 or 6 INCHES to 1 MILE

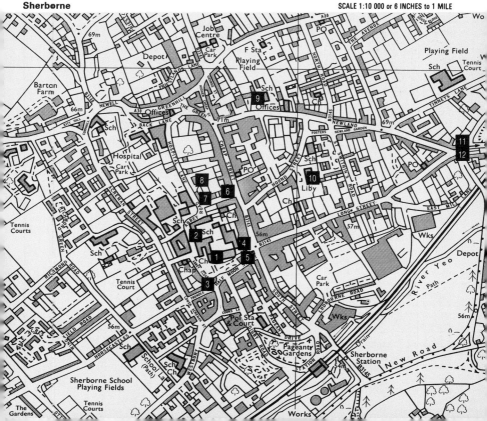

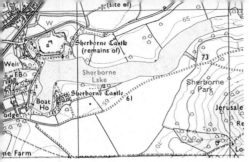

Sherbourne Castles SCALE 1:25 000 or 2½ INCHES to 1 MILE

then are some of Sherborne's most interesting town buildings, but in your walk around the town try not to overlook the many other Tudor, Stuart and Georgian buildings that contribute so much to its old-fashioned country atmosphere. The *Tourist Information Centre (10)* is located in Hound Street *(tel: Sherborne 81534)*

Sherborne's two castles lie to the east of the town centre, on the south side of the railway. *The Old Castle (11)* (EH) was erected in the early 12th century by Bishop Roger — that eminent builder bishop who, besides rebuilding the abbey, also built two other castles, one at Malmesbury the other at Old Sarum. In 1139 Sherborne Castle was seized by King Stephen, and it remained in the possession of the crown until 1592, when Queen Elizabeth granted it to her court favourite, Sir Walter Raleigh. In spite of some alterations he found it a most unsuitable place to live, and in 1594 decided to construct a new castle across the valley. After Raleigh's disgrace in 1603 both castles were confiscated by James I, and in 1617 were bought by Sir John Digby. During the Civil War the Old Castle was held for the king until 1645, when it was successfully besieged by Parliamentary forces led by General Fairfax, who then blew it up. The principal remain is the imposing four-storey Norman gatehouse, although portions of the keep, chapel and curtain wall also survive.

In 1660 the Digbys returned from exile in France and repossessed *The New Castle (12)*. Since then it has remained in Digby hands. The many towers and chimneys, and the covering of brownish stucco make it a rather austere building. The interior was refurbished in Jacobean style in the mid-19th century, although the Oak Room retains its original oak panelling of 1620. The beautiful grounds were landscaped by Capability Brown in the 18th century. He dammed the River Yeo to create the large lake which separates the old castle from the new. A stone seat near the lake is supposedly where Raleigh was sitting smoking a pipe when he was drenched by a servant who, being unaccustomed to this new practice, thought that his master was on fire. A Roman mosaic pavement, discovered at Lenthay Green to the south-west of Sherborne in 1836, has been reset into the floor of the Gothick dairy *(tel: Sherborne 813182)*.

Shillingstone (194) (ST 82-11) *5m NW Blandford Forum.* Exceptionally long main-road village situated on the southern slopes of the Stour Valley, between Hambledon Hill and Okeford Hill. Standing in a secluded spot north of the road is the church of the Holy Rood, a building of 12th century origin refashioned in the 15th century and enlarged in Victorian times. The most striking internal feature is the roof, redecorated at the turn of the century by

G.F. Bodley, perhaps better known as the architect of Washington Cathedral in the United States. Also of interest are the Norman windows, sited high up in the nave, and the Purbeck marble Norman font. In the belfry and porch are two ancient stone fragments on which are carved faces of powerful simplicity. From the churchyard there is an excellent view of Hambledon Hill ★. At the north end of the village stands an old market cross with an ornately carved modern shaft.

Shipton Gorge (193,194) (SY 49-91) *2½m E Bridport.* The second half of its name does not refer to any geological feature in the vicinity, but comes from the name of the Norman family who held the manor after the Conquest, the de Gorges. It is an unexceptional village situated in rolling countryside above one of the many small streams that feed the River Bride. The church of St Martin has retained its 15th century tower, but is otherwise a 19th century building.

Silton (183) (ST 78-29) *6m NW Shaftesbury.* Diminutive settlement on rising ground above the infant River Stour, close to the Wiltshire and Somerset borders. The small, mainly 15th century church has a delightfully airy interior, with well-restored wagon-roofs and stencil-painted walls. The north chapel has a tiny fan-vaulted roof and on the north wall of the nave there is a large monument by the fashionable sculptor John Nost to the 17th century judge, Sir Hugh Wyndham. Near the church is 'Wyndham's Oak', a massive oak tree under whose branches the worthy judge is believed to have often sat 'in peaceful contemplation'.

Sixpenny Handley (184) (ST 99-17) *10m NE Blandford Forum off A354.* A large sprawling village lying in a quiet hollow in the heart of the Cranborne Chase. Its unusual name has nothing to do with the late-lamented coin of the realm, but is in fact an amalgamation of the two medieval 'hundreds' of Saxpena and Hanlege. Despite its ancient name there is no air of antiquity about the village, for it was largely destroyed by a fire in 1892. One of the few buildings to escape this conflagration was the church, but it had already been disfigured by a heavy-handed restoration a few years earlier. However, the interior still contains an interesting 12th century font, and a very weathered Norman sculpture of 'Christ in Glory'. In the churchyard an inscription on a tombstone tells how poached deer were once hidden in the tomb beneath it.

South Perrott (193) (ST 47-06) *9m N Bridport.* Situated in the valley of the River Parrett, this attractive stone village sits partially astride the A356, with views north over the Somerset border. Sited close to some earthworks is the sizeable church, externally of the 15th century, but with four Norman crossing arches within. There appears to be little else of interest here except for two roundels of 18th century glass in the chancel north window.

Spetisbury (195) (ST 91-02) *3½m SE Blandford Forum.* This elongated village straggles along the busy A350 for more then a mile, squeezed between the River Stour, which here briefly divides into three separate channels, and the now disused Somerset-to-Dorset railway line. Although now subjected to much modern development it still possesses several attractive thatched cottages, including one that has been converted into a tea-room. A plaque on its wall proudly lists all the monarchs that have reigned since it was built in the 16th century. The long flint and stone church situated at the northern end of the village was, apart from its 14th century tower, largely rebuilt in 1859. Despite this, its interior is still worth visiting, as its contents include a fine 17th century pulpit, and an interesting late 16th century canopied tomb to John Bowyer. A small road at the other end of the village passes over Crawford Bridge, an appealing 15th century stone bridge of nine arches.

Stalbridge (183) (ST 73-17) *6m E Sherborne*. A small town on a gentle slope above the Stour, with modern buildings added to the old town, which was described by the famous 16th century antiquary, John Leland, as a 'praty uplandishe toune of one streate neately well buildyd'. Its greatest treasure is the 30-foot-high 15th century market cross, with its unusual stepped octagonal base supporting a weathered pedestal carved with figures from the Crucifixion and the Resurrection. The church stands on an elevated site at the north end of the town, its tall pinnacled tower a prominent landmark for miles around. Although heavily restored in the 19th century, it is a fine building, the contents of which include an old font shaped like a kettle-drum and two medieval altar tombs, one supporting the recumbent effigy of an emaciated corpse covered in a shroud.

Steeple (195) (SY 91-81) *4½m S Wareham*. Tiny hamlet attractively situated on an isolated knoll beneath the great ridge of hills which slice through the Isle of Purbeck ★. Except for two 16th century chapels, the church is largely 15th century, and has a most unusual barrel organ, and some heraldic stars and stripes, these being the coat of arms of the Lawrence family, collateral ancestors of George Washington. The manor house is largely 20th century, but incorporates some medieval work.

At the western end of high Ridgeway Hill there is a picnic site with spectacular all round views, close to the checkpoint at the entry to the Lulworth Range Area. From here it is possible both to visit Tyneham ★ and to drive across to East Lulworth ★ at certain times, but for details of access times, see note at foot of our Tyneham ★ entry.

Stinsford (194) (SY 71-91) *1m E Dorchester off A35*. The 'Mellstock' of Thomas Hardy's story *Under the Greenwood Tree*, Stinsford consists of a church and a few dwellings situated along a quiet country lane north of the River Frome. The church is much visited, for here, beside the graves of his two wives, lies the heart of Thomas Hardy, his ashes having been interred in Poets' Corner in Westminster Abbey. The church itself is 13th century in character, but it was ruthlessly restored in the 19th century. However, it retains a battered but impressive Saxon relief of a winged St Michael outside the tower, and within there is a square Norman font. Also see the plaques to William O'Brien and his wife Susanna, a daughter of the Earl of Ilchester who, much to the disgust of aristocratic society, married a professional actor

Thomas Hardy's stone in Stinsford Churchyard.

and dramatist. The Earl forgave his daughter on condition that O'Brien left the stage. This story delighted Hardy, and he used it several times in his writings.

Stoke Abbott (193) (ST 45-00) *6m N Bridport*. The 17th and 18th century stone and thatch cottages of Stoke Abbott, nestling along sunken lanes in a deep coombe of the west Dorset hills, make up one of Dorset's prettiest villages. It is overlooked from the west by Lewesdon Hill while to the north, Waddon Hill is topped by the remains of a small Roman fort. The church, a largely Victorian building which is beautifully positioned on a sloping site above a tiny stream, has a most exquisitely carved Norman font, but contains little else of interest. One of the rectors here in the 18th century was William Crowe, who is best known for his poem 'Lewesdon Hill', a verse apparently much admired by Coleridge and Wordsworth.

It was here in 1858 that James Searle murdered Sarah Anne Guppy, thereby earning himself an unenviable place in the record book, as being the last man in England to be publicly hanged — an event which Thomas Hardy is believed to have watched — but only from a safe distance with the help of a telescope.

Stour Provost (183) (ST 79-21) *5m W Shaftesbury*. A delightful village sited on high ground above the Stour Valley, just off the Sturminster Newton to Gillingham road. Its centre presents an attractive picture with many old yellow stone cottages and several 17th century farmhouses lining the main streets. The tower of the church is 14th century, and although the interior was over-restored by the Victorians, has an excellent 15th century oak panelled chancel roof and some good modern glass.

Stourton Caundle (183) (ST 71-15) *6½m E Sherborne*. Straggling up the slopes of a small valley, Stourton Caundle derives the first part of its name from the former Lords of the Manor, the Stourton family. Nothing remains of their fortified house, except a tiny 13th century chapel, now part of Manor Farm. Nearby, the church of St Peter dates back to the 13th century, with 14th and 15th century additions. On a canopied tomb-chest in the chancel, there is the recumbent alabaster effigy of a lady, which is said to be that of Agnes Fauntleroy, who died in the late 15th century. Also note the interesting Georgian font and cover, and the fine Perpendicular pulpit with linenfold panels.

Walk south, over Caundle Brook, to Stock

Gaylard (194) (ST 72-13). Here, in a splendid park populated by a herd of handsome fallow deer, is a simple 18th century house and a little church. This has some pieces of medieval glass, a 15th century stone altar and a fine 13th century monument of a cross-legged knight dressed as a crusader.

Studland (195) (SZ 03-82) 3m N Swanage. Unspoilt seaside village scattered over the tree-covered foothills between Studland Heath and the chalk heights of Ballard Down. Situated on a little knoll a few hundred yards from the sea is the most interesting church of St Nicholas. Entirely Norman except for the south porch and some of the windows, it is an exceptionally sturdy stone building with chancel, nave and low saddleback tower. Running along the south and north walls of the nave is a corbel table with grotesquely carved faces, and inside the dark interior there is a magnificent Norman chancel arch and stone vaulting of the same period. Note also the chalice-shaped 12th century font. A modern village cross, not far from the church, is covered with carvings of many unlikely objects, including a bomb, a violin and even the supersonic airliner, Concord.

Two large nature reserves maintained by the Nature Conservancy Council on Studland and Godlingston Heaths, contain many rare plants and animals, including all six of Britain's reptiles. At the centre of Studland Heath there is a large freshwater lagoon, called Little Sea, which in the winter is teeming with many different species of migrating ducks. There are several waymarked nature trails through the reserves.

Perhaps the most popular walk from Studland is that running westwards to the Agglestone Rock (SZ 02-82), an immense stone sited atop a small hill on Godlingston Heath. Some 17 feet high and weighing over 400 tons, legend has it that this is one of the stones the devil threw at Old Harry Rocks from the Isle of Wight. There are also splendid walks along Studland's superb beach towards the Sandbanks Ferry and over the heathland to the shores of Poole Harbour, and it should not be overlooked that Studland marks the eastern extremity of the Dorset Coast Path ★.

Sturminster Marshall (195) (SY 94-99) 6m SE Blandford Forum. An unexceptional village sprawling over a large area of ground in the Stour valley, with a medieval church rebuilt in 1802 and again in 1859. Architecturally it is an unremarkable building, but it does contain some interesting items, notably a Cromwellian funerary helmet, a painted wooded panel of King Henry VI, and two ancient coffin lids, one dated 1280. The road north from the church crosses a fine eight-arched bridge which still rests partly on its medieval oak piles.

Sturminster Newton (194) (ST 78-14) 7½m NW Blandford Forum off A357. Affectionately known to locals as 'Stur', this sleepy little country town is situated on sloping ground above the green watermeadows of the meandering River Stour, and is approached from the south by a fine 17th century stone bridge, which still displays its plaque threatening anyone who harms it with transportation (see also Witchampton ★). Writing in 1540, John Leland

1 The Quay
2 Mill Pond
3 St Mary's Church
4 Tithe Barn Museum & Art Gallery
5 Town Hall
6 Purbeck House
7 Mowlem Theatre
8 Tourist Information Centre
9 Grosvenor Hotel
10 Clock Tower
11 Swanage Railway Society

Swanage

SCALE 1:10 000 or 6 INCHES to 1 MILE

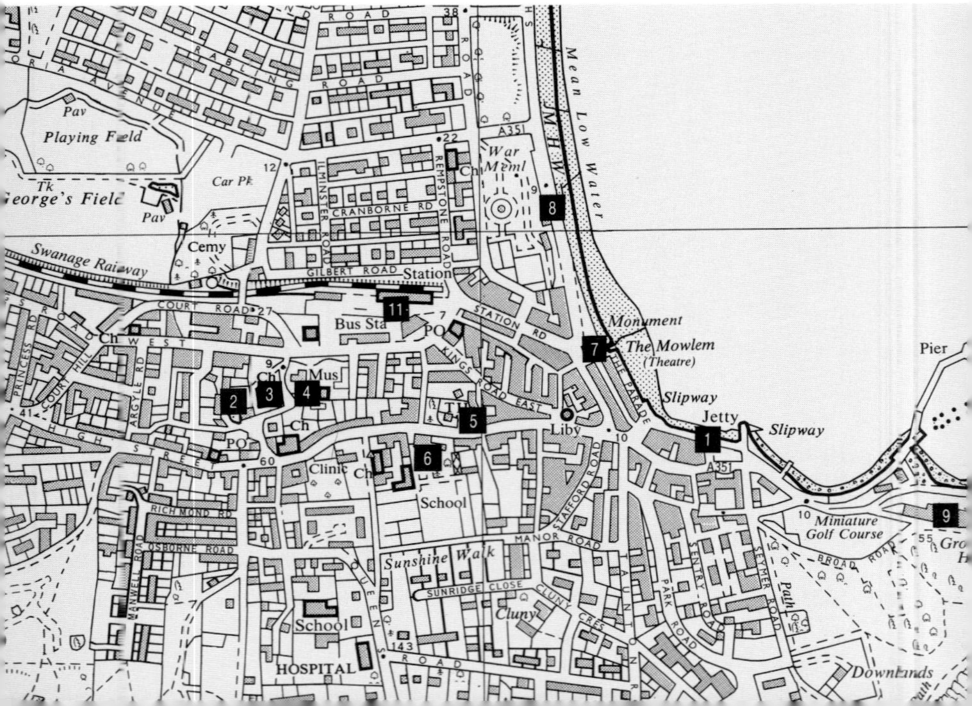

stated that 'the townlette is no great thing, and the building of it mene'. However, he did concede that this 'townlette had a very good market'. Since then the livestock market has continued to expand, so much so that today it is reckoned to be one of the biggest in the country, with possibly the largest calf market in Europe. The base of the 15th century market cross can still be seen in the square, although the market itself was transferred to a larger site around the Corn Exchange in 1900. In common with most other towns in Dorset, Sturminster Newton suffered badly from fires in the 17th and 18th centuries, but there are still a number of quaint old timber-framed thatched cottages, as well as several attractive bow-fronted buildings of brick, stone and cob. Of the original church built here in 1486 by John Selwood, one of the last Abbots of Glastonbury, only the tower, the outer aisle walls and the fine wagon roof survive. The rest of the fabric was rebuilt in 1824 by the Reverend Thomas Lane Fox, a man who it is said spent the greater part of his fortune of one hundred thousand pounds 'for the benefit of his parishioners'. It is a large building, imposing but rather characterless. There is little of interest inside, save for a well-carved lectern commemorating the Dorset poet William Barnes (see also Winterborne Came★), who was born in the parish in 1801. Behind the church lies the small stone school where Barnes was educated. His great friend Thomas Hardy resided in Sturminster Newton for two years, whilst writing *The Return of the Native*.

On the other side of the river, Newton has a charming row of 15th century cottages, with thatched roofs and exposed Tudor-style beams, while on the rocky outcrop of Castle Hill there is an ancient earthwork bearing the ruins of a late medieval house. Also in 'Stur' is Sturminster Mill, one of the few remaining working flour-mills in the county. Delightfully sited beside a weir on the River Stour, it dates from the 17th and 18th centuries and

was restored to full working order in 1981 after a period of neglect. Of especial interest is its water turbine which was fitted in place of the less-efficient traditional water wheel in 1904. *(Tel: Sturminster Newton 72275 or 73151.)* A footbridge over the weir enables visitors to walk from here across green fields to the town.

Sutton Poyntz (194) (SY 70-83) *3m NE Weymouth off A353.* Tucked away in a quiet nook at the southern end of White Horse Hill, this village frequently appears under the guise of 'Overcombe' in Hardy's story *The Trumpet Major*. Beside a large mill-pond are many charming stone and thatched cottages, some dating from the 18th and 19th centuries, others built in the 1930s by the architect who designed the New Victorian Cinema in London. Walk north-east to White Horse Hill, and return to Sutton Poyntz by dropping down to Osmington★, and returning along the path by the little River Jordan.

Swanage (195) (SZ 02-78). 'A seaside village lying snug within two headlands as between finger and thumb', is how Thomas Hardy describes the location of this cosy Purbeck holiday resort in his novel *The Hand of Ethelberta*. It is a most apt description, although since Hardy's brief stay here in 1875 it has greatly expanded. Until the mid-19th century the town's main business was the quarrying and exporting of Purbeck stone and marble from the cliffs to the south and west. Along *the quay (1)* are the remains of railway lines used to transport the stone to jetties, where it was loaded onto barges and shipped to London. Around the attractive *mill pond (2)* at the top of High Street are some lovely old grey stone quarrymen's cottages. Here also is *St Mary's Church (3)*, largely Victorian save for the solid 14th century west tower, and the *Tithe Barn Museum and Art Gallery (4)*. The stone industry figures predominantly here, with examples of the marble quarried locally and exhibits of old mining tools *(tel: Swanage 424768)*.

The town's reputation as a seaside resort was greatly enhanced by the visit in 1835 of Princess (later Queen) Victoria, but it was the coming of the railway in 1885 that made the place popular with the masses. The Victorian character of the town owes much to the work of John Mowlem and his nephew George Burt, local quarry contractors who made vast fortunes shipping Purbeck stone to the capital. When their ships returned to Swanage they carried much London stonework salvaged from demolished buildings, and they incorporated this in structures they erected in the town. To the *Town Hall (5)* of 1872 George Burt added the spectacularly carved mid-17th century entrance of the Mercers' Hall, Cheapside. In nearby *Town Hall Lane* there is the old-town lock up, a tiny building with a very old door held together by nails. Further up the High Street is *Purbeck House (6)*, a forbidding Victorian dwelling built in 1875 for George Burt, and now a convent. The walls are partly covered with stone left over from the Albert Memorial and in the grounds there is an archway originally erected at Hyde Park Corner in 1844.

The modern *Mowlem Theatre (7)* stands on the site of the Mowlem Institute of 1863. *King Alfred's Column* outside is a granite pillar crowned by cannon balls captured in the Crimea, and was erected by John Mowlem in 1862 to commemorate

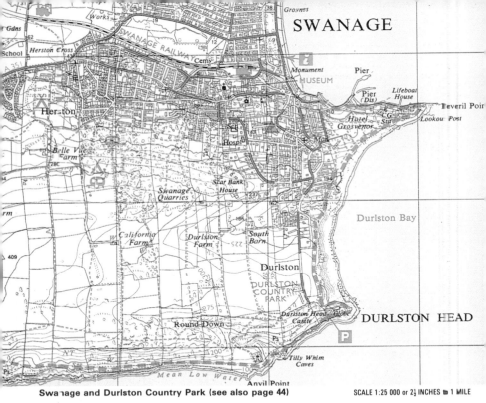

Swanage and Durlston Country Park (see also page 44)

SCALE 1:25 000 or 2½ INCHES ▪ 1 MILE

the destruction of the Danish fleet off Peveril Point in AD 877. *The Tourist Information Office (8)* is at The White House in Shore Street *(tel: Swanage 422835).* Two stone Ionic columns in front of the *Grosvenor Hotel (9)* probably originated from number 45 Regent Street. The gothic *Clock Tower (10)* to the east is yet another relic from London. It was set up in 1854 on the southern side of London Bridge as a memorial to the Duke of Wellington but was such an obstacle to traffic that it was dismantled and re-erected here (minus clock) in 1868. The railway line from Wareham was closed in 1972, but the *Swanage Railway Society (11)* has recently restored the station buildings and is running steam trains on a short section of relaid track. The Society hopes eventually to rebuild the line back to Wareham, and at the time of writing it hopes shortly to reach Harman's Cross (195) (SY 98-80).

The Dorset Coast Footpath passes through the town and gives two excellent walks, one south to Durlston Head, the other north to Ballard Down and Swanage Bay.

Old Harry's Rock. Durlston Country Park ★ contains the Great Globe, a 40-ton piece of Purbeck stone donated to the town by George Burt. Alternatively walk north-west onto Nine Barrow Down. Legend says that the nine Bronze Age round barrows which are over two foot high cover the graves of nine kings killed in battle. This walk passes Godlingston Manor, parts of which date from the 13th century.

Swyre (194) (SY 52-88) *4½ m SE Bridport.* Undistinguished village lying in a quiet valley between Beacon Knap and a small hill called the Knoll, with a largely rebuilt church. However, the 15th century tower remains intact, and inside there are two brasses to the Russell family, who lived at nearby Berwick House. It was a John Russell who in 1506 went to Wolfeton House to act as interpreter for the shipwrecked Archduke Philip of Austria and his Spanish wife (see also Charminster ★).

Sydling St Nicholas (194) (SY 63-99) *7m NW Dorchester off A37.* A quiet place remotely situated in the beautiful chalk valley of the Sydling Water, which is crossed here by several small bridges. There are many neat thatched cottages, a handsome mellow-brick Georgian house, and next to the church, the 18th and 19th century Court House. Sir Francis Walsingham, Secretary of State to Elizabeth I and founder of her 'intelligence service' once owned the village, and in the great tithe barn there is believed to be a beam carved with the date 1590 and the initials of his wife, Lady Ursula Walsingham. Sadly the barn now has a roof of corrugated-iron, but in most other respects is as impressive as any in Dorset. Standing on high ground above the village, and approached by a path beneath dark yews, is the gargoyled church, mainly 15th century, but with a chancel remodelled in the 18th century. The interior was spared the usual excesses of Victorian restoration, and retains a pleasant 18th century atmosphere, with box pews, 18th century tower screen, and numerous 18th and 19th century wall monuments to the Smith family. The massive 12th century font is thought to have been carved from a Roman capital.

Symondsbury (193) (SY 44-93) *1m W Bridport.* Nestles in a peaceful and well-wooded hollow beneath the rounded summit of Colmer's Hill. The village is noted for its thatchers, and many of its enchanting stone houses are roofed with thatch, including the picturesque Ilchester Arms, which has a skittle alley and table skittles. The church is mainly 14th and 15th century in origin, but its interior was ruthlessly scraped and re-pointed by over-enthusiastic Victorians. However, do not overlook the fine Georgian altar rails and the simple pulpit of the same period. Also of interest are the choir and altar stalls, with their modern carvings of various animals and flowers. West of the church, behind tall bushes, is the Old Rectory, an elegant Georgian house enlarged in the 19th century.

Tarrant Crawford (195) (ST 92-03) *3m SE Blandford Forum.* Here, at the end of a quiet track beside the delightful River Tarrant, is just a small church, a farm and its attendant buildings. The plain exterior of the stone and flint church conceals a delightfully simple and well-restored interior, with some of the most spectacular 14th century wall paintings in Dorset.

Tarrant Crawford was once the site of England's largest Cistercian nunnery, which was founded here in the mid-13th century by Bishop Poore, a native of the village and builder of Salisbury Cathedral. Poore is said to have spent some time here, and also King John's daughter, Joan of Scotland. After the Dissolution the nunnery was totally destroyed, much of the masonry being used in the building of the present Tarrant Abbey House and the great stone buttressed barn nearby.

Tarrant Gunville (195) (ST 92-12) *5½m NE Blandford Forum off A354.* Pretty settlement of traditional Dorset brick and flint cottages set among trees at the head of the narrow Tarrant Valley. The Tarrant is a 'winterborne', a stream or 'bourne' that only flows at certain times of the year, but here so much water is extracted that it now rarely flows at all, even in the wettest of winter months. Standing in a leafy spot above the village is St Mary's church, a large building with a squat Perpendicular tower. The interior was dulled in the mid-19th century, but the stencilled chancel decoration is rather fun. Among the memorials is one to Thomas Wedgwood, son of the great Staffordshire potter, and an early pioneer in photography. He was able to produce an image on a sensitized plate but died before discovering a means of making his images permanent — the secret of which was soon (in 1835) to be unravelled by Henry Fox-Talbot of Lacock Abbey in Wiltshire. Adjacent to the church is Gunville Manor, an imposing late 18th century house that once belonged to Thomas Wedgwood's

brother, Josiah Wedgwood II. The old thatched forge has a vintage AA tin sign on its north wall, one of only a few that have survived from the days when almost every village in the country had one of them.

The prominent gate piers almost opposite the Bugle Inn mark the main entrance to Eastbury House. This solemn block of Chilmark stone originally formed the west stable wing of a massive house designed by Sir John Vanbrugh for George Dodington, a founding Governor of the Bank of England. When Dodington died in 1720 his nephew, George Bubb inherited the estate and completed the house at a cost of £140,000, a vast sum in those days. On Bubb's death in 1762 the house passed to Earl Temple, who attempted to sell the house and its contents. However no buyer could be found, and in 1775 it was decided to demolish all but the two parallel ranges which made up the stable court. These were converted into living quarters, and for a while were occupied by Josiah Wedgwood's widow and her son Thomas, before being bought in 1897 by the famous Dorset hunting man, J.J. Farquharson.

Tarrant Hinton (195) (ST 93-11) *4m NE Blandford Forum.* This small village is greatly disturbed by traffic on the busy Salisbury to Blandford Forum road, but there is a pleasant group of thatch and whitewashed houses near the flint and stone church. This attractive building is all of the Perpendicular period, except for the chancel which was rebuilt in 1874. The most outstanding feature within is the Easter Sepulchre in the chancel. This exceptionally delicate piece of early Renaissance work carries the initials of Thomas Weever, rector here between 1514 and 1536. Note the two dainty angels flanking the recess, and also the 17th century communion rail which was originally made for Pembroke College, Cambridge.

Tarrant Keyneston (195) (ST 92-04) *2½m SE Blandford Forum.* Straggling beside the cressy Tarrant stream, this long village takes its name from the Kahaynes family, Lords of the Manor in the 12th and 13th centuries. It has several attractive thatched cottages and an inn called 'The True Lovers Knot', but its unenviable situation on a wide and straight section of the B3082 has led to it being described by local wits as having the 'fastest High Street in the West'. The church was largely rebuilt in 1852, and its only redeeming features are the embattled 15th century tower and a white painted south door. Set astride the B3082, half a mile north-west of Tarrant Keyneston, is Buzbury Rings, an Iron Age earthwork of unknown purpose, but possibly built for the protection of livestock rather than for defence.

Tarrant Monkton (195) (ST 94-08) *5m NE Blandford Forum off A354.* Pretty, well-cared-for village with thatched, colour-washed cottages lying in peaceful country astride the River Tarrant, which is here spanned by a narrow and picturesque three-arch packhorse bridge, a reminder of the days when Tarrant Monkton was on the main London-to-Weymouth route. There is a ford beside the bridge, and this is usually passable throughout the year. Standing opposite the excellent Langton Arms inn is the church, all Victorian although incorporating some material from the ancient church, including several 14th and 15th century windows. Four simple wooden crosses in the north-east corner of the churchyard mark the graves of four unknown First World War German soldiers who died of influenza in the prisoner-of-war camp at nearby Blandford Camp.

Tarrant Rawston (195) (ST 93-06) *3m E Blandford Forum.* Minute hamlet in a delectable stretch of the broad Tarrant Valley. Here in a farmhouse garden will be found a small 15th century church with a Jacobean pulpit and a small west gallery.

Tarrant Rushton (195) (ST 93-05) *3½m E Blandford Forum off B3082.* Attractive little hamlet tucked between the sparkling river and the slopes of a chalk down, with a flint church pleasantly sited amongst trees and well-mown lawns. It dates back to the mid-12th century, and has a Norman chancel arch and three remarkable hagioscopes (or squints) — holes in the wall between the aisle and chancel, to allow views of the main altar from places where it could not otherwise be seen . Built into the chancel west wall are two earthenware jars on their sides. These strange vessels do not contain anything, but were apparently installed to improve the building's acoustics. The vast aircraft hangar on the down above the village is all that remains of Tarrant Rushton Airfield. This played a prominent role in the Normandy and Arnhem landings, and after the 1939-45 war was taken over by one of the great aviation pioneers, Sir Alan Cobham, to develop the technique of refuelling aircraft in flight. Both he and Lady Cobham are buried in the village below, and there is an attractive memorial to them in the church.

Thorncombe (193) (ST 37-03) *10m N Lyme Regis.* Set in rolling hills to the east of the Axe River, countryside more Devonian than Dorset in character, this is an austere little place. The church was totally rebuilt in 1867, but retains a handsome 16th century pulpit and an exceptional 15th century life-size brass to Sir Thomas Brook and his wife Joan. Holditch Court, two miles to the south-west, is part of a late 14th or 15th century semi-fortified manor house. It is possible to walk south from here passing Sadbarrow, a fine neo-classical house built in the late 18th century.

Tincleton (194) (SY 77-91) *4m E Dorchester.* A scatter of houses and a small 19th century chapel in meadowland beside the River Frome. The chapel is plain from the outside, but inside has much to please the eye, including an elaborately carved alabaster reredos, several well-carved wall monuments and an unusually shaped Norman font. Peeping through trees a little to the east is a stately mid-19th century neo-Tudor manor called Clyffe House. This is not open to the public, but can be seen from a path which skirts past its grounds. Walk south from here, across meadowland, to Woodsford Castle ★ .

Todber (183) (ST 79-20) *4½m SW Shaftesbury.* Many of its houses are constructed of the biscuit-coloured stone extracted from the quarries between here and Marnhull ★ . Most of the quarries are now

no longer worked, but they are clearly discernible by their steep grassy banks. The church was rebuilt in 1879 at the expense of the Marchioness of Westminster, and although there is little of interest inside, the little saddleback tower incorporates fragments of medieval masonry. A 19th century cross in the churchyard is partly made up of Anglo-Saxon fragments.

Toller Fratrum (194) (SY 56-97) *8m NW Dorchester off A356.* There is a sense of seclusion in Toller Fratrum, a hamlet of grey stone buildings lying at the end of a narrow cul-de-sac between the downs and the valley of the little River Hooke. From the 14th century until the Dissolution of the Monasteries in 1539 the village belonged to the Knights Hospitallers, or the Brethren of the Order of St John of Jerusalem (hence its name, the 'Toller of the Brothers'). In 1540 the manor was purchased by John Samways, and it was he who built the beautiful manor house and the accompanying thatched stable block. The house has two immense twisted chimney-stacks and a number of stone finials carved as heraldic beasts, among them a monkey holding a mirror. Further curious carvings are to be found on the stable block, including one of a small boy playing the bagpipes! Behind the stables is the little church, an unprepossessing 19th century building dedicated, unusually, to St Basil. Inside there is an exceptional Norman font, carved with a large number of lively faces and figures, some of them inverted. The stone carving set into the east wall of the chancel portraying St Mary Magdalene washing Christ's feet, is also Norman in origin.

Toller Porcorum (194) (SY 56-98) *9m NW Dorchester off A356.* The district hereabouts has long been associated with pigs, and this place, the 'Toller of the Pigs', has been known as Swyne Toller and Hog Toller. It is beautifully situated in the remote, well-wooded valley of the River Hooke, but alas does not exhibit as much character as its delightful name would have led us to expect. The church, sited on a small hillock, has a stout 15th century tower, but the rest of the fabric was heavily restored in Victorian times. The stem of the font was probably fashioned from part of a Roman altar pillar or a Norman capital, and has been 're-worked' with spirals at three corners, and a ram's head at the fourth.

Tolpuddle (194) (SY 79-94) *7m NE Dorchester.-* Long main-road village with a delightful mid-17th century manor house looking southwards over lush meadows watered by the River Piddle. The stone and flint church dates in part from the mid-13th century, but was much altered by a restoration in the mid-19th century. Within the dark interior there is a tiebeam roof of the 14th century and a carved Purbeck marble coffin-lid of a 12th century priest. On a small sloping green east of the church there is an ageing and sickly sycamore, propped up by wooden posts. It was under this tree that the 'Six Men of Dorset' regularly met to discuss ways of improving the lot of the local farm workers. In 1833 their leader, George Loveless, formed a 'trade union' for the agricultural labourers of the village, in itself not an unlawful act, as trade unions had been made legal in 1824. However, the local landowners, believing that such associations threatened their authority, determined to smash this little band. In February of 1834 Loveless and five others were arrested on the charge that they had 'participated in the administration of an illegal oath.' They were tried at Dorchester Crown Court, found guilty and sentenced to seven years transportation to Australia. Almost at once a huge campaign was organized to obtain the release of the 'Tolpuddle Martyrs', as they had become known, and in 1836 the men were granted pardons and returned to England. Only James Hammett returned to Tolpuddle, and his grave may be seen in the churchyard. In 1934 the Trades Union Congress erected six cottages in memory of the 'Martyrs', and one of these contains the Tolpuddle Martyrs Memorial Museum. With the aid of photographs and documents this tells the story of the six men and the rise of agricultural trade unionism. Other memorials to the 'Martyrs' in the village are the thatched shelter on the green, the gateway to the Methodist Chapel, and the cottage which was the home of Thomas Stanfield, one of the 'martyrs'.

Trent (183) (ST 59-18) *3m NW Sherborne.* This is a lovely village spread out over sloping ground close to the Somerset border, with many old yellow and grey stone houses and cottages, some of them thatched. The glorious church, mainly 13th century, has a fine 14th century tower with a spire, a very rare feature in Dorset, where most of the spires are of much later date. Apart from the addition of extremely unpleasant glass in the north and south windows, the interior was well restored by the Reverend William Turner in 1840. Among its many treasures are a fine set of 15th century carved bench-ends, an early 17th century pulpit of Dutch origin, a remarkable 15th century rood screen, said to have come from Glastonbury Abbey, several 14th century effigies, and some fine pieces of medieval glass in the east window. There are also many fine post-medieval wall memorials, including one to Francis Wyndham, who hid Charles II after his flight from Worcester in 1651. Grouped round the church are a handsome collection of stone buildings, the best of which is the Chantry, built for the local priest in the late 15th century. Of similar date are Dairy Farm and Church Farm, while Turner's Almshouses were built in convincing Tudor style in 1846. Also belonging to the church group is the manor house where Charles II hid in 'an old well-contrived secret place' for two weeks.

Turnworth (194) (ST 81-07) *6m W Blandford Forum.* Thomas Hardy was very fond of this modest hamlet, and described it as 'lying in a hole a narrow cleft beneath the wooded slopes of Shillingstone Hill and Bell Hill'. Its small church, with graceful flint and ash ar 13th century tower, was rebuilt in 1869 by G.R. Crickmay. He engaged as his assistant Thomas Hardy, who by this time was a qualified architect living in London. It was Hardy who designed the capitals and possibly the bearded heads serving as corbels. Some twenty years later the novelist returned to this church to read the lesson for his great friend, the Reverend Thomas Perkins. On Ringmoor, half a mile north-west of here, are the earthwork remains of an Iron Age and Roman settlement (ST 80-08), which are reached by walking through beautiful woodland owned by the National Trust.

Tyneham (194) (SY 88-80) *6m SW Wareham.* During the Second World War a vast tract of land, stretching from Lulworth Cove ★ to Kimmeridge ★, was requisitioned by the War Office and used as a training ground for the British and American troops preparing for the invasion of Europe, and after the war this was retained by the army for use a tank and artillery range. However, in 1974 the Ministry of Defence decided to allow the public access to the more picturesque areas of the range, *although only at certain times of the year**. One such area is the beautiful Tyneham valley, situated between Whiteway Hill and Gadd Cliff. Now deserted and partly derelict, the village of Tyneham is one of the most evocative places in Dorset. Its Victorian

Tyneham ... Dorset's 'Deserted Village'.

church has been restored and now contains an interesting exhibition illustrating the story of the village. Close by is a cream-coloured, pre-war telephone box, complete with an ornate cupola roof. The Elizabethan manor house to the east is almost a ruin, but for an excellent account of what this and the village were like before the army moved in, read 'Tyneham — A lost Heritage' by Lilian Bond. There is a large car park in the village, and it is possible to walk west through a wooded valley to Worbarrow Bay, where there is an excellent bathing beach.

*The road from the checkpoint near Steeple ★ down to Tyneham, and also across to East Lulworth ★, is normally open for one week at Easter, one week at the Spring Bank Holiday, from the first week in July until the first week in September, two weeks at Christmas and all but six weekends a year. This information is correct at the time of compilation, but it is best to check in the Friday edition of the Bournemouth Evening Echo, *or the* Dorset Evening Echo, *for times for the following week.*

Up Cerne (194) (ST 65-02) *9m N Dorchester off A352.* Here is a church and a manor house delightfully sited beside a lake in a secluded hollow of the chalk downs. Except for the 15th century chancel, the church was entirely remodelled in 1870, but its contents include a Norman Purbeck marble font and a medieval sculpture of the Madonna over the porch door. The manor dates from the early 17th century, but like the church was extensively altered and restored in Victorian times.

Upton (195) (SY 98-93) *2m NW Poole.* This expanding residential suburb of Poole lies on low ground north of Lytchett Bay, and is bounded on three sides by the busy A35. It has one interesting building — Upton House, a large early 19th century Italianate mansion set in a small park overlooking Holes Bay. Since 1976 it has been run by Poole Council as a Country Park, and the house and the park, which includes wildlife ponds, a nature trail and a picnic area, are now open to the public.

Upwey (194) (SY 66-84) *3m N Weymouth*. Straggling down the Ridgeway towards Weymouth, this long thin village — 'the upper town on the River Wey' — has what is claimed to be 'the only genuine wishing-well in Southern England'. In the past it was much visited by holidaymakers from Weymouth, among them George III, who drunk the water from a gold cup, which later became the original Gold Cup of the Ascot Races. Close by, there is a handsome Perpendicular church with an elaborately carved Jacobean pulpit and three unusually carved wooden panels, possibly belonging to the plinth of an earlier pulpit. Nineteenth-century Upwey Mill was the model for 'Overcombe Mill' in Hardy's novel *The Trumpet Major*. The best walk from here heads westwards on to Friar Waddon Hill, where it is possible to link on to our **Walk 5.**

Verwood (195) (SU 08-08) *9m NE Wimborne Minster*. Undistinguished suburb of Bournemouth occupying a large area of heathland on the eastern edge of the Cranborne Chase. The church was constructed at the end of the 19th century, and is not of great interest to the visitor. At Brambles Farm, just to the north of Verwood, will be found the Dorset Heavy Horse Centre, with its working horses in stable and in harness, and its parades of horses and displays of horse-drawn farm machinery. There is also a pets' corner, cafeteria, shop and picnic area *(tel: Wimborne 824040)*.

Wareham (195) (SY 92-87). The gateway to the Isle of Purbeck, this charming old town is pleasantly sited on a small rise between the Rivers Piddle and Frome. In earlier times Wareham was an important port, for the Frome was then navigable from Poole Harbour as far as its quay. In 876 the Danes made it their headquarters for an attack upon Devon and Dorset, but their fleet was wrecked by a storm in Swanage Bay in 877. Several years later King Alfred captured the town and incorporated it into a chain of fortified burghs he built to protect his kingdom against Viking raids. The massive earth walls thrown up around the perimeter still survive in places, but nothing remains of the stone wall that once crowned these banks. At a place on the west rampart known as Bloody Bank, several followers of

The Quay at Wareham.

1 Castle	5 Priory House	9 Red Lion Hotel
2 King's Arms	6 Holy Trinity Gallery	10 Town Museum
3 The Quay	7 Black Bear Inn	11 Strech's Almshouses
4 Lady St Mary's Church	8 Town Hall	12 St Martin's Church

Wareham   SCALE 1:10 000 or 6 INCHES to MILE

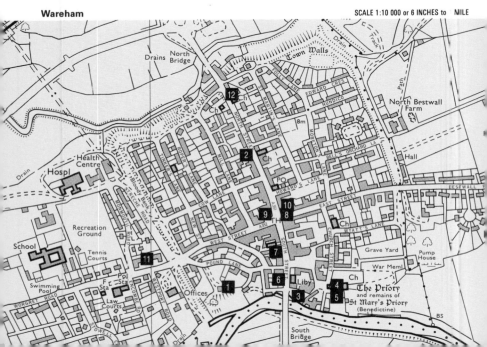

The Duke of Monmouth were hanged after his defeat at the Battle of Sedgemoor. In the early Middle Ages the town expanded and during the seige of Calais in 1347 it supplied King Edward III with three ships and 59 men. However, during this century Wareham was superseded as a port by Poole, and the Norman *castle (1)* fell into decay, an earth mound in the south-west corner being its only surviving remains. During the Civil War Wareham changed hands several times until Parliament finally took it in 1644. Sir Anthony Ashley-Cooper, the Parliamentary commander, considered razing the town, but it was spared at that time, only to be devastated by a great fire over a hundred years later, in 1762. The few thatched houses that remain, including the 17th century *King's Arms (2)* in North Street, mark the limits of the fire.

The best starting place for a walk through the town is the attractive and usually busy *Quay (3)*. *The Church of the Lady St Mary (4)* is reached through a passage, and though its Saxon nave was sadly destroyed during rebuilding in the 1840, it is still worth visiting for its ancient relics. The 12th century ead font is one of only 38 in the country and has twelve figures on its sides, presumably of the twelve apostles. There are some 6th or 7th century engraved stones, two of which are believed to have been supports for a Roman altar, a Saxon stone coffin said to have contained the body of King Edward the Martyr, and two 13th century Purbeck marble effigies of knights. Note also the beautiful late-13th century window in the chancel. The famous Dorset historian, John Hutchins, was rector here at the time of the fire in 1762, and although his house was consumed by the flames, thankfully most of his precious manuscripts were saved by his wife. Behind the church the 16th century *Priory House (5)* stands on the site of a 12th century priory, founded as a cell of Lire Abbey in Normandy. Returning back to the Quay turn right into South Street. *Holy Trinity Church (6)* on the left has been converted into an art gallery. A little further north is *The Black Bear Inn (7)*, a handsome early 19th century structure complete with a striking statue of a black bear on its columned porch. One particularly gloomy legend relates that if ever this bear were to fall, then the world would come to an end. Behind iron railings opposite is the stone-fronted Manor House, dated 1712 on the lead roof.

The point where the four main streets intersect is known as The Square and is dominated by the Victorian *Town Hall (8)*, looking decidedly out of place with clock tower and thin spire. On its other side is the *Red Lion Hotel (9)*, a typical post-fire house constructed in simple red-brick style. *The Town Museum (10)*, adjacent to the Town Hall, has a magnificent and probably unique collection of material associated with Lawrence of Arabia, who spent his last years at Clouds Hill ★. There is also a display of copies of silver pennies made at Wareham Mint in the 10th century.

Situated well to the west of the Square, beyond West Street and at the beginning of Worget Road, are *Strech's Almshouses (11)* of 1741. Their attractive belfry and cupola were salvaged from the 18th century town hall. Now retrace your steps to the Square and turn left into North Street where, at the junction with Cow Lane, there is a large stone chimney-breast which belongs to a 16th century house called Anglebury. 'Anglebury' was the name Thomas Hardy gave to Wareham and the town

figures prominently in his book *The Hand of Ethelberta*.

Standing on a cutting at the top end of North Street is *The Church of St Martin (12)*, one of the oldest churches in the county. Parts of this sturdy building date from the early 11th century, and the tall narrow nave and chancel are typical of this 'Anglo-Saxon' period. The north aisle was built in the 13th century and the short saddle-backed tower was added in the 1500s. The outstanding items inside are the 12th century paintings and the splendid recumbent effigy of T.E. Lawrence (Lawrence of Arabia), by Eric Kennington. A footpath at the end of East Street leads to the River Frome, and it is possible to walk a considerable distance along the north bank.

Wareham Forest (194,195) (SY 87-92 etc.) *Starts 1m N Wareham*. Wareham Forest is administered by the Forestry Commission, who started planting here in 1924. There is a waymarked nature trail through part of the forest, which begins several miles north-west of Wareham and ends, most conveniently, opposite the 'Silent Woman', an 18th century inn situated about 150 yards further along the road. On this walk you could be fortunate enough to see some Sika deer, as there is a large herd in this area of the forest. Incidentally, the Silent Woman Inn is said to have derived its name from a former landlady who had her tongue cut out by a ruthless band of smugglers to prevent her from revealing their secrets.

Warmwell (194) (SY 75-85) *5m SE Dorchester*. Compact little village sited in a depression between heathland and the coastal downs, with an appealing manor house built by Sir John Trenchard of Wolfeton in 1618. In the mid-17th century it was the home of the scholar and prophet John Sadler, who it is claimed, predicted not only the Great Plague and the Fire of London, but also the Monmouth Rebellion. The church has a fine square medieval tower, but the rest was heavily restored in 1881. In the Second World War Warmwell was the home of a forward fighter station, and in the churchyard there are many memorial tombstones to R.A.F and U.S.A.F pilots who sadly failed to return from sorties over enemy territory. Nothing now remains of the airfield from which they flew on their often-fatal missions.

West Bay (193) (SY 46-90) *1½m S Bridport*. Situated in a gap in the cliffs where the River Brit enters the sea, this tiny artificial harbour serves as the port of Bridport ★. Such was the problem with silting-up that the harbour was never able to accommodate ships of large tonnage, and today most of the boats moored here are for pleasure use, although it still handles limited commercial traffic, notably timber. In the late 19th century the authorities decided to turn the village into a holiday resort, a move deplored by Frederick Treves, who found the village charming as a 'nursery-tale harbour', but as a seaside resort a 'pitiable mockery'. Despite these harsh words something of the old flavour of West Bay still persists, especially around the delightful thatched Bridport Arms Hotel on the east side of the quay. On the East Cliff there is an 18-hole golf course with fine views of Portland and the West Dorset and Devon coastline.

West Bexington (194) (SY 53-86) *6m SE Bridport*. A small road from Swyre leads southwards to end at a car park immediately in front of Chesil Beach ★. Here lies West Bexington, a tiny village consisting of several hotels and a few houses. It is an unexceptional place, but there are good walks north and south along the seemingly endless pebble beach. There is also a path leading up from the northern end of the village to Limekiln Hill (NT).

West Chelborough (194) (ST 54-05) *15m NW Dorchester*. An exceptionally lonely little settlement sited at the end of a narrow road on the northern side of Chelborough Hill, with views north out over several small wooded valleys. The most remarkable feature to be found in the plain 15th to 18th century church is the early 17th century monument to a lady of the Kymer family. Her effigy is shown lying awkwardly beneath untidy bedclothes with her young daughter by her side. Although crudely carved the whole composition is of tender and moving simplicity.

West Knighton (194) (SY 73-87) *2½m SE Dorchester off A352*. Situated on rising ground at the edge of heathland, West Knighton, like its southern neighbour Broadmayne, has expanded considerably in recent years. However, a pleasant 17th century farmhouse and a few old houses remain at the centre of the village. Here also stands the mainly 13th century church, a delightful little building with a well-restored Victorian interior containing pine box pews, benches and gallery.

West Lulworth (194) (SY 82-80) *9m SW Wareham*. A long village situated in a narrow valley which curves round to meet the sea at the ever-popular Lulworth Cove ★. It is a pleasant enough place, with a great many stone cottages, several hotels and a largish church built in 1870 by Hicks of Dorchester in whose office Thomas Hardy first trained as an architect. At the southern end of the village there is a massive car park, which in the summer months is invariably packed with cars of the visitors to Lulworth Cove ★.

West Milton (194) (SY 50-96) *3m NE Bridport*. Three high hills provide shelter and seclusion for the few buildings of West Milton, which bunch about a small stream. St Mary Magdalene church stands on a south-facing slope at the western end of the village, and was built in the 19th century to replace the old church of which nothing remains save the Perpendicular tower.

West Parley (195) (SZ 08-97) *3m N Bournemouth*. The old village of West Parley lies along a quiet cul-de-sac, close to the River Stour and well away from the housing estates which have sprung up to its north. The church, mainly 19th century with fragments of Saxon and Norman masonry, has an attractive wood-framed porch and some excellent 17th and 18th century woodwork.

West Stafford (194) (SY 72-89) *2m E Dorchester*. A delightful village sited on low, watery ground south of the meeting place between the little South Winterborne stream and the River Frome. There is a friendly inn, The Wise Man, a pretty red-brick rectory and several attractive stone and thatch cottages. The interior of the church has altered little since its mid-17th century restoration, and contains some exceptional fixtures and fittings of that period. Especially noteworthy are the simple oak benches, the fine plastered wagon-roof of the nave, the chancel screen, and the canopied oak pulpit. There are also some admirable 17th and 18th century mural monuments, including one to Canon Reginald Southwell Smith, who was rector here through almost the whole of Queen Victoria's reign.

Half a mile to the east is Talbothays Lodge, a late 19th century building designed by Thomas Hardy for his brother Henry. In Hardy's novel *Tess of the d'Urbervilles*, West Stafford is called 'Talbothays'.

Weymouth (194) (SY 67-79). Fine holiday town with something to offer every member of the family. The wide Esplanade, backed by splendid Georgian and Victorian terraces, follows the curve of Weymouth Bay, known as the Naples of England because of its blue water.

Modern Weymouth is actually an amalgamation of two boroughs — Weymouth itself on the south side of the River Wey, and Melcombe Regis on the north. Old Weymouth is mentioned in a Saxon charter of the reign of Athelstan, but it was during the reign of King Henry VIII that the town grew in importance when *Sandsfoot Castle (1)*, and then Portland Castle were constructed to protect the Portland Roads from hostile Spanish and French vessels. Sandsfoot Castle is now a ruin, all of the gun emplacements having been destroyed by sea erosion, but parts of the barracks, storerooms and gateway remain. Melcombe Regis is chiefly remembered as the place where it is believed that the Black Death entered England in 1348. Prior to their union in 1571 the two boroughs were connected by a ferry worked by a rope but afterwards a wooden bridge was built, the ancestor of the present *Town Bridge (2)*, opened in 1930 by King George VI. It is a steel and concrete structure that can split in two and rise, though it now rarely does so.

During the Civil War Weymouth was the scene of considerable fighting, and a cannon ball embedded in the wall of a house in *Maiden Street (3)* is said to have lodged there during one skirmish. When the town was retaken by Parliament in 1644 the government ordered the fortification of Nothe Point. On cessation of hostilities the defences were demolished but in 1860 it was decided to construct a new *Nothe Fort (4)*. This great circular stone building held 10 nine-inch guns in massive casements and had accommodation for 200 troops. The period between 1650 and 1750 saw Weymouth decline as a port but in the mid-18th century the new fashion of sea bathing revived the town's fortunes. In 1780 the Duke of Gloucester, brother of King George III, spent the winter here and built himself a house, now the *Gloucester Hotel (5)*. In 1789 the Duke persuaded the King to come to the town to try sea bathing for his health, and he

Weymouth Harbour.

continued to come here until about 1805. The royal court's presence attracted the wealthy and fashionable, and the town expanded rapidly. The **King George III Statue (6)**, in the centre of the town was erected by the grateful inhabitants in 1809 to celebrate the fiftieth year of his reign. It is of Coade stone and shows the king in coronation robes. From here walk northwards, passing **Gloucester Row (7)**, the best of the many Georgian terraces. It was built about 1790 by James Hamilton and features a splendid wrought iron balcony. Opposite is the colourful **Jubilee Memorial Clock Tower (8)** of

1 Sandsfoot Castle (off map to south)
2 Town Bridge
3 Maiden St.
4 Nothe Fort
5 Gloucester Hotel
6 King George III Statue
7 Gloucester Row
8 Jubilee Memorial Clock Tower
9 Royal Crescent
10 Victoria Terrace
11 Belvedere
12 Waterloo Place
13 Black Dog Inn
14 St Mary's Church
15 Guildhall
16 Town Museum
17 Ferry Terminal
18 Tourist Information Centre & Pavilion Theatre Complex
19 Trinity Church
20 Trinity Rd.
21 Trinity St.
22 High West St.
23 Nothe Gardens
24 Lodmoor Country Park (off map to north)
25 Radipole Lake

SCALE 1:10 000 or 6 INCHES to 1 MILE

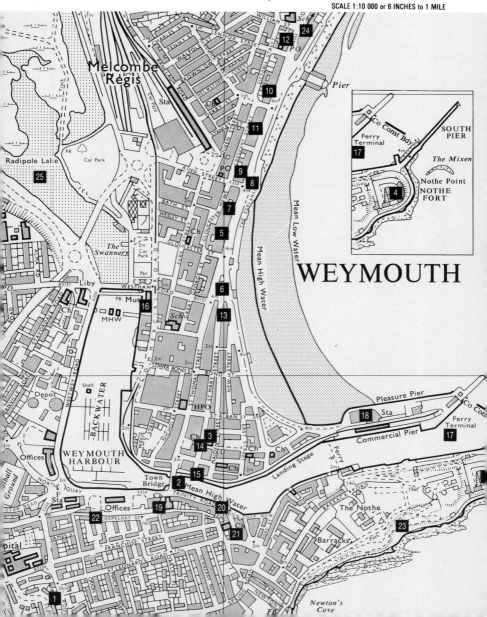

1887 while a little further up is *Royal Crescent (9)*, planned as a crescent but built as a straight terrace. The grander *Victoria Terrace (10)*, built in the mid-19th century, stands between two more Georgian terraces; *Belvedere (11)* and *Waterloo Place (12)*.

Visitors should retrace their steps to the statue of King George III and continue into St Mary's Street. *The Black Dog Inn (13)* on the left has a 16th century two-storey stucco entrance, and was the scene of a brutal murder in the 1700s. In one of the three bars there is a collection of ships' crests and Naval hat bands from all over the world. Towards the end of the street is the Georgian *St Mary's Church (14)*. Of Portland ashlar, it was designed by James Hamilton, and has a short clock tower and cupola surmounted by a golden ball. The excellent altar-piece depicting the Last Supper was painted by Sir James Thornhill, a Weymouth man who was MP for the borough in the early 18th century. The impressive *Guildhall (15)* was built in Classical style in 1836-7. A former school in Westham Road houses the *Town Museum (16)*. Here is a treasure chest belonging to Archduke Philip of Austria and his wife, stormbound here in 1506 (see Charminster★), but pride of place is devoted to the bathing machine used by King George III. Before crossing the Town Bridge into Old Weymouth look at the pleasant red-bricked warehouses that line the north side of the quay. Note also the railway line embedded in the quay, which allows trains to carry passengers to the *Ferry Terminal (17)* situated on the south side of the pier. The small harbour is very busy in the summer months with pleasure boats and fishing smacks mooring besides great channel ferries. *The Tourist Information Centre* is in the *Pavilion Theatre Complex (18)* on the north side of the pier *(tel: Weymouth 72444)*.

Trinity Church (19) in Old Weymouth is a pre-Victorian Gothic building which has a much larger interior than the facade indicates. To the right is *Trinity Road (20)*, lined with quaint late 18th and early 19th century cottages. *Trinity Street (21)* has more pleasing Georgian dwellings and two Tudor fronted houses, the Old Rooms Inn with boldly projecting porch, and numbers 2-3, open to the public on several days of the week. At the top end of the *High West Street (22)* is the modest Old Town Hall, sixteenth century in origin but largely rebuilt in the 1770s and again in 1896. Nearby is the Boot Inn, a much altered 17th century tavern with an interesting collection of boots in the single bar. *Nothe Gardens (23)* lie on the south side of the promontory known as The Nothe, and there are good views across Weymouth Bay.

To the north of the town, off the A353 road, is *Lodmoor Country Park (24)*. Among the attractions here are the Weymouth Butterfly Farm, the Sea Life Centre, a Miniature Railway and 'Model World'. The Butterfly Farm is set in a wildflower meadow and contains butterflies from all parts of the earth, as well as a great variety of insects *(tel: Weymouth 787770)*. The Sea Life Centre claims to have the largest display of native marine life in Europe. There are many exciting static exhibits including a mock-up of a ship's bridge and a mini-submarine. *(Tel: Weymouth 788255)*. The marshy ground to the north is home for many species of birds and is justifiably popular with bird-watchers.

Just to the north of the town (but on our map) is *Radipole Lake (25)*, now a nature reserve containing a large colony of swans as well as numerous other birds.

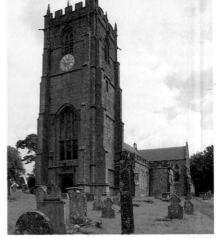

Whitchurch Canonicorum's splendid Perpendicular church tower.

Whitchurch Canonicorum (193) (SY 39-95) *5m NE Lyme Regis off A35*. Lost in a tangle of narrow tree-lined lanes on the eastern side of the Marshwood Vale, Whitchurch Canonicorum, so named because in medieval times it was divided between the Canons of Salisbury and Wells, has one of Dorset's finest village churches. This dates back to the Norman period, although the splendid Perpendicular tower and the porch are its finest exterior features. The interior, with its 15th century roof and stone flagged floors, was treated sympathetically by the Victorian restorers, and retains a wealth of interesting treasures. Foremost among these is a complete stone shrine containing the bones of the Patron Saint of the church, St Wita or St Candida. Little is known of this saint, but it is believed that she was a Saxon killed during a Danish raid in the 9th or 10th century. Her plain 13th century tomb in the north transept, is pierced by three holes through which crippled pilgrims would thrust their diseased limbs in the hope that they would thereby obtain a cure. The capitals of the 13th century arcade columns are carved with an unusual variety of designs, and one of the Early English arches is enriched with bold zigzag patterns. Other items of interest in this fascinating church are a Jacobean pulpit, a fine early 17th century limestone altar tomb, and a brass to the famous Elizabethan admiral, Sir George Somers.

Whitcombe (194) (SY 71-88) *2m SE Dorchester*. Just a farmhouse, a pretty group of thatched cottages and a church, all set alongside the A352 in gently undulating downland. Standing in a field a little apart from the rest, the 12th to 15th century church is noted as the place where the dialect poet William Barnes, as rector of both this and the neighbouring parish of Winterborne Came★, preached both his first and last sermons. Now disused, it is lovingly preserved as a memorial to Barnes by the Redundant Churches Fund, and the contents of its unspoilt interior include fragments of two Anglo-Saxon crosses, a 13th century Purbeck marble font and an impressive 15th century wall painting of St Christopher.

It is possible to walk west from here, over Cote Hill and down into Winterborne Came★, where Barnes had his rectory.

Wimborne Minster (195) (SU 01-00). Dominated by the twin towers of its Minster, this pleasant little market town lies on low ground between the Rivers Stour and Allen. Archaeological evidence suggests Wimborne was first settled by the Romans, although the earliest recorded date in the town's history is AD 705, when Cuthburga, sister of King Ina of the West Saxons, built a Benedictine nunnery here. In the early-11th century it was destroyed by the Danes, but in 1043 Edward the Confessor created a college of secular canons on the old monastic site. During the Dissolution the college was dissolved, but fortunately the **Minster (1)**, unlike the other collegiate buildings, was spared from destruction.

It is a most imposing building with a curious mottled appearance resulting from the use of two different coloured stones, one pale grey and the other rich brown. The oldest part of the church is the massive 12th century central tower, which was once crowned by a spire. However, this fell during a service in 1602, miraculously without loss of life or injury. The rest of the building dates from the 13th, 14th and 15th centuries.

Before entering the church glance up at the west tower to see the famous Quarter Jack. Originally the figure was a monk, but since Napoleonic times the task of striking the quarters has been entrusted to this brightly coloured grenadier. It is sad to report that he has recently stopped striking,, but he is remembered in a Thomas Hardy poem entitled 'Jack o'Clock':

> How smartly the quarters of the hour
> march by

that the jack-o'-clock never forgets -
— just so did he clang here before I came,
And so he will clang when I am gone.

The most striking architectural features inside the Minster are the eight elaborately decorated Transitional-Norman arches of the nave and the four massive Early Norman piers and arches of the central crossing. The baptistery beneath the west tower contains a number of interesting items, including a fine Norman font of Purbeck marble and a tablet to the famous Dorset smuggler Isaac Gulliver, who spent his final days in a large house in West Borough. Here also is a remarkable early 14th century orrery or astronomical clock, showing the sun, moon and stars revolving round the earth. It was carefully redecorated in 1979. One of the oldest objects in the church is the Saxon chest in the north choir aisle. The fine Renaissance monument to Sir Edmund Uvdale (1606) was carved by an Italian sculptor, and shows him reclining in a most relaxed manner. The unusual raised tomb in the south choir aisle contains the remains of Anthony Ettricke, Recorder and Magistrate of Poole, who committed the Duke of Monmouth for trial in 1685. Ettricke was convinced that he was going to die in 1693 and he had this date carved on his coffin, but in fact he lived for another ten years and the date had to be altered to 1703. Another of the Minster's many fine monuments is the Beaufort Tomb in the presbytery. On it are the alabaster effigies of John de Beaufort, Duke of Somerset, and his wife, Margaret. Their daughter Margaret, Countess of Richmond and Derby and mother of Henry VII, founded the Grammar School in 1496. A corbel at the head of

1 Minster
2 Dean's Court
3 Tourist Information Centre
4 Priest's House Museum
5 Walford Mill
6 St Margaret's & St Anthony's Chapel

Wimborne Minster

SCALE 1:10 000 or 6 INCHES to 1 MILE

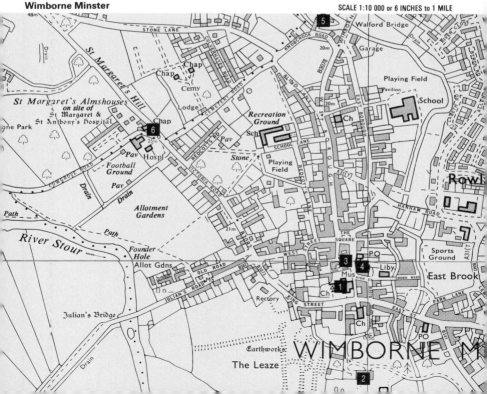

this tomb shows a bearded Moses holding the Tables of the Law. Nearby a small 15th century brass tablet set in a mutilated Purbeck slab records that King Ethelred (not the 'Unready') was killed fighting the Danes on Cranborne Chase and buried here in 871. The only medieval glass in the Minster can be seen in the middle lancet of the great east window. It shows the 'Tree of Jesse', and is reputed to have been made by Flemish craftsmen in the 15th century. In a room above the vestry is one of the largest chained libraries in the country. Founded in 1686 by the Reverend William Stone for the free use of the citizens, it contains 185 works in 240 volumes, including three Breeches Bibles, a Polyglot Bible and an original edition of Sir Walter Raleigh's *History of the World*. The library's oldest book is a religious manuscript written upon vellum in 1343. Those wishing to explore the Minster in even greater detail are strongly advised to purchase the informative colour guide book.

The prevailing architectural style of the town is Georgian, and many fine buildings of this period may seen in the Square and West Borough. However, the most splendid 18th century town house is *Dean's Court (2)*, which was originally the Deanery to the Minster. The lovely 13-acre garden contains the Henry Doubleday Research Association's Sanctuary for Threatened Vegetable Species. For opening times contact the **Tourist Information Centre (3)** in Cook Row (tel: Wimborne 886116). The facade of the **Priest's House Museum (4)** in the High Street is also Georgian, although it hides a much older structure dating from the 16th century.

Directly north of the Minster is the Cornmarket, the old heart of the town, now paved to form a pleasant pedestrian precinct. A fixed iron rod inside the White Hart Inn was used to handcuff offenders waiting to serve their sentence in the stocks which stood outside (now in the museum). In the High Street will be found the William Walker Glass Studio where regular demonstrations of glass-blowing are given (tel: Wimborne 880940).

Half a mile north of the town centre is *Walford Mill (E)* , recently converted into a craft centre (tel: Wimborne 841400). Walford Bridge is basically a much enlarged medieval packhorse bridge. *St Margaret's and St Anthony's chapel (6)*, on the main road to Blandford, is a former leper hospital chapel dating back to the 13th century.

Wimborne St Giles (195) (SU 03-12) *9m N Wimborne Minster*. Glorious little village lying in the valley of the River Allen, with church and alms-houses overlooking a broad green, and beyond it, an attractive village sign. Close by, the sparkling river feeds a seven-acre serpentine lake in the great park of St Giles House. This vast mansion was built in 1651 by Sir Anthony Ashley Cooper, later the first Earl of Shaftesbury, and although its exterior has been heavily Victorianised, the interior retains the flavour of the 1750s, when it was extensively redecorated and re-furnished. There is also a remarkable Shell Grotto of the same period in the park, but neither park nor house are open to the public.

The lovely mellow-brick almshouses were built by the 1st Earl in 1624 and are attached to the Georgian church, which was perhaps built by one of the Bastard brothers of Blandford Forum ★. Its interior was Gothicised by G.F. Bodley in 1886-7, and after

a disastrous fire in 1908, it was beautifully restored and enlarged by Sir Ninian Comper, one of the 20th century's outstanding church decorators. Many of the furnishings are by Comper, including the stained glass (except for some 16th century German glass in the south window), font cover, west gallery, and the magnificent rood screen. There is also a superb collection of monuments and memorials to the Ashley family, the most spectacular of which is a fantastic, brightly painted 17th century canopied tomb to Sir Anthony Ashley.

Winfrith Newburgh (194) (SY 80-84) *8½m SE Dorchester off A352.* Four roads meet at Winfrith Newburgh, yet there is little through-traffic to disturb the peace of this picturesque self-contained brick and stone village set under high wooded downs. A small clear stream, the Winfrith, flows between the road and the church of St Christopher. The latter lies among beautiful lime-trees at the southern end of the village, and has a 15th century tower with some delightfully grotesque gargoyles. The rest of the fabric was rebuilt in 1854, and is not of great interest to the visitor. Just beyond the church there is an attractive red-brick manor house, while Winfrith House stands at the other end of the village, a handsome 18th century building.

The Atomic Energy Research Establishment is situated about a mile north of here, on Winfrith Heath (SY 81-86). Opened in 1967, it is well screened, with only the two cooling towers being visible from the main A352 road.

Winterborne Came (194) (SY 70-88) *1½m SE Dorchester off A352.* A mile from its meeting with the Frome, the South Winterborne stream flows through the peaceful well-wooded park of Came House, a swagger mid-18th century mansion designed by Francis Cartwright for John Damer, younger brother of Lord Milton of Milton Abbey ★. Next to the house, surrounded by tall broad-leaf trees, is Winterborne Came's enchanting little 15th century church. This has a 16th century rood screen, a 17th century altar tomb with alabaster effigies, and an ornately decorated Jacobean pulpit. It was from this pulpit that Dorset's other great literary figure, William Barnes, preached for nearly a quarter of a century. He is buried in the churchyard, his grave marked by a simple Celtic cross inscribed with the words: 'In memory of William Barnes. Died October 7th 1886 aged 86 years. For 24 years rector of this parish'. The old rectory where he lived is half a mile north-east of here, just off the A352. It is a gorgeous thatched and pink-washed building, built in the ornamental-cottage style in the early 19th century.

William Barnes was born at Bagber, near Sturminster Newton in 1801. His formal education finished at the age of 13, and in 1818 he was articled to a solicitor in Dorchester. Five years later he moved to Mere in Wiltshire, where he became a schoolmaster. In 1827 he married his Dorchester sweetheart Julia Mills, the daughter of an excise officer, and the subject of many of his poems. Returning to Dorchester in 1835, he set up his own school in South Street, and the young Thomas Hardy would often come here to question the poet on points of grammar. In 1847 he took Holy Orders and three years later obtained a Cambridge divinity degree. Tragically his beloved wife died in 1852, and his school, unprofitable at the best of times, was soon forced to close. Fortunately in 1862 he was offered the rectorship of Winterborne Came and Whitcombe★, and was also granted a Civil List pension of £70 a year. In the idyllic surroundings of this parish he continued to write poetry, right up to his death in 1886.

Barnes was an exceptional character. His mastery of languages was quite phenomenal, it being said that he was familiar with at least sixty-five different tongues, including Welsh, Persian, Russian, Italian, Hebrew and Hindustani. He could play four instruments, was an excellent wood-engraver and wrote on a wide range of subjects, from archaeology to geology. However, it is for the poems written in the dialect of Dorset that he his best known. For inspiration Barnes drew on the places and characters of his county, and it is said that no one, not even Hardy himself, describes 19th century Dorset better. Perhaps his best known poem is Linden Lea:

Let other vo'k meake money vaster
In the air o' dark-room'd towns,
I don't dread a peevish measter;
Though noo man do heed my frowns.
I be free to goo abrode,
Or teake agean my hwomeward road
To where vor me the apple tree
Do lean down low in Linden Lea.

Winterborne Clenston (194) (ST 83-02) *6m SW Blandford Forum off A354.* Here, in the narrow valley of the tiny Winterborne stream, is a delightful collection of buildings, consisting of a church, a few cottages, several barns and a wonderful Tudor manor house. The latter, the ancestral home of the de Winterborne family, was beautifully restored in 1955, and has a striking five-sided gabled staircase turret. Inside there is much Tudor plasterwork and Jacobean panelling and also an extremely rare stone candle holder set into a wall. The house is open by written appointment only. Nearby there are two splendid barns, one thatched, the other roofed with tiles of two different colours, creating a wonderful chequered pattern. Within the tiled barn there is a magnificent hammerbeam roof which may have come from Milton Abbey★ after the Dissolution in 1539.

Clenston's comely little mid-19th century church stands on its own, some way down the valley. Built of flint and stone with a small broach spire, it is more attractive from without than within, although the chancel windows contain some good pieces of early-Victorian glass.

Winterborne Herringston (194) (SY 68-88) *1m S Dorchester.* Hidden in its beautiful park of ash, chestnut and elm, Herrington House is a large building which was constructed of Portland stone in the 16th century. Although much altered and enlarged in the 19th century, the interior has retained many of its original features, including a wonderfully exuberant barrel-vaulted plaster ceiling embellished with a great number of heraldic birds and beasts. It is, however, not open to visitors. A few earth platforms and a wall built of masonry salvaged from an ancient church are all that survive of the medieval village at Winterborne Farringdon, half a mile east of here.

Winterborne Kingston (194) (SY 86-97) *5½m S Blandford Forum off A354.* Undistinguished settlement on a minor road junction in the Winterborne valley, which here has become broader and flatter. The oldest part of the church is the stubby 14th century flint and stone tower. The rest of the building was heavily restored in 1873, although the architect G.E. Street did retain some of the old fabric, including several 15th century windows. The Georgian font has a fine dome-shaped oak cover crowned with a large pineapple finial.

The village lies on the line of the Roman road that ran from Badbury Rings★ to Dorchester, and on the undulating downs to the west there is at least one long barrow and several round barrows — evidence of occupation by Neolithic and Bronze Age peoples.

Winterborne Monkton (194) (SY 67-87) *1½m SW Dorchester off A354.* Quiet hamlet beneath the slopes of Maiden Castle★, with a small 16th century church pleasantly sited amongst trees, on the edge of a sloping field. Its interior was over-restored in Victorian times, but do not overlook the moving and unusual late 19th century alabaster effigy of a long-haired young girl, Ellerie Williams of Winterborne Herringston★, the next village down the valley.

Winterborne Stickland (194) (ST 83-04) *6½m SW Blandford Forum.* This Winterborne village straggles along the valley road for more than a mile, and is overshadowed to the east by a 500-foot hill upon whose summit stands a tall radio mast. Over the south doorway of the pleasant Early English church there is a 14th century tympanum, while of interest inside is the massive mid-18th century black marble tomb of Thomas Skinner. There are several charming flint and brick thatched cottages grouped around the church, but the rest of the village has been considerably disturbed by modern development.

Winterborne Tomson (194) (SY 88-97) *6½m S Blandford Forum.* Here, in a tiny walled churchyard close to a handsome 17th century farmhouse, is one of our favourite Dorset churches. It is a diminutive 12th century single-cell structure with a semi-circular apse and a tiny wooden bellcote. Beneath its charming plastered wagon roof there survives a complete set of 18th century wooden fittings, bleached almost white with age. After falling into disuse, this enchanting building was exquisitely restored in 1936 by A.R. Powys, brother of the talented writers, Theodore, John and Llewelyn Powys, in memory of Thomas Hardy, the money for the restoration being raised by the sale of some Hardy manuscripts. Do not miss this gem of a church.

Winterborne Stickland.

Winterborne Whitechurch (194) (ST 83-00) *4½m SW Blandford Forum.* Partly astride the A354, this expanding village in a hollow of the downs, has an endearing flint and stone church. This is of 13th century origin, and has a rugged central tower which is supported by shafted pillars, their capitals carved with bold winged faces. The interior is very bright and airy, with much colour-stencilling over the tower arches and at the top of the pillars. Some of this colouring is medieval, but most was added around 1882 by the vicar's wife. There is an elaborate and most unusual 15th century font with heraldic shields on all four corners, and a 15th century pulpit, said to have come from Milton Abbey when it was restored in the last century. During the Commonwealth the vicar here was John Wesley, grandfather of the the great John Wesley, founder of the Methodist faith.

Winterborne Zelston (195) (SY 89-97) *6½m S Blandford Forum off A31.* Picturesque village hidden down a quiet cul-de-sac, with delightful thatched and colour-washed cottages overlooking a clear chalk stream, which is crossed here by a pretty little hump-backed bridge. A gravel path just beyond the bridge leads to a rather severe church. This was drastically restored by the Victorians, and is not of great interest to visitors.

Winterbourne Abbas (194) (SY 61-90) *4m W Dorchester.* Lying at the head of the South Winterborne valley, with high downs around it, this undistinguished village is much disturbed by traffic on the busy Dorchester to Bridport road. The church of St Mary is mainly 13th century in origin, although the fine gargoyled tower dates from the 15th century. Its rather shapeless interior contains several interesting items, including a Norman font, a north-gallery dated 1701, and an exceptional mid-14th century piscina.

There is a well-preserved Bronze Age stone circle called Nine Stones (EH) (SY 61-90) half a mile west of the village, to the south of A35. This consists of nine upright sarsen stones arranged in a rough circle about 25 feet in diameter. Winterbourne Poor Lot Barrows (EH) (SY 59-90), a fine group of bowl, bell and disc barrows, are situated a mile and a half beyond, to the north of the A35.

Winterbourne Steepleton (194) (SY 62-89) *3½m W Dorchester off A35.* A pretty grey stone village, beautifully situated in the narrow South Winterborne Valley between Loscombe Hill, North Hill, and the higher, wooded Lambert's Hill to its north. There is a late 19th century manor house, a charming Tudor farmstead and a church with a fine 14th century spire. The rest of St Michael's is 12th and 13th century, except for the Saxon nave which has a superb 10th century sculpture of a flying angel set into its south wall. The interior has been Victorianised, but retains several items of interest. These include an early 12th century font, a Jacobean west gallery, and a superb brass to Daniel Sagittary, who died in 1756. See also the scant remains of medieval wall paintings on the nave walls.

Witchampton (195) (ST 98-06) *4m N Wimborne Minster.* Considered to be one of Dorset's most attractive villages, Witchampton lies on a wooded

hillside above the Allen stream, which is here crossed by a bridge, complete with a notice threatening deportation to anyone who damages it — an interesting relic of sterner times, and one of several examples in this area. There are many black and white thatched cottages, a fine old manor, which has several medieval features, and the buttressed ruins of a medieval tithe barn. Opposite Abbey House, a beautiful 16th century brick house is the church, pleasantly situated above its sloping churchyard lawns. The interior was well restored in 1833, and its contents include an ancient font and a 17th century tablet, whose inscription includes the cheering lines: 'There's no rest like that within the urn'!

Woodcutts (184) (ST 97-17) *11 NE Blandford Forum.* Little more than a farmhouse and one or two cottages remotely sited on sloping ground beneath the high chalk escarpment bordering the northern edge of the Cranborne Chase. Just under a mile to the north-west of Woodcutts, by way of a bridlepath, is the site of an ancient Romano-British farming settlement, which was excavated in 1884 by one of the founding-fathers of scientific archaeology, General Pitt-Rivers. Many of the finds and a model of what the village must have looked like can now be seen at Salisbury's excellent town museum, part of which is specially devoted to Pitt-Rivers and his work.

Woodsford (194) (SY 76-90) *4m E Dorchester.* Small hamlet lying in green pastures beside the River Frome at a point where it is crossed by a ford with a church rebuilt in the 19th century, and a farmhouse from Tudor times. A quarter of a mile to the west is Woodsford Castle (SY 75-90), a magnificent fortified manor house beneath a vast thatched roof, and now in the care of the Landmark Trust. Possibly one of the oldest castles to have been continuously lived in throughout its history, Woodsford officially became a castle in 1337, when Edward III gave its owner, William de Whitefield, permission to crenellate (or fortify). In 1368 it passed to Sir Guy de Bryan who gave his name to Hazelbury Bryan★. It originally had five round towers, one in each corner and a fifth one in the centre of the east wall, but only that in the north-east corner remains. It is open by written appointment only. *(Write to the Landmark Trust, Shottesbrooke, Nr Maidenhead, Berkshire.)*

Woodyates (184) (SU 02-19) *11m NE Blandford Forum.* The famous coaching inn where George III liked to stay when travelling to Weymouth has long since disappeared from this tiny roadside hamlet. In the 18th century the landlord of the inn was Robert Browning, a great-grandfather of the famous Victorian poet. It was here, many years earlier, that the luckless young Duke of Monmouth, fleeing from Sedgemoor, abandoned his exhausted horse and continued on foot, only to be captured at Horton Heath★, only a few miles to the south. Walk east from here to join the footpath running along the northern side of the great earthwork of Bokerley Dyke★, to link with Walk 12.

Wool (194) (SY 84-86) *4m W Wareham.* Writing in 1906 Frederick Treves described Wool as 'once a pretty enough village, but the railway has contaminated it'. However, even today the old village still retains considerable character, especially Spring Street, where attractive thatched cottages lie behind a broad grass verge. Despite remodelling in 1865, Wool's Church of the Holy Rood retains elements of earlier sanctuaries; the north arcade and the triple chancel screen are 13th century, the stout tower 15th century. The church's proudest possession, a fine altar-frontal made from pieces of medieval vestments, is now in Dorchester Museum.

Seventeenth-century Woolbridge Manor, now a hotel, stands on the north bank of the River Frome, close to one of the loveliest medieval bridges in Dorset. Once the home of the Turbervilles, this beautiful stone and brick house was the fictional setting for Tess's tragic honeymoon in *Tess of the d'Urbervilles*. The open coffin in which the sleep-walking Angel Clare placed his beloved Tess is still in the grounds of the ruined Cistercian Abbey at Bindon (SY 85-86), a mile to the east of the manor. (As far as we are aware the abbey grounds are still not open to the public.)

Wootton Fitzpaine (193) (SY 36-95) *3½m NE Lyme Regis*. Well spread-out village attractively situated in a little valley running south between heavily wooded Wootton Hill and Coney's Castle Hill (NT), which is crowned by the ramparts of an Iron Age settlement. The cruciform church was drastically altered by those over-confident Victorians, and is of little interest to visitors, although its position beside the park of Wootton House is worth savouring. The house itself is a modest mid-18th century building, restored and enlarged at the turn of the century.

There is a waymarked forest walk near Wootton Hill (SY 35-97), and our own **Walk 1** starts from the car park below Coney's Castle Hill (SY 37-97).

Worth Matravers (195) (SY 97-77) *3½m W Swanage*. A bare niche in the hillside above Winspit Bottom is the setting for Worth Matravers, one of the most attractive settlements in the Isle of Purbeck ★. For hundreds of years Worth Matravers was one of the main centres for the quarrying of Purbeck stone, and the church and all the houses and cottages are built of this grey, rather austere stone. Most of the quarries that pit the country around the village are now deserted, but a few are still worked, including one on St Aldhelm's Head. The Square and Compass takes its name from the tools of the stonemasons' craft, and this inn was used by the quarrymen as their trading point. After Studland the church here is the most complete Norman church in the county. Its memorable features are the beautifully ornate 12th century chancel arch, the richly carved corbel table of the same period, and the early 13th century tympanum depicting 'the Coronation of the Virgin'.

If possible walk south to the quarry at Winspit, once the largest cliffside quarry in the district. From here, stone would be lowered directly onto sea barges and then transported round the coast to Swanage, where it would be transferred onto larger vessels bound for London. Now disused, the quarry is a favourite roosting place for many different species of bats. From Winspit walk east to Seacombe Quarry, and then return to Worth Matravers by way of the footpath along Seacombe Bottom. Note the extensive strip lynchets on either side of Winspit Bottom and on the west side of Seacombe Bottom. For further details see our **Walk 11.**

Wraxall (194) (ST 56-01) *10m NW Dorchester off A356*. Delightfully situated in a wooded basin below Rampisham Hill, Higher Wraxall consists of a few charming thatched cottages and a pretty Jacobean manor house. Equally diminutive is Lower Wraxall, sited beside a clear chalk stream to the south. Its tiny church, with Norman nave and 13th century chancel, has an attractive 17th century wall memorial to William Lawrence and a brass to Mrs Lawrence, who died in 1672.

Wyke Regis (194) (SY 66-77) *½m SW Weymouth*. Small town lying on hilly ground between the Isle of Portland and Weymouth, with fine views southwards of the former. The lofty tower of All Saints church, an impressively spacious Perpendicular building sited 260 feet above sea level, is a prominent landmark for mariners entering Portland Harbour and West Bay. Around the church are two churchyards crammed with the graves of sailors who perished in the treacherous waters off Chesil Beach ★.

Wynford Eagle (194) (SY 58-95) *8m NW Dorchester*. Here, in one of Dorset's most isolated valleys, is a fine 17th century manor house, with a stone eagle perched upon its central gable. The name 'Eagle' was derived from the Norman knight William De Aquila, the Eagle, of Pevesney Castle, who held the manorial rights here after the Conquest. In 1551 the manor passed to the Sydenham family, the most famous member of whom was the eminent 17th century physician, Thomas Sydenham. Considered to be the founder of British clinical medicine, Sydenham was one of the first doctors to treat his patients in a scientific manner, and not according to dogma and superstition.

The small church was rebuilt in 1842, but reset in the west wall there is a Norman tympanum with curious carvings of two 'wyverns in opposition' (a wyvern is a winged dragon with a serpent's tail). However, Wynford Eagle's real charm lies in the wonderful sweeping line of its hillsides, broken here and there by prehistoric cultivation terraces; and in the clear stream that flows across the fields and below the manor garden. See also **Walk 4**, which starts from Wynford Eagle.

Wytch Farm Oil Field (195) (SY 98-85 etc.) *5m E Wareham*. The largest onshore oil field so far developed in Britain is sited beneath heath and marshland on the northern shore of the Isle of Purbeck. It is hoped that its probable expansion will not detract unduly from the flavour of this unique area.

Yetminster (194) (ST 59-10) *5m SW Sherborne*. Large village lying in low watery country close to the Somerset border, and possessing a wealth of picturesque yellow stone houses. Most of these date from the first part of the 17th century, but one or two were constructed as early as the 15th century. The village school was founded by the famous scientist Sir Robert Boyle in 1697. The tall embattled tower of the handsome 13th to 15th century church has some fine gargoyles and a charming golden weathercock. Its bright interior is full of interest, with 15th century painted wagon-roofs, 16th century benches, a Norman font, and some good monuments, including a mid-16th century brass to members of the Horsey family.

Motor and Cycle Tours

Tour 1
Lyme Regis and the Eastern Fringes

55 miles. Apart from its early and late stages, this route follows quiet country roads for most of its course. Although few really steep hills will be encountered, the cyclist will find quite enough work to keep the muscles in trim. The quality of the countryside will provide ample compensation, but this must be said of almost all our Dorset routes.

Our route heads north from Lyme Regis and follows north-eastwards, close to Dorset's borders with Devon and Somerset, calling at lovely Forde Abbey, itself only yards from the latter county. Now eastwards across rolling downland country, and through Broadwindsor, before turning south and west, passing the handsome manor house of Mapperton, and the little town of Beaminster. We now turn south, dropping down towards the sea, passing through the fine old town of Bridport, before running parallel with the coast, partly along the busy A35. After several diversions to the lovely, cliff-lined shore, we return to Lyme Regis.

Start from the pretty seaside town of **Lyme Regis**, itself only just inside the border with Devon. Leave north-westwards on the A3070 Axminster road, soon passing into the neighbouring county. The attractive Devon village of Uplyme soon appears on right, and after 2m go over X-rds onto B3165. After less than a mile turn third right onto minor road (Sign — Wootton Fitzpaine), passing back into Dorset. Head for **Wootton Fitzpaine**, a scattered village in a small valley, and turn sharp left beyond cemetery. Near Coney's Castle (earthworks of Iron Age settlement) pass car park which is start of **Walk 1**.

In Fishpond Bottom hamlet, turn right, then left, and finally right, heading north-eastwards with Lambert's Castle (earthworks of Iron Age settlement) above to left. (To explore Lambert's Castle (NT) now turn left and left again onto B3165, for car park on left). For main route, bear right and right again onto B3165, through **Marshwood**, a village with fine views from its churchyard, before turning left at Birdsmoorgate X-rds onto minor road. Turn right at first X-rds, and bear left in small village of **Thorncombe**.

After 1m, turn right at T-junction (but turn left, and then straight not left, if you wish to visit the fine 16th and 17th century house of **Forde Abbey**, under 1m). Return to main route and then turn right onto B3162 at Maudlin Cross, keep on B3162 through unexceptional Drimpton, and into the steep-sited village of **Broadwindsor**, much loved by William Wordsworth's sister, Dorothy. Turn left twice in **Broadwindsor** and head north-eastwards on B3164. Now straight, not left, joining A3066 for a short time before

SCALE 1:190 080 or 3 MILES to 1 INCH

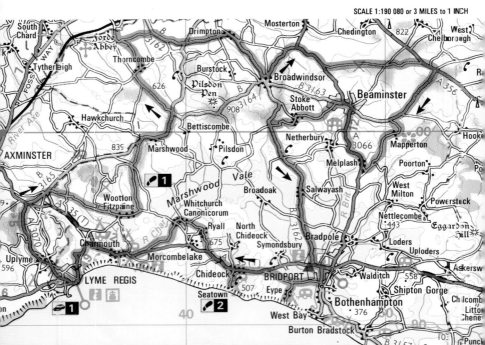

Lyme Regis Harbour ... a view from the Cobb.

bearing left just before it enters a tunnel, onto minor road heading eastwards. Pass Buckham Down Car Park and Picnic Site, fine views south towards the coast. Over diagonal X-rds on Beaminster Down, bear right onto A356, and soon turn right onto B3163 (Sign — Beaminster). After 1m track on left to Toller Whelme church.

After 1m, take 2nd left turn to **Mapperton**, with church and beautiful 16th and 17th century manor house down to left after ¾m. Turn right at next X-rds, and then bear right onto A3066 in **Melplash** (but turn left for church, an excellent mid-19th century neo-Norman building). Head north on A3066 into the small and delightful town of **Beaminster**, with its fine church. Beyond church bear left onto B3163, and before end of town turn left onto minor road (Sign — Stoke Abbott). Keep through pretty stone and thatch village of **Stoke Abbott**, turning right at far end, well beyond church, and then turn left at X-rds onto B3162, heading southwards for **Bridport** (5m).

In charming, largely Georgian town of **Bridport** turn left onto A35, and soon turn right by Town Hall, onto B3157. Well beyond

church, turn right onto minor road, and then over small X-rds (unless you wish to visit the shore at **Eype's Mouth** — under 1m). Back on main route, bear left **with great care** onto A35. Now through pretty stone and thatched village of **Chideock**. Keep on A35 unless you wish to turn left to visit the shingly shore at **Seatown**, which is at the start of our **Walk 2**. There is also a good walk westward from here to the National Trust's **Golden Cap** cliff country.

Keep westward on A35 from **Chideock**, but after 1m bear right off A35, and then keep through Ryall hamlet before bearing left by the Five Bells Inn in **Whitchurch Canonicorum**. Do not miss the church beyond on right, with its splendid Perpendicular style tower, and interesting interior. Straight, not right in village, over X-rds (Sign — Charmouth), and bear right with care onto A35.

Keep on A35 through delightful Georgian-flavoured seaside village of **Charmouth**. (But turn left if you wish to go to beach — a great favourite of Jane Austen's). Well beyond village fork left onto A3052, and keep on this until reaching **Lyme Regis**, thus completing Tour 1.

Tour 2

The Upper Frome Valley and the Downlands of Eggardon

40 miles. There are several steep hills to be tackled on this route, but it follows minor roads for all but about five miles, and with some fine downland country along the way, it makes a rewarding journey for cyclists.

Our route heads north-eastwards from Bridport plunging almost immediately into remote hilly country, and does not turn southwards until it has penetrated Somerset for a mile or so. It almost entirely encircles the great parklands surrounding Melbury House before heading southwards again, now down the Frome Valley to Maiden Newton. From here our route runs westwards through a splendid downland area, passing through the remote hamlet of Wynford Eagle, and the delightful villages of Powerstock and Loders before returning to Bridport.

Start from the fine, largely Georgian town of **Bridport**, noted for centuries for the manufacture of ropes and fishing nets. First head northwards on the A3066, and at the end of the residential suburb of Bradpole, turn right at X-rds. Soon turn left at T-junction and go north-eastwards up small valley. Now take second left, and over small X-rds, following signs to North Poorton. Turn left in South Poorton, right in tiny hamlet of **North Poorton**, and up steep hill into woodlands. Fork right near end of woods, again climb steeply, and over X-rds in high country.

Drop down into valley, over X-rds in Higher Kingcombe hamlet, and climb out of valley before bearing right and then left by radio masts. Now cross A356 with care and go down into **Rampisham** with its pretty thatched Post Office and creeper-covered inn. Bear left in village and head up valley, keeping straight through Uphall hamlet. Now turn right to cross small Benville Bridge, and turn left before going over offset X-rds. After ½m, earthworks of Castle Hill up to left: probable site of a medieval castle. Straight, not left at Clarkham Cross, and after crossing into Somerset, keep straight through Closworth, small village with over-restored Perpendicular-towered church, and site of 19th century bell-foundry.

Turn right onto A37, following course of

SCALE 1:190 080 or 3 MILES to 1 INCH

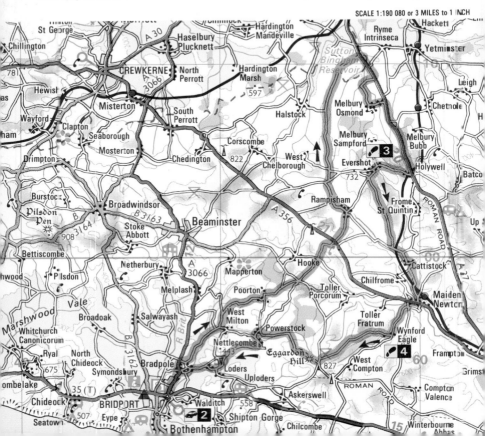

'Elbow-streeted Cattistock'.

Roman road running from Ilchester to Dorchester Soon back into Dorset, and then turn right off A37. Loop through delightful, thatched **Melbury Osmond**, the village where Thomas Hardy's father and mother were married in 1839, and which is on the course of our **Walk 3**. Then turn right, rejoining A37, keeping on this for 2½m before turning right at X-rds, going through Holywell hamlet just beyond. Turn left in large village of **Evershot**, but go straight ahead if you wish to visit its small spired 15th and 19th century church. Start of our **Walk 3** is at the eastern end of the village. Climb out of **Evershot**, and bear left at X-rds at top of hill.

Along ridge and then drop down to valley, to turn left at X-rds and over railway line. Now in valley of the River Frome. Straight, not left and then through 'elbow-streeted' **Cattistock**, not missing the fine, largely 19th century church. Turn right with care onto A356 in small town of Maiden Newton with its interesting partly Norman church, cross bridge over River Frome, and soon bear left off A356. Almost immediately turn right at small X-rds, and follow up valley to turn right in **Wynford Eagle**, an attractively sited downland hamlet which is the start of our **Walk 4**.

Now climb steeply out of valley, and after 2½m turn left near Shatcombe Lane Picnic Site (to right). Almost immediately turn right at X-rds, and the great mass of **Eggardon Camp** soon to left. Fine views from the vicinity of this twenty-acre Iron Age settlement. Earthworks of medieval Powerstock Castle on left before entering delectable stone and thatch hillside village of **Powerstock**. Now turn left by church (fine south doorway), then left again at end of village, before turning right in neighbouring hamlet of Nettlecombe. Up over Welcome Hill, and down steeply before turning left to go through quiet village of **Loders**, with its unspoilt little church to left. Bear left near Bradpole church and soon turn left onto A3066 to return to **Bridport**, thus completing Tour 2.

Tour 3

The Blackmoor Vale and the Hills of North Dorset

57 miles. Once away from the over-busy A30, this route heads off along minor roads into the flattish country of the Blackmoor Vale, and in its early stages is ideal for cyclists who do not wish to exert themselves. While the southern section running up onto the north face of the Dorset hill country presents several challenges, the splendid views northwards, out over the lush countryside of the Blackmoor Vale more than compensate for the occasional efforts involved.

Our route starts at the busy little town of Sherborne, and heads eastwards, and then south, to encompass almost the whole of the lovely Blackmoor Vale. In doing so, it passes a fine manor house at Purse Caundle, a lovely old watermill at Sturminster Newton and several attractive villages. Although never entirely losing touch with the Vale, it then climbs from time to time, on to the quiet country above the heavily wooded scarp-face of the Dorset hills, before finally turning northwards near the tiny village of Batcombe, and heading home towards Sherborne. However before finally returning, the route loops around to the north and west of its eventual destination to take in the interesting Worldwide Butterflies at Compton House, and the lovely manor house at Sandford Orcas. And so to Sherborne, to complete our journey.

This tour starts from the beautiful town of **Sherborne** with its fine abbey and wealth of other medieval buildings, and heads eastwards on the busy A30. After crossing into Somerset, turn right, off A30, at the entrance to Milborne Port. Now go straight, not right near woodlands, and turn left at T-junction. Turn left in village of **Purse Caundle**, church with interesting interior on right and fine, gabled manor house on left. Turn right with great care, rejoining A30, but soon turn right off A30, heading for Stalbridge. Up steep hill, then straight, not left and straight, not right before climbing hill up into small town of **Stalbridge**.

Over X-rds in **Stalbridge** crossing A357, noting fine 15th century market cross. Keep straight out of village, and after 2m, turn right at T-junction beyond Gibbs Marsh Farm.

Turn right and over bridge crossing River Stour before entering scattered village of **Marnhull**. Over offset X-rds by Marnhull's splendidly towered church, joining B3092, and head southwards on B3092, through unexceptional **Hinton St Mary**, to quiet little town of **Sturminster Newton**, with its delightful watermill (see below).

Straight, not left in **Sturminster Newton**, and over bridge crossing River Stour, before turning left onto A357. (Do not miss a visit to the watermill, near bridge to right.) Through woods, good car park down road to left. Access to Fiddleford Mill House from here (See **Fiddleford**). Keep on A357 through **Fiddleford**, and then turn right at New Cross Gate X-rds off A357. Through village of **Okeford Fitzpaine**, pleasantly sited beneath Okeford Hill, and go straight, not left just beyond. After 1m fork left, climb steeply up hill, and straight, not right near top. Pass Ibberton Hill, with picnic facilities on left, and then good viewpoint car park on left before bearing right at diagonal X-rds (but fork left if you wish to use our **Walk 8**, which starts to left after ¼ mile). Straight, not left at next Y-junction, and then bear left at **Bulbarrow Hill**. Earthworks of Rawlsbury Camp up to left just beyond. Pass woodlands on right and down steep hill through Stoke Wake hamlet.

Straight, not left twice, and turn right in Park Gate hamlet, before entering widespread village of **Hazelbury Bryan**. Straight, not left and straight, not right, by well-restored and interesting church, then bear left twice, before forking right at end of this very 'spread-out' village. After 1½m turn right at T-junction, straight through Westfields hamlet, bear left at entry to Brockhampton Green hamlet, bear right beyond Sharnhill Green hamlet, and over X-rds, crossing B3143 in **Buckland Newton**, a village which lies in a fold of the hills which face northwards over Blackmoor Vale.

Turn right by **Buckland Newton** church,

High summer at Okeford Fitzpaine.

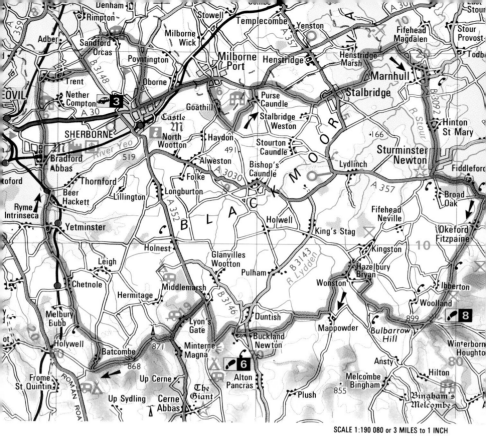

SCALE 1:190 080 or 3 MILES to 1 INCH

turn left at end of village, and bear left up steep hill. Turn sharp right, (but go straight ahead for ¼m for layby on left which is start of our **Walk 6**), down steep hill, through Cosmore hamlet and turn sharp left with care onto A352 in Middlemarsh hamlet. Straight, not right, well beyond Lyon's Gate hamlet, and then turn right, off A352, where this main road turns to left.

Turn left beyond woodlands and along pleasant open road. Straight, not right just beyond Batcombe Car Park (fine views to north from here over the densely wooded scarp-face to the Blackmoor Vale). After 1½m turn right, down small, very steep road, and through minute village of **Batcombe**, with its interesting and beautiful church. Now head north for Chetnole, going left at 1st T-junction, right at 2nd T-junction, and left and right at Hell Corner. Bear right at entry to Chetnole, an unexceptional village lying on the delightfully named Wriggle River.

Go northwards to **Yetminster**, a large village with a wealth of yellow stone houses. Keep straight through (but turn right if you wish to visit the handsome 13th to 15th century church). Over X-rds at end of village and turn left at T-junction beyond railway

bridge. Straight, not left just before crossing the infant River Yeo over its 16th century hump-backed bridge. Now turn left into **Bradford Abbas**, and immediately right (unless you wish to visit the church, a fine 15th century building, with many interesting features within). Head straight out of village northwards, over small X-rds and cross A30 with great care (but turn right and take first turn left if you wish to visit Worldwide Butterflies at Compton House (see **Over Compton**).

Over next small X-rds (but turn right if you wish to visit **Over Compton** or Nether Compton). Fork right and then turn right beyond church in attractively spread-out **Trent**, one of the villages where Charles II hid during his flight from the Battle of Worcester. Keep straight through village, eventually to turn left onto B3148 about 1m beyond. Take first turn right, off B3148, then turn right by glasshouses, before turning right and bearing left in **Sandford Orcas** (but turn left in village if you wish to visit the church or the lovely early-16th century manor house). Straight, not left at next junction, climb steep Holway Hill, right at small X-rds, before bearing right onto B3145 for the short return to **Sherborne**, thus completing Tour 3.

Tour 4
Maiden Castle, Abbotsbury and the Bride Valley

52 miles. There are very few steep hills on this route, and the use of A roads is limited to about six miles in all. The B3157 between Abbotsbury and Bridport, being a coast road, can be rather busy at holiday times. However, the quieter and more hilly return journey from Shipton Gorge onwards provides some wonderful stretches of country which will be especially appreciated by cyclists.

Our route takes us first to the massive earthworks of Maiden Castle, before heading southwards over downland country, almost as far as the coast. Those wishing for an early encounter with the sea can divert to Weymouth and rejoin the main route near Langton Herring, by using the B3157 northwestwards from Dorchester. The main route heads westwards behind Weymouth, and then runs parallel with the fascinating Chesil Beach and the lagoon behind it, the West Fleet, at the end of which will be found the fascinating Abbotsbury Swannery. Beyond this is lovely Abbotsbury village, with St Catherine's Chapel, and the Tropical Gardens beyond. The route now largely follows just behind the coast to salty West Bay, before heading inland to Bridport, where it turns eastward for a journey over downlands and up the valley of the little River Bride. Beyond this idyllic countryside, we are up onto the downs again, passing the Hardy Monument, with splendid panoramas and fine opportunities for walking, before returning to Dorchester.

This tour starts from the pleasant old county town of **Dorchester**, a market centre with a largely Georgian flavour. We start out southwards on the A354, Weymouth road, but within less than a mile from its centre, there is an option to fork right to visit the splendid earthworks of the great Iron Age settlement of **Maiden Castle**, the largest of its kind in Europe. Resuming the journey southwards on the A354, fork right off A354, about 1m beyond the Maiden Castle turn, and through minute **Winterborne Monkton**. Now bear left onto B3159, pass attractive **Upwey** church, and take 1st turn to left. Straight, not right, joining A354, and after 1m turn off A354 at second right **with great care**, onto minor road.

Straight, not left, and extensive Came Wood now on left, partly concealing line of round barrows. Now turn right at X-rds, and then turn left at top of steep hill, near point where Dorset Coast Path comes in from left. Now drop down through **Sutton Poyntz** with its large mill-pond, and turn right onto A353 in busy village of **Preston**. After ½m, bear right off A353, down Littlemore Road, keeping row of shops on left. (But keep straight on A353 if you wish to visit **Weymouth**, and rejoin main route near Langton Herring, using the B3157 Abbotsbury road, out of Weymouth.) After 2m turn left with care onto A354 in Broadwey, and after ½m turn right, off A354 (Sign — Nottington). Turn right in Nottington, and straight, not left at entry to Buckland Ripers hamlet. After 1¾m turn left onto B3157, and soon turn right off B3157 (Sign — Langton Herring).

Straight, not left at entry to **Langton Herring** (unless you wish to visit church or walk down to coastguard cottages overlooking the Fleet (see **Chesil Beach ★**). Turn sharp left in Rodden hamlet, and after 2m St Catherine's Chapel visible ahead (See **Abbotsbury ★**). **Abbotsbury** Swannery Car Park on left, and after ¼m massive tithe barn on right at entry to highly attractive village of **Abbotsbury**. Stop here to walk round and to walk up to St Catherine's Chapel. Bear left onto B3157 in centre of village, and after ½m bear right keeping on B3157 (but go straight ahead if you wish to visit Abbotsbury Sub-Tropical Gardens and beach).

Pass Abbotsbury Castle (Iron Age earthworks) on right, and keep on B3157 for 1m beyond it, before turning right between two bungalows (opposite turn to left for **West Bexington** Beach). Bear left in the delightful thatched village of **Puncknowle**, and turn left at end of village (Sign — Swyre). Turn right in **Swyre**, onto B3157 and follow this road through the colourful village of **Burton Bradstock**, with its interesting church, and fork left off B3157 1m beyond, to enter **West Bay**, Bridport's little harbour and busy holiday village in its own right.

Head north from **West Bay** (Sign — Bridport), and after 1m go half right at roundabout (but go ahead left if you wish to visit **Bridport**). Now head north again to 2nd roundabout, to turn right onto A35 (Sign —

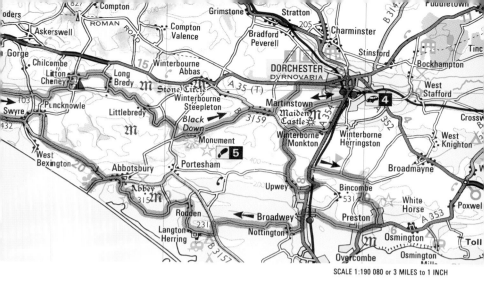

SCALE 1:190 080 or 3 MILES to 1 INCH

Dorchester). Keep on A35 for 1¼ m and then turn right with care onto minor road. Fork left in **Shipton Gorge** village, bear left by church, and then straight not left at end of village. Straight, not right at 1st junction, and turn left at 2nd junction just beyond Bredy Farm (but dont miss a visit to the 'Old Farming Collection' here — see **Burton Bradstock**), and bridge over litle River Bride. Now in the Bride Valley. Over X-rds and straight, not right before re-crossing River Bride, then straight not right twice, before entering widespread village of Litton Cheney. Through village, passing church up to left, and follow out (Sign — Long Bredy), with downland above to left. Straight, not left, through **Long Bredy** (birthplace of Nelson's Captain Hardy), turning left at end of village.

West Bay.

Pass delightfuly situated **Littlebredy** with handsomely-spired church on right, and many ancient burial mounds on the surrounding hills. Soon fork right near Bridehead, source of the River Bride, pass Littlebredy Farm, up onto downs and turn right at Y-junction. Pass woodlands on left and turn right at T-junction onto open road across downland. Sharp left at diagonal X-rds, and beyond woodlands, **Hardy Monument** on right. Car park here is start of our **Walk 5**. After 2¼ m turn right onto B3159 at entry to the long, thin village of **Martinstown** (or Winterborne St Martin). At end of village turn left, off B3159, and soon fork right keeping on wider road. Turn right with great care onto A35, and follow into **Dorchester**, thus completing Tour 4.

Tour 5

A Land of Two Giants, One Ancient and One Literary

47 miles. Reasonable for cyclists. Starting gently up the valleys of the Frome and the Sydling Water, this route then crosses several valleys and the steep downland ridges dividing them. But once beyond Bere Regis the flatter country of Wareham Heath and the Piddle Valley provides an easy run home to Dorchester.

Our route first heads north-westwards from Dorchester up the Frome Valley, and then northwards beside the little Sydling Water stream to Sydling St Nicholas. Now west to the delightful village of Cerne Abbas, with its fine church, its abbey gatehouse, and its splendidly endowed giant, cut in chalk on a hillside above. Then west again, and north-west across high downland ridges and the quiet valleys between them, before heading southwards to the wooded heathland country between the valleys of the Piddle and the Frome. We then follow up the Piddle Valley past lovely Athelhampton Hall, before

running through the great Puddletown Forest, with its colourful Rhododendron Mile, and nearby Forest Walk. Beyond the forest country, on its western fringes, we pass close to Thomas Hardy's modest birthplace, at Higher Bockhampton, and within a brief distance, before returning to Dorchester itself, encounter the quiet churchyard where the heart of this outstanding literary giant was buried.

This tour, like Tour 4, starts from the delightful old County town of **Dorchester**, but starts out on the A37, Yeovil road, for about ¼m before forking right to cross the River Frome, to divert to **Charminster** with its handsomely pinnacled church tower and interesting Wolfeton House. Fork left and turn left in **Charminster**, and over X-rds beyond the church before joining the A37. Now follow A37 north-westwards up the Frome Valley, past Stratton, and after 1¼m turn right with care, onto minor road under railway bridge, to follow up the valley of the Sydling Water, which is alongside on right.

Bear right, keeping up valley, and eventually into **Sydling St Nicholas**, stopping to look round the unspoilt, largely 15th century church. Bear right at end of village, and soon bear right again, before climbing steep hill. Track on left along ridge makes fine walk. Now start dropping down to next valley, fine view of **Cerne Abbas** Giant on hillside ahead. Turn left onto A352, and car park on

SCALE 1:190 080 or 3 MILES to 1 INCH

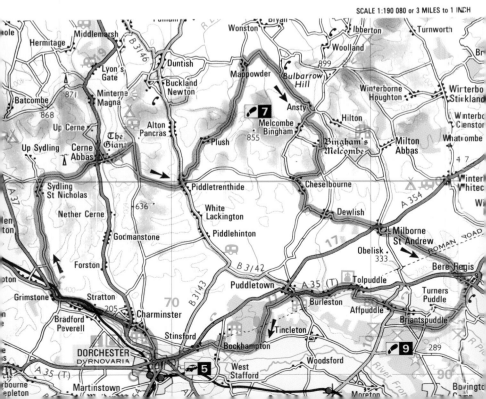

Thomas Hardy's Birthplace at Higher Bockhampton.

right with good view of Giant and explanatory notice, about ¼m ahead. Turnabout here and fork left to go through attractive and interesting village of **Cerne Abbas**. Bear left in village, fine church up to left, and soon go straight, not right (Sign — Buckland Newton) to leave village. Turn sharp right at top of steep hill (Sign — Dorchester), fork left at diagonal X-rds (Sign — Piddletrenthide), and eventually down steep hill into **Piddletrenthide**.

Turn left onto B3143 in long, thin village of **Piddletrenthide**, and after short distance take second right, off B3143 (but go straight ahead to visit church, with its fine Perpendicular tower). Up steep hill out of village, and after 1¾m through the minute village of **Plush** (a possible alternative start for our **Walk 7**), with its hospitable Brace of Pheasants Inn. After 1¼m pass Folly hamlet, which is the main start for our **Walk 7**, and head north to **Mappowder**. Turn right well beyond church, and bear left at end of village. Straight, not left, joining wider road leading to Higher Ansty (see **Ansty**). Turn right in Higher Ansty, right again at Ansty Cross, pass Fox Inn (good cold buffets here), and turn left just beyond at Lower Ansty. After 1m Bingham's Melcombe church over to right, and ¼m beyond turn right and through ford. Soon turn left (but turn right and then go ahead through gates to visit Bingham's Melcombe Church). After 1m turn right at X-rds, and then bear left twice in straggling village of Cheselbourne.

Well beyond Cheselbourne turn sharp left, up over small hill and drop down into attractive little **Dewlish** village, to go over X-rds by church. Over Devil's Brook and climb hill out of village, then down past woods to eventually bear left with care onto A354 at entry to **Milborne St Andrew**. Almost immediately turn right at X-rds, pass turn on right to church with its Norman doorway and its handsome tomb of John Morton, and over offset X-rds at end of village. After 3m, straight, not right, under bridge beneath A35, and turn left into large village of **Bere Regis**. Turn right near the splendidly roofed church, and leave village southwards on minor road.

After ½m fork right, soon over X-rds and over River Piddle (or Trent). Over 1st X-rds on wooded heathland, and turn right at 2nd X-rds (but go straight ahead for Cul-pepper's Dish Car Park and Picnic Site which is start of our **Walk 9**). Turn left in **Briantspuddle**, and after ¼m, war memorial and 20th century thatched cottages on left. Straight, not left, joining B3390 at entry to thatched village of **Affpuddle**. Straight, not right in village, leaving B3390 and church soon on right.

Turn right, over two branches of River Piddle, with manor house on left, at entry to **Tolpuddle**. Turn left with care onto A35 by Memorial Shelter on village green, the original meeting place of the famous 'Tolpuddle Martyrs'. Church on left and at end of village, TUC Memorial Cottages on right. Keep on A35, through Burleston hamlet and after ½m the lovely **Athelhampton Hall** on right. Take **2nd** left in busy **Puddletown** village, off A35, and onto minor road leading into Puddletown Forest. Soon enter 'Rhododendron Mile', best seen in early summer, Forest Walk on right. Bear right at small T-junction just beyond woodlands, and after 1½m over X-rds. (But turn right to visit Hardy's Birthplace (NT) at **Higher Bockhampton**, and/or to walk Thorncombe Wood and Black Heath Nature Trails.) Over small X-rds (but turn left to visit **Stinsford** Church, where Hardy's heart is buried), and bear left with great care onto A35 to return to Dorchester, thus completing Tour 5.

Tour 6

The Stour and Tarrant Valleys and the Western Confines of Cranborne Chase

55 miles. Reasonably easy for cyclists. Our route passes into hilly country only a mile or so beyond its start from Blandford. However, once beyond Bulbarrow Hill it drops down into flatter farming country, and only climbs significantly again when it enters the hill town of Shaftesbury. We then have a few miles of the A350 to contend with before climbing steeply beyond Fontmell Magna up on to Cranborne Chase, and a further climb up through woods beyond Ashmore. From here there is a fine run down the Tarrant Valley, with only about four miles of the A350 to be tackled at the very end.

Our route heads westwards from Blandford into hilly, wooded country, passing through the delightful estate village of Milton Abbas, the fine church of Milton Abbey, before going up over Bulbarrow Hill, with its splendid views out over the Dorset countryside. Now steeply down to less dramatic farming country, and through unspoilt villages like Woolland and Ibberton, before visiting Sturminster Newton, with its charming old watermill. From here the route heads northeastwards to the delightful old hill town of Shaftesbury before turning south to skirt the western bastions of Cranborne Chase for a while. But we soon accept the challenge provided by this outstandingly beautiful downland country, and climb up into it to visit Win Green over in Wiltshire and Ashmore, Dorset's highest village. And now we turn south-east and south to run down the Tarrant Valley, passing though a succession of small villages and hamlets, the names of most incorporating the word Tarrant. And so, over the Stour and to make a further change of direction to return northwestwards up its valley to return to Blandford.

This tour starts from the delightful Georgian town of **Blandford Forum**, leaving southwards on the A354, across the Stour, before turning first right onto a minor road not far beyond the gates of the famous Bryanston School. Pass woodlands on right and after about 2m, fork left in further woods, and then straight, not left at end of woods. Bear left at entry to long, valley-village of **Winterborne Stickland**, and beyond church, turn 2nd right and climb steadily out of valley. After 2m bear left, and soon enter **Milton Abbas**. Turn right, and drop down very attractive main street, lined with white, box-like thatched cottages, with church and Hambro Arms Inn both on left.

Fork right at bottom of **Milton Abbas**, with slight glimpses of lake down to left, and after ½m, car park for **Milton Abbey** to left — fine church, with mansion which is now a well-known public school. Continue up valley through beautiful, partly thatched **Hilton**, being sure to visit the church with its treasures brought from Milton Abbey, and well beyond village, bear right and turn right, to climb fairly steeply, with woods soon on right. Fork left beyond woods with steep slopes of **Bulbarrow Hill** up to left (but go straight ahead for a short distance for start of our **Walk 8**). Now bear left and soon fork right to drop down steep hill to small village of Woolland.

Woolland church on left, and take next turn right to move to Ibberton. Bear right and turn left at T-junction at entry to pretty, partly thatched village of **Ibberton**, nestling beneath steep downland slopes. Keep through village (but turn right if you wish to visit the attractively sited church), and straight not left at end of village. After ¼m, straight not left again, and turn left at entry to Belchalwell Street hamlet. Now through minute village of **Belchalwell**, with pleasant little church over to right.

Turn left at T-junction in The Common hamlet, and bear right twice, before entering Newton, now almost part of Sturminster Newton. Turn right with care onto A357, and beyond working watermill on left, turn off A357 onto B3091 to enter **Sturminster Newton** (Sign — Shaftesbury). Through this quiet little country town, turning right at T-junction, keeping on B3091, and keep on this road for 8m to reach the very attractive hill town of **Shaftesbury**.

Turn right and bear right in **Shaftesbury**, and well beyond centre, bear round to right at large roundabout onto A350, heading southwards (Sign — Blandford). Keep on A350 through **Compton Abbas**, but in large village of **Fontmell Magna**, with its pottery and substantial Victorian church, turn left at X-rds, off A350. Beyond village, up steep wooded hill and turn left at X-rds onto wider road. At end of woods on right, turn right off wider road and bear right. Compton Airfield (see **Compton Abbas**) soon on left, with viewing area. After 1½m, fork left, and after 1m turn sharp right onto B3081. (But go straight over diagonal X-rds into Wiltshire, and take 1st turn right if you wish to visit Win

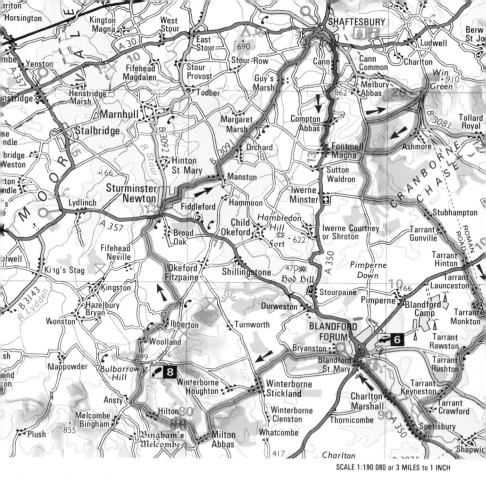

SCALE 1:190 080 or 3 MILES to 1 INCH

Green, a National Trust downland area, with car park, walking opportunities and many distant views.)

Main route now heads south on B3081, but almost immediately fork right onto minor road, and head through the delightful downland village of **Ashmore**, with a pretty duckpond at its centre. Bear right near duckpond and eventually drop down into valley (good path through woods to left) and up through dense woodlands. Now turn left onto wider road at X-rds (the same X-rds at which we turned left, after coming up from Fontmell Magna), and head southwards along fine ridge road, with good views to right. Straight, not right, and then turn left at X-rds by Hill Farm (Sign — Tarrant Gunville).

Down pleasant valley with woods first to right and then to left, and through Stubhampton hamlet, into the Tarrant Valley, before going through the quiet, brick and flint village of **Tarrant Gunville**. Straight, not right, and inn soon on right, with impressive gates of Vanbrugh's Eastbury House beyond on left. Through small village of **Tarrant Hinton** before crossing the A354 with great care at offset X-rds. Through Tarrant Launceston hamlet, and at entry to pretty **Tarrant Monkton**, turn right through watersplash, and immediately bear left, and left again by church. At end of village recross the Tarrant stream and turn right at X-rds to continue down valley.

Keep right at Y-junction, and pass hamlet of **Tarrant Rawston**, with minute church in farmyard to right. Bear left at next junction, keeping in Tarrant Valley, and straight, not left. (But turn left and left again if you wish to visit attractive little church of **Tarrant Rushton**.) Over X-rds crossing B3082, into long, straggling village of **Tarrant Keyneston**. Turn left at T-junction (Sign — Spettisbury) and after ¼ m straight, not left, just before small bridge. (But turn left if you wish to visit delightful little church of **Tarrant Crawford**.) After ½ m turn right and after another ½ m, over fine old Crawford Bridge, crossing River Stour, before turning right with care onto A350. Follow A350 through **Spetisbury**, Charlton Marshall, with its interesting church, and **Blandford St Mary**, to return to **Blandford** thus completing Tour 6.

101

Tour 7

Up the Allen Valley to the Cranborne Country

36 miles. With the exception of one comparatively steep hill, a short one just beyond Gussage St Michael, this route traverses some of Dorset's easiest countryside, and should be very suitable for cyclists. There are however several stretches of exposed downland roads, and it would be preferable to cycle over this route when the weather is reasonably quiet. Main roads have mostly been avoided, but both motorists and cyclists should take care when joining the fast and often busy A354, Salisbury to Blandford road.

Our route sets out from Wimborne Minster northwards, and goes through a series of attractive villages, closely following the course of the little River Allen back to the downland country where it rises. Once beyond the busy A354, it passes through more downland country, passing the southern borders of the great Rushmoor Park once the home of the Pitt-Rivers family. From here it passes through Farnham and Woodcutts, both having associations with the famous General Pitt-Rivers, the true pioneer of modern British archaeology. Once beyond Sixpenny Handley, we cross the A354 and head south-east over more open country, and then southwards to the delightful villages of Cranborne and Wimborne St Giles before passing the little Norman church of Knowlton, built within the earthworks of a Bronze Age circle. From here we go south again, through the western fringes of the New Forest heathlands before finally returning to Wimborne Minster.

This tour starts from the busy market centre and colourful holiday town of **Wimborne Minster**, with its fine Minster Church, heading north on the B3078. After 4m, turn left at X-rds, and over bridge crossing little River Allen (don't miss sign on bridge threatening 'Transportation for Life' for anyone caught harming it). Beyond bridge bear right at entry

SCALE 1:190 080 or 3 MILES to 1 INCH

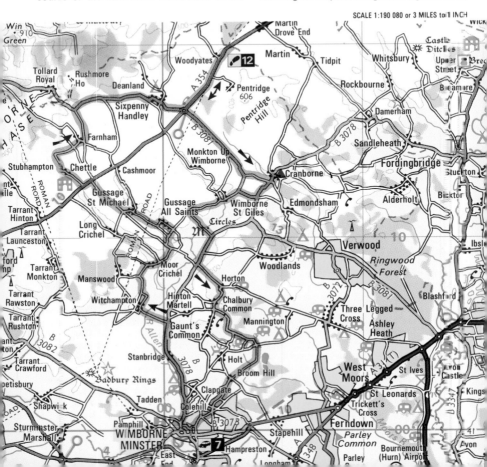

Almshouses and church at Wimborne St Giles.

to delightful village of **Witchampton**, and straight not left beyond well-restored church. Turn left just before gates of Crichel House, and soon turn right at T-junction, with woods now on right. Bear right by farm, and turn right at T-junction before going through estate village of **Moor Crichel**.

Straight not left at end of village, turn left at T-junction, and soon right, before crossing stream. Turn left by thatched cottage at X-rds known as Amen Corner, and into **Gussage All Saints**, passing finely proportioned manor house and church with 14th century tower. Cross stream beyond church and follow this up valley to village of **Gussage St Michael**. Straight, not right by church, and up steep hill before turning right at X-rds, with long barrow to left. Pass two more long barrows on right before turning left with great care onto A354 (traffic can be very fast here).

After ⅓m turn right with care, off A354, and soon enter partly thatched village of **Chettle**. Straight, not left, unless you wish to visit church and/or handsome, Baroque-style Chettle House. Bear right at end of village and again, well beyond village, before going over X-rds and into pretty thatched village of **Farnham**. Turn right beyond church, and soon turn left, to leave village northwards.

After 1m turn right onto B3081, and go straight not right in **Woodcutts** hamlet, with its distant memories of archaeological pioneer, General Pitt-Rivers. Bear left at entry to delightfully named **Sixpenny Handley**, keeping on B3081, and well beyond village over A354 at roundabout, keeping on B3081

(but bear left onto A354, and go about 2½m for layby on left which is start of our **Walk 12**). Soon cross the **Ackling Dyke**, marking the line of a Roman road which ran between **Badbury Rings** and Salisbury, and onto pleasant open road. At 3m beyond roundabout, turn left off B3081, and when woods appear on left, keep a lookout for lovely prospect of Cranborne Manor down to left. Just beyond, turn right onto B3078 (but turn left if you wish to visit the charming village of **Cranborne**).

Now head south-westwards out of **Cranborne** on B3078, after 1m turn right onto B3081, and after ¾m turn left off B3081 (Sign — Wimborne St Giles). Enter delectable **Wimborne St Giles**, attractive church and mellow-brick almshouses on left. Straight, not right by village sign on right and stocks on left, and fork left beyond stream. After 1¼m turn left, and after 1m **Knowlton** church and earthworks on left, just before route turns right onto B3078.

Turn left at offset X-rds by the Horton Inn, onto minor road, and in **Horton** village turn right by church, and Horton Tower soon appears on left. Now fork left, and turn left at X-rds in Chalbury Common hamlet, and then straight not right at entry to woodlands. Bear right in Lower Row hamlet before going over X-rds at Higher Row. After ½m bear right, but car park on left is start of an interesting forest walk. Straight, not right, at entry to Broom Hill hamlet, and then over X-rds. After ¼m straight, not right by inn, and then over X-rds by church in Colehill, before following in on minor roads to the centre of **Wimborne Minster**, thus completing Tour 7.

Tour 8
West Purbeck, Lulworth and the Dorset Heathlands

45 miles. There are a few steep little roads in the Purbeck Hills around Creech and Kimmeridge, and the downland country beyond Lulworth Cove also provides a few challenges. But in the main cyclists will find this a reasonably easy route to follow, with long stretches of level roads running across the heathlands around Clouds Hill and Bovington Camp. The return from Wool Bridge to Wareham follows the often busy A352, and cyclists might prefer to take the quieter minor roads running parallel with it to the south.

Our route first heads southwards from Wareham over partly built-up heath country, passing the attractive Blue Pool, before climbing into the Purbeck Hills. Then south again, to the sea at deeply inset Kimmeridge Bay and the lovely Smedmore House above it, before heading north to Steeple, where a choice of routes may be available (if the army ranges are open to the public when you come this way). Our main route continues north-

wards, pass the Gothick folly of Grange Arch, and the fine mansion of Creech Grange, and runs in a wide sweep around the fringes of the army ranges to return to the coast at the dramatic Lulworth Cove. Now north and west through downland country just behind the coast, before heading north towards the wooded heathlands, known as Egdon Heath in Hardy's Wessex novels. Here are walking and picnicking opportunities in plenty, and our route also passes Clouds Hill, the cottage where Lawrence of Arabia spent his last years, and the fascinating Bovington Tank Museum. And finally we pass close to lovely Wool Bridge, before returning to Wareham.*

This tour starts from the delightful little town of **Wareham**, with its Georgian flavoured streets and its small quay on the River Frome, just upstream from Poole Harbour. First head southwards on the A351, but after 1¼m fork right off A351 beyond Stoborough (Sign — Furzebrook). After 1½m entrance to the beautiful **Blue Pool** on left, then straight, not right at T-junction (Sign — Church Knowle) before climbing up over steep ridge with hairpin bend. Down steep hill and eventually over X-rds (but turn left if you wish to visit unspoilt **Church Knowle**). After 2m main route now turns right at entry to small thatched village of **Kimmeridge** (but bear left and go through Kimmeridge if you wish to visit Smedmore House and/or Kimmeridge Bay (Toll Road) — 1¼m ahead).

The Blue Pool, near Wareham.

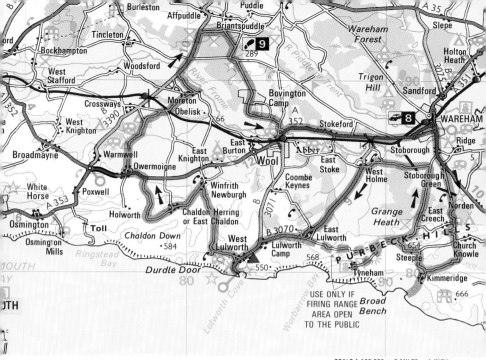

SCALE 1:190 080 or 3 MILES to 1 INCH

Beyond **Kimmeridge** village, down steep hill, over small stream and up steep hill, before turning left at T-junction. Turning to **Steeple** church on left, and ¼ m beyond turn right, and at top of hill turn sharp right by Steeple Picnic Place. But bear left and **if firing range area is open to the public** (see **Tyneham**) go through military check point to visit the 'deserted village' of **Tyneham**, and/or to drive across range for 'short-cut' to **East Lulworth** (see below). Having turned sharp right on main route, the Grange Arch (see **Creech**) soon on right (best visited on foot from Steeple Picnic Place).

Down hill through woods and straight, not right at T-junction by gateway of the lovely **Creech Grange** on left. After 2½ m turn left beyond Stoborough Heath, after 2m straight not right, and then bear left onto B3070. Keep through **East Lulworth** on B3070, with entrance to Lulworth Castle (not open) on right just beyond. Turn left at T-junction near Army Gunnery School, keeping on B3070, and go through **West Lulworth** to arrive at car park for the beautiful **Lulworth Cove** (very crowded in summer).

Now turnabout and fork left off B3070 in **West Lulworth**, bear left by church (Sign — Durdle Door), and after ¾ m straight not left (but turn left if you wish to visit the massive natural archway of **Durdle Door**). Now head inland and after 2½ m, turn left at T junction by church in picturesque **Winfrith Newburgh**. Fork left and immediately bear left by the Sailor's Return Inn in **Chaldon Herring**,

and through West Chaldon hamlet before turning left with care onto A352.

After 1m, turn right with care off A352, and through attractive village of **Owermoigne** before passing entrance to Moigne Court on right. After 1¼ m turn right in woodlands, and bear right at T-junction before passing over railway line. Bear right near entry to village of **Moreton**, last resting place of Lawrence of Arabia, and then turn left and left again (but go straight ahead to visit church — dont miss the beautifuly engraved windows). 1m beyond Moreton, turn right onto B3390, over River Frome and over X-rds keeping on B3390. Now into wooded heathland and turn right, off B3390 by Affpuddle Heath Car Park. After ¾ m Cull-peppers Dish Car Park and Picnic Site on right — this is starting point of our **Walk 9**.

Now turn right at X-rds, bear right at T-junction, turn left at next T-junction, and after ¼ m turn right (Sign — Bovington Camp). **Clouds Hill** (Lawrence of Arabia's Cottage — NT) on left just beyond. Keep through Bovington Camp, and at 1¾ m beyond Clouds Hill, the very interesting **Bovington Tank Museum** on left. Now straight, not left, then turn right at T-junction, and bear left (but walk down right if you wish to visit the historic **Wool Bridge** (Wool was 'Wellbridge' in Thomas Hardy's *Tess of the D'Urbervilles*). Immediately beyond this turn, bear left with great care onto A352, to return to **Wareham**, thus completing Tour 8.

Tour 9
Poole Harbour, East Purbeck and the Bankes Inheritance

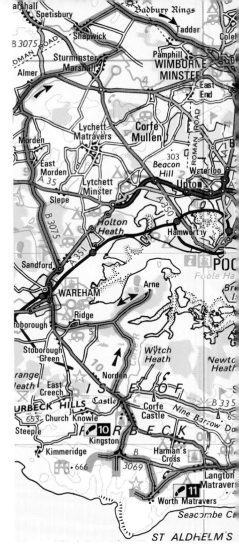

65 miles via Sandbanks Ferry, or 77 miles avoiding ferry. Apart from a few small hills in the Isle of Purbeck, this is a largely level route. However, many sections are unavoidably busy.

This tour starts from the busy coastal town of Bournemouth, one of Britain's finest holiday resorts. Before setting out ensure the the Sandbanks Ferry is operating (if in doubt telephone Poole 708282). If the ferry is closed, or if there are likely to be long delays, use A35, and A351 to move to Swanage, possibly diverting to the interesting town of Poole, on the way. It will then be possible to join the route here, or at the minor road north of Studland.

Assuming that use of the Sandbanks Ferry is to be made, set out westwards from Bournemouth centre, after 2m bear left at gyratory system onto B3065, and then turn left at **Poole Harbour** shore onto B3369 (but turn right if you wish to visit **Poole**). Over Sandbanks Ferry and into the Studland Heath country. Nature Reserve to left, and 2½m beyond ferry, car park to left with access to shore (Nature Trail starts from here). Bear right in unspoilt village of **Studland** with its interesting Norman church, joining B3351 for short time. ½m beyond village, fork left off B3351, bear left at Y-junction and follow into lively seaside resort of **Swanage**.

Turn right onto A351 in lively resort of **Swanage** (but go straight ahead if you wish to visit **Durlston Country Park** — 1¼m ahead). Follow out of Swanage on A351, but after 1½m fork left onto B3069, and through stone and thatch village of **Langton Matravers**, museum on right. After 1m fork left off B3069 and turn sharp right in the grey stone village of **Worth Matravers** (but go straight ahead if you wish to visit the interesting Norman church). Car park on left is start of our **Walk 11**. After 1m turn left onto B3069, and keep on this road through beautifully situated **Kingston**. (But turn left and left again for toll road towards Chapmar's Pool, or turn left and go beyond the impressive Victorian church for toll road towards Swyre Head).

1m beyond **Kingston**, bear left onto A351 at entry to the highly popular village of **Corfe Castle**. Car park down to left before church — use this to explore village and visit castle. This car park is also the starting point of our

Walk 10. Keep out of village on A351, and after ½m turn right onto minor road. After 2½m, partly over wooded heathland, turn right and through woodlands to the tiny settlement of **Arne**. Use car park and explore on foot down to **Poole Harbour** shore at Shipstal Point.

Turnabout in **Arne**, back through woodlands, straight not left twice, straight not right twice, and turn right onto A351 in Stoborough. Over bridge crossing River Frome at entry to pleasant old town of **Wareham**, soon turning left to keep on A351 (but go straight ahead if you wish to explore town). Bear round to right at large roundabout, over next two roundabouts, keeping on A351, and after ¾m, bear left at roundabout onto B3075. Soon through open heath and woodland, with Gore Heath Picnic Place and Car Park on right after 1¼m.

The Foreland or Handfast Point

Ballard Point

Swanage Bay

SWANAGE
Peveril Point
Durlston Bay
DURLSTON HEAD
Tilly Whim Caves

)R ST ALBAN'S HEAD

Over offset X-rds, crossing A35 with great care, keeping on B3075. Keep on B3075 for 3m, and then bear right onto A31. Over small X-rds, straight not left near East Almer Farm, and ¼m beyond, go straight not right, onto minor road, leaving A31. Over X-rds with great care, crossing A350 and into **Sturminster Marshall**. Go straight through village, with church on left, and bear left immediately beyond bridge over River Stour. Now go straight, not right, three times, and turn right near the church in pretty, partly riverside village of **Shapwick**.

Straight not right twice in **Shapwick** and after 1m, turn right with care onto B3082. Almost immediately, a turn on left to the car park for **Badbury Rings** (NT), fine Iron Age earthworks, with walking and picnic possibilities. Now along the B3082, here down a splendid avenue of beech trees, and keep on B3082 into Wimborne. (But do not miss a visit to splendid **Kingston Lacy House** (NT), entrance on right after about 2m.

Turn left at 1st traffic lights in busy, but delightful **Wimborne Minster**, and follow through town, bearing left, and then right three times before turning left onto B3078 (Signs — Poole). Now bear right at two roundabouts, joining A31 (Signs — Ringwood). (But follow signs to 'Tropical Bird Garden', if you wish to visit the attractive **Merley Tropical Bird Garden**.) After 2m bear right at roundabout onto B3073 (Sign — Hampreston), after 2m bear 1st left at 1st roundabout by Longham church, and immediately bear 2nd left at 2nd roundabout, onto minor road (Sign — Hurn Airport). Over X-rds at traffic lights crossing A347, and after ¼m, straight not right (but turn right if you wish to visit **West Parley** church — ¾m). Bear round to right at small roundabout near commencement of Hurn Airport, and after 1 ¼m entry to airport on left. Turn right at T-junction beyond river bridge, and follow all signs to Christchurch, to arrive at roundabout intersecting with A35 in **Christchurch**.

Bear right at roundabout onto A35, (but go over roundabout, if you wish to visit the charming old town of **Christchurch**, and/or go east beyond town on B3059, eventually turning right, to explore down to **Mudeford Quay** and **Mudeford Beach**). But main route heads west from roundabout, on A35 for 1m before turning left onto B3059, and not far beyond, a turn to **Hengistbury Head** on left (Car Parks and Nature Trail). Now follow B3059 to rejoin A35 in Boscombe, by turning left, and follow this into **Bournemouth** centre, thus completing Tour 9.

Walks

Walk 1

Wooded Hills and Ancient Earthworks in Dorset's Far West

Allow 3 hours

This walk takes you along ridges high above Marshwood Vale and the coast above Lyme Bay and affords splendid views at almost every point. Starting from the Iron Age fort of Coney's Castle the route takes you south over gently sloping fields to Wootton Fitzpaine, along a pleasant valley up to the woods, over Wootton Hill, where there are fine views across to Lambert's and Coney's Castles and back along a farm track round the base of Coney's.

(A) Start from the car park at Coney's Castle (NT) (193) [SY 37-97]. To reach this use **Tour 1**, or turn south off the B3165 about 7 miles north-east of Lyme Regis at the splay-entranced side road containing a telephone kiosk, which is about a quarter of a mile west of the Bottle Inn, **Marshwood** (SY 38-99). At Fishpond Bottom, take the second left and then the right fork up the hill. The car park is on the left. Leave the car park at the NT sign (which is on **Tour 1**) and go out onto the road. Turn left and walk half a mile down the road to a concrete drive on the right, signposted to Great Coombe Farm.

(B) Ignoring the concrete farm road, take the next gate on the right after the turning and cross the field diagonally left, aiming at two trees in the far hedge. Go over a double stile and cross the next field in the same direction, aiming at the sea in a 'V' below as soon as it becomes visible. After a gate the same line across the third field brings you into the bottom corner.

(C) Go through the gate to your right (but

Wootton Fitzpaine Church.

keep straight down the road if you wish to visit **Wootton Fitzpaine**, and rejoin our route at **(D)**) and walk along the left hand hedge and through the gate in front of you. Keep along the right hand side of the next hedge and through the gate on the left, just before the corner. Then walk diagonally downhill to the houses at the bottom where there is a stile onto the road. This is part of **Wootton Fitzpaine**.

(D) Turn right and walk along the road for about a quarter of a mile. When the road starts to drop downhill watch for a hydrant sign on your left. Turn left onto a farm track here which leads to some barns. At the end of the first building follow the track to the right and continue along it for about 250 yards. On a curve, before the track goes through a gate, there are two gates on your right. Take the second one and follow the headland straight along to a plank bridge in the top corner and straight on beside a stone wall on your right. Turn down to the little red-roofed barn and turn right, passing it on your left. Continue to the stile in the next hedge. Cross the next field diagonally left and exit by the gate in the corner with the remains of stiles on each side. Go down to the next gate to your left, through this, turn right and walk along the left hand side of the hedge, parallel to the stream. After going through another gate walk absolutely straight across the next field and you should hit the bank of a small stream at a point where you can see the stile on the other side. Cross to this, over it and turn left to the next waymarked stile. Follow the path along a bank and through the trees to the next stile. Then drop down the bank and continue half right along the bottom, aiming at some ruined buildings and over a waymarked stile.

(E) Pass between the first two buildings and a third on your left and, when the track turns right uphill, leave it and go through the gate ahead, along the bottom of the field for about 15 yards and over the concrete bridge on the left. Turn right and go through the gate 20 yards ahead and continue parallel to the stream along the next two fields. Towards the end of the third, turn right through the gap spanning the stream and out onto the road.

(F) Cross the road, go through the hunting-gate and walk up the field, aiming at the nearest telegraph pole. Follow the same line to the far hedge, then turn left and walk along it to the gate on the right. Go through this and up the right hand side of the hedge, into the next field and straight across to the gate onto the road. About 20 yards up the road to the left there is a sign to 'Marsh Farm' which points up a stony track forking left. Follow this track for a quarter of a mile. After passing a pig farm it becomes grassy and,

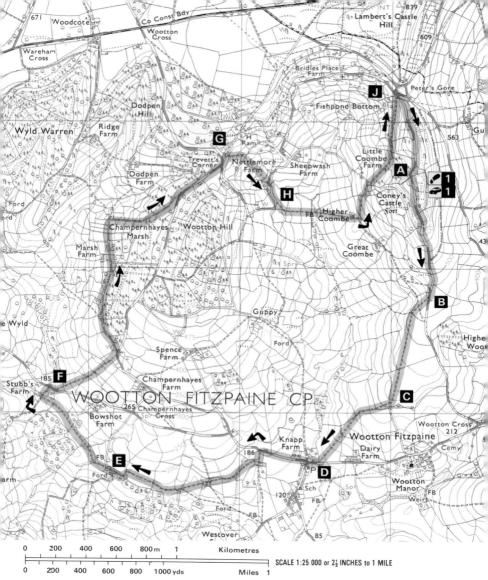

when it begins to drop downhill, veering left, leave it and take the right turn up into the wood Follow this up as it runs into a wider one and leads you out onto the road on Wootton Hill. Continue left, up the road until, at Trevett's Corner, at its junction with a right turn signposted 'Fishpond', it curves left. Here you leave it and keep straight on up a lane for a few yards.

(G) Opposite Tempest House take the farm road to the right and when faced with two gates, take the red one on the right (towards Nettlemore Farm). Once through it, climb over the wooden rails on your left and walk straight down the side of the field. After the next gate walk diagonally right, crossing the slope, **not** going down it to the gate at the bottom, but to the one ahead. Then, continue in the same direction, cross the next field diagonally left until you spot a hunting-gate bringing you out onto the road. Turn right and go through the first gate you come to on the left after about 200 yards.

(H) Cross the field diagonally right and once through the gate walk down the green track to the footbridge at the bottom and up to Higher Coombe Farm. Go through the farmyard and turn left along a stony track leading uphill. The track takes you for half a mile along the side of the valley.

(J) At the end of the track, turn hard right onto the road and walk back up to the starting car park at Coney's Castle **(A)**, thus completing Walk 1.

109

Walk 2

Coast and Country — including Thorncombe Beacon and Eype Down

Allow 2½ — 3 hours

This walk takes in part of the Dorset Coast Path, crosses a wild common, follows two ancient, hollow lanes and returns across quiet fields. It is in 'close' country with steep valleys and round hills and affords glorious views of the hills and coast in all directions. Use stout footwear as some sections are very muddy.

(A) Start from the car park at **Seatown**, (193) (SY 42-91), which is on **Tour 1**, having turned south off the A35 at **Chideock** Church. Leave the car park from its SE corner and walk straight up to the NT stile, following the green track round the scrub to the top. Then continue along the coastal path over Ridge Cliff and Doghouse Hill to the summit of Thorncombe Beacon.

(B) Sit here awhile and take in the fine views, westwards to the Devon coast beyond Golden Cap, and eastwards to Bridport, Chesil Beach and Portland. Leaving the Beacon, instead of following the coastal path all the way downhill, turn off it to make for a tumulus down on your left. Pass this on your left, keep round the contour and over a stile in the hedge on your left.

(C) Follow the well-defined path ahead, away from the coast, passing a wood on the right, then uphill along a broad track, leaving this when it goes off to the right and continuing along a green track between gorse and brambles. This is Eype Down and below to your right you can see the hamlet of Higher Eype and beyond it a great mass of caravans between here and Bridport. At the bottom of the slope is a 4-pointer signpost.

(D) Turn left, signed 'Chideock and Quarry Hill', and follow the green path down,

SCALE 1:25 000 or 2½ INCHES to 1 MILE

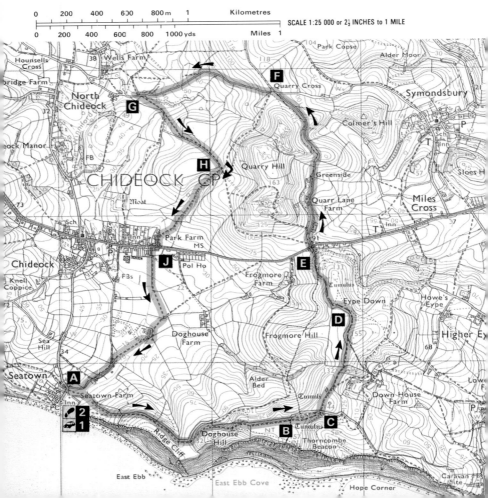

Sweeping downland above Seatown.

keeping to the main track as it curves this way and that. As soon as you sight the main road below, aim at Quarry Hill rising behind it to the north, and at a small, grey roof down on the road. The path ends at a short section of lane. Turn right and walk down it, then down the road into which it runs and you emerge onto the A35.

(E) Cross A35 with great care and enter Quarr Lane immediately opposite and follow it for about ¾ mile. When the surface runs out after the last house, it becomes first a green track and then sometimes a stony one through little gorges and sometimes a barely discernible green path through overgrown bracken and grass. But keep the high hedge on your left all the way and watch out first for glimpses of Quarry Hill up to the left and then Colmer's Hill on the right, crowned with seven spindly trees. Seconds after passing a hollow-lane leading back down to your right, you come out onto an open green space with another lane going left. This is Quarry Cross.

(F) Turn left into Hell Lane and follow it downhill, through several muddy patches, for about ¼ mile, until two gates cross the track. After going through the first gate, go round to the right to see the small fishing lake, then back through the second gate and on down the lane. After an open space, a tiny stream appears beside you from your left. Now watch out for a waymarked stile on the left.

(G) From the stile turn sharp left and cross the field, aiming to the left of the tree belt until you see the next stile. From here your path south-eastwards along the next four fields is waymarked with numbered arrows. Follow No. 7 until, at the base of Quarry Hill, a signpost at the gate on your right indicates footpaths 9, 10 and 7.

(H) At this point it would be worth climbing at least part of the way up Quarry Hill using the rights of way shown on our map, and back via the stile high up to your left. It is sometimes called Quar Hill, the old Dorset word for 'quarry' and it was once the source of limestone which was taken downhill on horse-drawn sledges.

(H) At the signpost, turn right through the gate and follow the old sledge-track downhill (Footpath 9). As you go, look half-right over Chideock to the wooded Langdon Hill which runs up to **Golden Cap**, and further right, to Hardown Hill above Morcombelake. Follow the waymarks to a large corrugated-iron building and, just before some new houses, turn left onto concrete and down to the road. You are now in the attractive village of **Chideock**, which is well worth exploring. Turn right and walk along the road to the telephone kiosk.

(J) Cross the road and after going slightly westwards, go straight down the footpath signed 'Seatown'. At the end of path, skirt the right-hand edge of a cultivated field and turn left along its bottom to a gate on the right. Through the gate and straight across the next field to the signpost on the far side. Then follow the footpath signs round the sewage works via two metal kissing-gates, and over two footbridges crossing the River Winniford, Wynreford or Chid. Now out onto a narrow concrete road and keep straight on, watching for an unmarked stile in the fence on the left. Over stile and down towards a little red building at the bottom. Skirt this and you are back in the carpark at **Seatown (A)**, thus completing Walk 2.

Walk 3
Melbury Country — Parkland, Deer and Horses

Allow 4 hours

This is a walk that is at almost all times wet and muddy and the going is sometimes difficult. The wearing of wellington boots is recommended and inexperienced walkers are advised not to try it. Starting from the village of Evershot the walk crosses Melbury Park where herds of red deer can be seen and, with luck, a white hart. Passing close to Melbury House, the seat of the Earls of Ilchester, with its associated stud, to the hidden village of Melbury Osmond, it then heads westward along grassy lanes and over fields beside ancient woodlands to Lewcombe. Here a short diversion leads past Lewcombe Manor House to one of the smallest churches in the country nestling in the woods beside the old farmhouse. Turning southwards for the return to Evershot the walk crosses a ford and fields to Girt Farm. Here the countryside opens up to give a panoramic view over the vale with its small dairy farms divided by woods and hedges and overlooked by the medieval earthworks of a motte and bailey on Castle Hill.

Evershot ... a village of considerable character.

(A) Park on the side of the road at the eastern end of the village of **Evershot** (134) (ST 57-04), which is on our **Tour 2**, and is also eight and a half miles south of Yeovil via the A37 and minor road from Holywell. Start the walk northwards along the tarred drive into Melbury Park which is entered after 100 yards through gate pillars crowned by heraldic lions. Follow the drive past two cattle grids to the back of Melbury House. Turn left (unless you wish to visit **Melbury Sampford** church) and follow the drive due north between fields of horses from the stud, to the picture-book village of **Melbury Osmond**. Turn left down a lane half way up the hill through the village, opposite Rock Cottage.

(B) Walk down this lane, which soon turns into a green lane, to a gate where a farm track joins from the right. Follow the farm track straight on to enter a field. Continue straight across two fields, keeping the wood on your left in the second field, to a hunting gate in the top left hand corner. Go through the gate and turn immediately right to follow a very wet and boggy path down to a delightful stone bridge over a stream. Cross a narrow field and, ignoring a gate into the field on the right, proceed straight ahead to a hidden gate into the field at the top of the rise. Cross this field and follow a green lane to join the road.

(C) Turn left and follow the road for 200 yards then left again over a cattle grid down the drive towards Lewcombe House. Immediately after passing a cottage on the right there is a stile on the right into the field **(D)**.

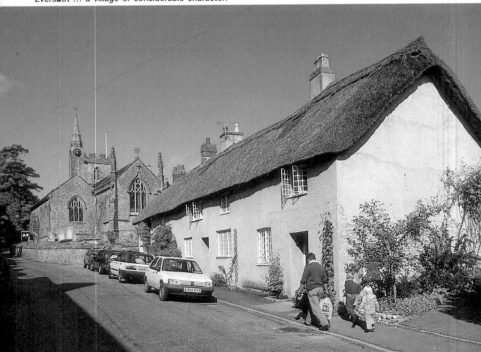

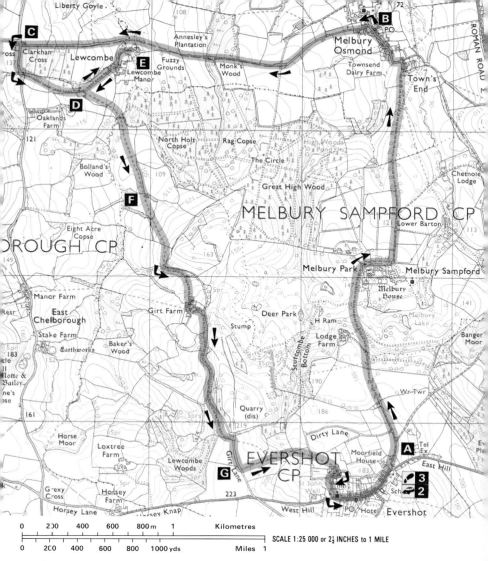

For the diversion to Lewcombe Manor with its tiny church (E), continue along the drive over another cattle grid, turning left at the back of the Manor House and follow the drive down to the church and old farm house.

(D) Returning to point (D), go over the stile (now on left) and walk diagonally across two fields via a gate to another stile by the river in the bottom right-hand corner of the second field. Cross the river via a ford, which is sometimes quite deep, and climb the steep bank to the rails into the field above. Care should be taken here as this bank is very slippery. Go southwards over a long field to a gate in the left-hand corner.

(F) Now across the next two fields to join the farm track leading to Girt Farm. Good view over the vale to the right. Passing through the farmyard turn left past the front of the farmhouse and follow the farm drive. Good views of medieval earthworks of Castle Hill over to left. At the top of the hill the drive turns right and after 250 yards enter the field on the left via a stile.

(G) Walk along the top of the field with a hedge on the left and go through a gate into the next field and cross this to a stile into a lane. Cross the lane into the next field and, leaving barns on the right, follow the fence round to a gate to enter a lane between a cottage down to a road near the entry to **Evershot**. Turn right and follow the road to the church. Tess's Cottage opposite is associated with Hardy's *Tess of the d'Urbervilles*. Turn left at the church and walk through the village, perhaps calling at the Acorn Inn before returning to the starting point, to complete Walk 3.

Walk 4
Wynford Eagle Downland Country

Allow 3 hours

This walk passes through parts of Dorset's wonderfully unspoilt countryside, where cereal crops grow, cattle and sheep graze, and the hand of man is still only lightly felt. Here is a land of picturesque valleys and rolling hills. You will be walking mostly on broad downland ridges, with fine views out over the rolling countryside beyond. Apart from the odd tractor and driver, encounters with fellow men are seldom made, save in the two villages nestling in the valleys below.

Note: There are no footpath signs, or waymarks **anywhere** on this walk, so please follow the directions carefully.

(A) Park in the small hamlet of **Wynford Eagle**, which is on our **Tour 2**, and which lies about 1½ miles south-west of Maiden Newton on the road to **West Compton**. The hamlet consists of little else than Manor Farm and its associated buildings, and it is possible to park on the waste ground beside a large barn which is on the east side of the road a few yards south of the turning signposted 'Askerswell & Bridport' (194) (SY 584-959). Retrace your steps a few yards, turn right by the post box and follow the track up the hill. When you come to a chalk pit, immediately in front of you, turn right.

(B) This is a well-defined farm track, with the hedge on your left. When you reach the crest of the hill, you can pause and enjoy the

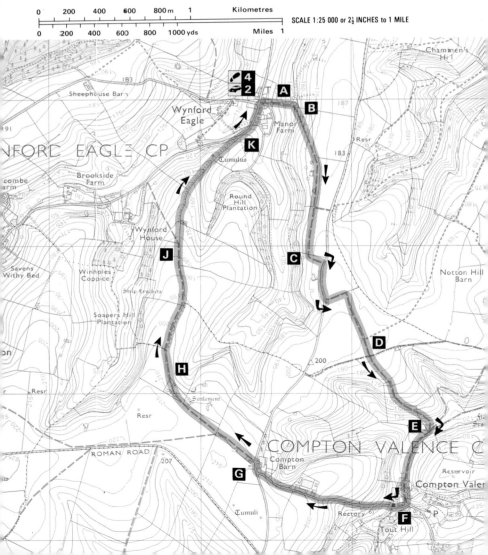

Wynford Eagle ... an unspoilt downland hamlet.

view into the valley, on your right. If you turn further to your right, almost behind you, you will notice a cluster of radio masts on the skyline to the north-west. This is the Rampisham BBC Transmitting Station (ST 54-01). Proceed along the track, and pass Hill Barn on your right. When the track turns to the left, keep straight on across the field. When you come to the wire fence — along which some vegetation grows — you will find a distinct gap to go through.

(C) Turn left and uphill bearing slightly right of the fence, and you will come to a hunting gate which leads you on to a tarmac road, known as Greenford Lane. Turn right along the road, and proceed for about 250 yards. You will see a barn, on the left-hand side of the road, and two gates, just before it. Take the left-hand gate and proceed through the field, with the hedge on your right. When the hedge comes to an end, turn right and follow another hedge on your right. As you come level with the copse on your right pause to enjoy the view on your left, looking down a lovely V-shaped valley to the hills beyond.

(D) When you reach the end of the copse, go through the gate and bear right until you come to a wire fence ahead of you. Follow this fence and you will come to a gate at the end of the field. Once through the gate, carry on forward, **not** down the track to your left. Aim for the right-hand side of the wood on the skyline, and once over the contour slope you will see a metal gate in the corner of the field ahead of you. Go through the gate and a few yards further you will find another metal gate on your left. Go through this gate, then continue steeply downhill, with the fence on your right, into the bottom of an attractive dry valley. Now walk over soft, pleasant downland turf.

(E) On reaching the valley bottom turn right through a metal gate. A few yards further on go through another metal gate on your left, continuing forward with the fence now on your right, towards a well-defined

track you can see ahead. Go through the gate at the end of the field, onto the track which will lead you into Compton Valence and through a farmyard.

(F) When you reach the tarmac road, turn right in centre of Compton Valence, beautifully sited in a hollow with swirling downland above on every side, and faint signs of prehistoric, Roman and medieval field systems within the rectangle formed by its approach roads. Now proceed along the road past the church (not of exceptional interest) on your right. Continue up Church Hill Lane, noticing the cultivated shrubs and flowers along the bank on your right. When you reach the top of the hill, pause and look back to admire the views on both sides of the road.

(G) Turn right at T-junction, with a large stone barn on your right, and you will see some farm buildings on the other (left) side of the road. At the far end of these buildings, turn left off the road, go through the gate and proceed through the field, following the hedge on your right. When you reach the end of the field go through the fence and turn right, following the wire fence on your right for about 100 yards. When you reach the end of this field go through the gate on your right and immediately through another one on your left and proceed along a faint track. At the next gate and fence leading off to the right, turn right, following the fence on your right.

(H) At the end of this field, go through the metal gate on your right, and immediately through a hunting gate on your left. Follow the hedge on your right, and at the end of the field, you will join a well-defined track, leading downhill to **Wynford Eagle**.

(J) Follow this track, which will eventually bring you to a tarmac road. **(K)** Go through the gate and, taking in the view to your left of the meandering stream and meadows, turn right. Walk down the road into **Wynford Eagle** hamlet, which will shortly lead you to the starting point **(A)**, thus completing Walk 4.

115

Walk 5

The Hardy Monument and the Portesham Downland Country

Allow 5 hours

This walk introduces you to Black Down, with its extensive views across to Somerset in the north, Weymouth, Portland and White Nothe to the south-east and Golden Cap beyond Bridport to the west. The hilltop is privately owned but open to the public for quiet enjoyment. It is topped by the monument erected by public subscription in 1844 to commemorate Admiral Sir Thomas Masterman Hardy, commander of Nelson's flagship HMS Victory. Standing 70 feet high this monument, which is now owned by the National Trust, is a landmark for miles around. The first half of the walk takes you east along a chalk ridge past a series of Neolithic round barrows, affording spectacular views in all directions, and returns over three grassy hills and up through Benecke Wood.

(A) Start at **The Hardy Monument** (which is on our **Tour 4**) on the west side of the road running south-west from Martinstown to Abbotsbury (194) (SY 613 876). Walk up to the Monument and facing it with your back to the sea, take the narrow footpath which leaves from the stones at the left-hand end of the row of small wooden posts crossing your line of vision. Aim at the wooden signpost on the other side of the road saying 'Inland Route'. To avoid 400 yards of road, cross the stile and follow the narrow path round the left-hand side of the little hill and back to the road. Otherwise, turn right onto the road and walk downhill for about 450 yards. Be careful as this road is very busy, particularly at weekends and holiday times.

(B) Turn right at the signpost saying 'Inland Route. Corton Hill'. Continue along the wide track, sometimes stony, sometimes grassy, sometimes just a headland path with hedge, with wall or fence on your right. After about 2 miles two pylon lines cross your path, then a few scattered tumuli on your left, then a hunting gate which leads you round behind one of a pair of tumuli in front of its mate. Ahead you can see a second pair of tumuli and when you reach them, turn through the gate on your right.

SCALE 1:25 000 or 2½ INCHES to 1 MILE

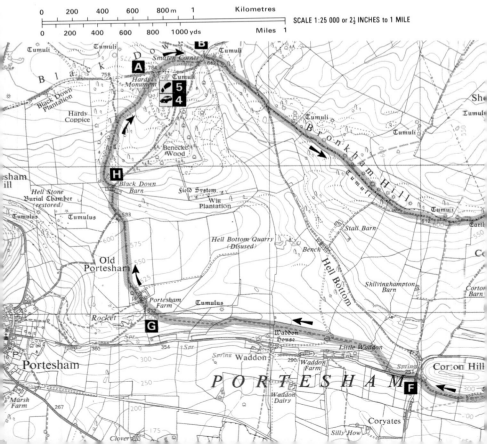

(C) Turn right and walk back along the top edge of the field and then turn left and go down its side. Keep to the same line when crossing from the cultivated to the grass land (but if necessary, go across to the gate on the left and back). Then continue downhill, along the top edge of the little green valley on the left. Go through a gate and then follow the track down to the end of the field, keeping the fence on your right. Turn left, walk along the bottom of the field, turn right at the end and walk through a farmyard and out onto the road. This is Friar Waddon, once a village which was recorded in Domesday Book as being held by a French religious house. Now only a farmstead, it was among the last in Dorset to run pure-blooded Longhorn cattle — hence the abnormal width of the door-ways to some of the older byres.

(D) Here you can **either** turn left along the road for about 20 yards and take the stony farm track running diagonally up Friar Waddon Hill. At the top, turn right round the tumulus and, leaving it on your right, walk straight along the top of the hill, through a gate and along the left-hand side of a wall. Make for the pylon lines ahead and then drop down the hill to the right and over a stile onto the road. Turn left. (See **(E)** below).

(D) Or you can turn right on leaving Friar Waddon Farm and walk along the road as it curves round to the left to a gap between the hills with a farm road coming up from the left to join the road.

(E) Turn left onto the farm road, take about 10 paces and leave it to the right through a narrow gap with a tall rock cliff on the right. This leads you down through a tiny gully to a stile, after which you follow the contour of Corton Hill round to the right, keeping above the telegraph post between you and Corton Farm below. Continue round the base of the hill, keeping to the narrow path to avoid

Corton Farm, beneath Friar Waddon Hill.

putting a foot down an old badger set, and following the yellow waymark signs on two or three tall posts. The path round the hill brings you down to a T-junction on the road by a stone stile.

(F) Walk a few yards down the leg of the 'T' to the first gate on the right and, glancing back at the dramatic slope of Corton Hill towering above you, make your way uphill by zig-zagging up the strip lynchets to the top of the ridge and continue along it, aiming for a square concrete structure. This is way-marked, and following the yellow arrow straight ahead, keep along the ridge, over a stile, keeping the wall on your right. At the end of the field, bear right and left again, still on left-hand side of wall. Keep the same line along this and two more scrubby fields, over waymarked stiles, to a corner flanked by two stone walls. Here you have to negotiate some rusty barbed-wire, a heap of fallen stones and a rickety wooden rail into the next field. Then face half right and walk up the field where you can see some farm buildings (Portesham Farm), to the gate in opposite corner.

(G) Turn right onto the concrete farm road and keep straight on, passing the farm on your right, and follow the farm track up a rise and then downhill to Black Down Farm.

(H) Now take the signposted path from behind the barn uphill through wood to the the Monument, taking the right fork at the stone marker in the clearing; through more wood, then a well-defined path through the bracken and uphill aiming at a prominent bush on the skyline to complete Walk 5 back at the **Hardy Monument (A)**.

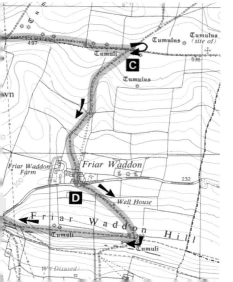

Walk 6
Wooded Watershed Country at the Head of the Cerne Valley

Allow 3½ hours

This walk provides a mixture of hilltops, wooded lanes and farmland paths, with intimate views across the Piddle and Cerne valleys and more distant prospects northwards into Somerset and Wiltshire from the downland watershed country of Telegraph Hill and Dogbury. It passes Minterne Parva, the tiny hamlet of Up Cerne, with its largely 16th century manor house, and also the banked enclosure of Dogbury Camp. It may be muddy in parts, so stout footwear is advisable.

If not using our **Tour 3**, which passes close to the start point, travel south on the A352 from Sherborne. After about 7m, take a left fork at Middlemarsh signed 'Dorchester Alternative Route'. The starting-point layby is on the left, about 2m beyond Middlemarsh, and about ¼m beyond a minor road coming in from the left.

(A) Start at the large layby on the east side of the road on Watts Hill (194) (ST 673-040). Take the lane running downhill (south-eastwards) from the back of the layby and follow it until another lane joins it from the right, with a barn in the corner. Turn into this, turn right at the next T-junction and continue to another barn on the left.

(B) Go through the gate on the left and walk round the hedge on your right to a stile. Over this and cross the next field diagonally, aiming to the right of the clump of trees ahead. Then over a stile, across the road and over a second stile waymarked with a footpath sign. Follow the hedge on your right about half way round, to a wide gap; go through and walk straight down to a gate into a belt of scrub and then down to the next gate, into a large field. Here you walk down diagonally, aiming half right at a dead tree (hopefully still here) in the nearest (projecting) corner. The gate here leads you onto a track running alongside a hedge on the left and when you emerge from the field, keep on it, alongside a beech hedge to a lane crossing. This is Minterne Parva.

(C) Turn left, passing Minterne Parva Farm on your right and follow the lane down to the main road (A352). Turn left along A352 for 200 yards and then right into minor road which brings you to the minute hamlet of **Up Cerne**, with its interesting little church, and its gabled manor house, built in the 16th century by Sir Robert Meller as an extension of an existing medieval hall.

(D) Turn right near the church and follow the made-up road, with a small stream alongside, to a house and Great Pond on your left.

(E) Turn right by Great Pond onto the green track, cross the valley, and follow the track to the left at beginning of woodland. Where the track forks, take the right-hand one to climb the hill and when you reach the T-junction at the top, take the narrow path to the left and continue along the ridge for about ½m. Sadly the views from the ridge are not good, but eventually there will be few glimpses between small trees on the right. Now start to watch for a hunting gate in the right-hand hedge which you will see when the path has opened out into a clearing.

(F) The hunting gate brings you out into a field. Turn left and walk round the edge and down the side to a gate on your left. Once through this, follow the left-hand edge of the next two fields and out onto an open space alongside a road, with a small hardstanding on its edge.

(G) Turn left onto the road, walk 200 yards uphill and continue straight on into a green lane (having first paused to survey the panoramic view from Telegraph Hill across the valley into Somerset and Wiltshire). The green lane curves downhill and round the base of High Stoy to a narrow minor road with woodland rising up to right. Turn right and follow this for about 1 mile down to the main road (A252).

(H) Cross the A352 with great care and enter the stony track on the opposite side, marked 'Unsuitable for vehicles'. This track leads up to Dogbury Down, crossing the earthworks of Dogbury Camp hidden in the trees on both sides. Follow track carefully, ignoring one lane leading down to the right, and eventually when reaching the minor road, turn right and walk back to the starting-point layby left **(A)**, thus completing Walk 6.

Church and lake at Up Cerne.

Walk 7
Chalkland Ridge Country

Allow 2 ½ hours

This relatively short walk provides superb views, especially northwards to the Blackmoor Vale. There are also delightful glimpses from the long chalkland ridges, out over the little valley in which the minute village of Plush lies. Here, in countryside which contains the very essence of the Dorset hills, will be found an interesting nursery specialising in orchids, and a pleasant inn which will provide welcome refreshment for walkers following this route.

(A) Unless starting from **Plush** (see note at end , start from the lane crossing at Folly (194) (ST 72-03) (which is on our **Tour 5**) on the minor road from Piddletrenthide to Mappowder, about 3 miles north of Piddletrenthide and 2 miles south of Mappowder. The little house on the west side of the road used

to be a drovers' inn called The Fox and the lane crossing the road here was one of a network of drovers' roads which ran all over the hills we shall be walking on. Walk up the lane on the east side of the road for about a quarter of a mile to a very overgrown fork going half right with a gate at the end.

(B) Go through this gate and follow the track round to the right and rising gradually up to the top of Lyscombe Hill. Continue along the top of the down for about half a mile, keeping an eye on the splendid view across the valley to your right and passing a small wood on your left, until you encounter a wire fence crossing the path.

(C) Turn right along this fence to the bottom corner of the field and through into the next field with a turn to left and right. Then down the left side of the next fence to a wooden bar-stile on the right. Over this and follow the hedge on your right round the top of the slope. Continue along the lefthand side of the hedge until you spot a bar stile in it. Do not cross it, but turn left and walk straight downhill to a stile in a wire fence crossing from left to right. You are now looking at the tiny village of **Plush**. Once over the stile you will spot a green track running diagonally

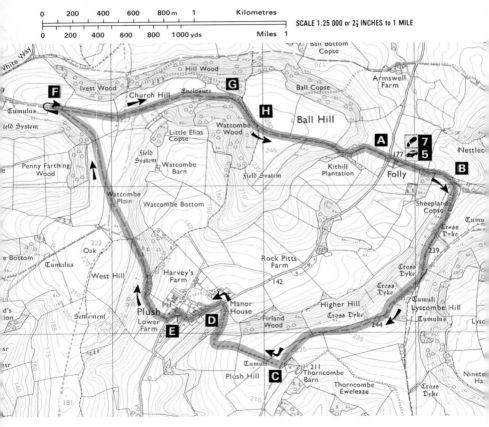

The Brace of Pheasants Inn, Plush.

downhill to the right. Walk down it to the gate at the bottom and out onto the road.

(D) Turn left and walk along the road, keeping left at the T-junction in front of the Brace of Pheasants, an inn which is well-known for its excellent food and for its spectacular recovery from a disastrous fire in the seventies. About 100 yards past the inn you will see a wide farm track on your right running uphill through trees.

(E) Walk up the track to the top where you emerge into the open. Look at the very special view of sweeping downland and valley to your right. Walk straight ahead, on a faint green track, curving round to pass an earthwork on your right and follow the contour round between some more earth-works, aiming at a gap in the hedge ahead. Once through this, aim at a gate ahead and stop to look over it at the fine view across Blackmoor Vale.

(F) Do not go through the gate, but turn right and walk along the hedge. Cross over to explore the remains of an ancient settlement on the right. Nothing is known about this, but, as you are on an old drove road, there must be some connection. Stay on the right hand side of the field to investigate an old dewpond, now sadly puddled by cattle, and leave the field by the gate just beyond the pond.

(G) Cross a small clearing and follow the path into the wood, watching out after 200 yards for a gate on the left and a sign to Folly fixed to a tree.

(H) Leave the wood by this gate, walk down the left hand side of the field to a gate giving onto a track and follow this down to the road to the point where you started **(A)**, to complete Walk 7.

Note: With the landlord's permission to park, perhaps following a drink or a meal, this walk could be started from the Brace of Pheasants at Plush **(D)** *following the same circle.*

Walk 8

Abbot's Country, and Beyond to the Devil's Brook

Allow 4 hours

This walk starts from Bulbarrow Hill, the second highest point in Dorset and takes us south along a downland ridge, with spectacular views to the west and south-west. After a dramatic view of Milton Abbey to the east we take to the fields along a pleasant valley to skirt the village of Hilton, before going up through woods over a ridge and down to Bingham's Melcombe. We return through the hamlet of Aller, through Hilton again and up Hilton Bottom, a quiet valley enclosed by two grassy ridges.

(A) Start from the top of **Bulbarrow Hill** (194¹ (ST 77-05), which is close to the routes of both our **Tour 3** and **Tour 6**. If not using one of these tours, travel west from the crossroads north of Shillingstone on the A35⁷, go through Okeford Fitzpaine keeping along the valley to Belchalwell Cross. Here a signpost directs you left uphill to Bulbarrow. Drive along the top of the hill, passing the large car park and viewpoint on your left. Just after the viewpoint keep straight on, taking the left fork ahead, and park on the wide green verge on your left (ST 778-054), under a large tree, a few yards after passing the entrance to the radio masts on the right.

(A) Walk a short distance west along the road until you see a signpost pointing down a bridleway on your left. Take the bridleway, go through the gate and follow the grass track (called the Ice Drove) all the way down the ridge, keeping the fence on your left all the way.

(E) When you meet a thick hedge crossing your route, go through the gate ahead, turn left and follow the track into the wood to another gate with a stile beside it.

(C) Once through the gate you are in the Green Hill Nature Reserve. You turn right and follow the (sometimes overgrown) little track alongside the hedge on your right and down to the road. Before reaching the bottom, look half left across the valley where you can see **Milton Abbey (E)**. If you have time, turn left and walk along the road to have a closer look.

(D) Otherwise turn right and walk along the road for about 700 yards to the entrance to a tree-lined drive. Turn left down the drive.

(F) Just before the drive rises to enter the wood, turn right through a gate into the last field on your right. Keep along the bottom of the next three fields, with the hedge on your right, cross a concrete bridge at the end of

the third, turn sharp left through a gate, and continue in the same direction, hedge still on the right, to the end of the fourth field.

(G) Go through the gate and leave the track immediately by another gate on the left. Follow the hedge on the right and take the fenced off path along the left of a wall, continuing until the track meets a tarmac road. The signpost on the left indicates a bridleway to Aller.

(H) Turn left, through a hunting gate, straight up to a gate into the wood, through this and straight up the path ahead to the top of the wood (you can see daylight through the trees at the top as you look up from the gate). Go over the stile at the top of the path and straight on across the field to the gate onto the road.

(J) Cross the road and go through the gate on the opposite side. Turn half right and walk downhill, aiming at the right-hand end of a belt of trees, then at a stile. Over the stile and drop down the bank onto the lane.

(K) Turn left and walk down the lane until it meets a road coming in from the right. Turn right along this.

(L) After about 100 yards the road veers right again. Leave it here and go through the gate in front of you and walk across the field to the slightly complicated footbridge you can see below. Cross this and keep straight on, passing St Andrew's Church on your left and the entrance to 15th century **Bingham's Melcombe** Manor House on your right. It is not open to the public.

(M) Follow the drive as it turns right and then leave it and continue in the same direction up a wide mown grass strip with a wall on your right. Notice the incredible yew hedge, wonder how it gets to be trimmed, and catch occasional glimpses of the manor house over the wall. Just before the mown grass strip comes to an end, turn through the last gate on your left and follow the hedge along the bottom of the field, downhill and then up to a stile. Over this and follow the hedge as before.

(N) When you come to a gate on your right giving onto a track running downhill, take this down to the stream (the Mash Water). You can either negotiate the ford and walk up to the next gate, or walk a little way along the stream to your left, use the footbridge and then turn right through the hedge to another gate into the same field. Walk up the field aiming at the gate ahead. This leads to a short green track and out onto a lane which brings you to the road. Turn right onto the road and walk through the hamlet of Aller.

(O) Where the road veers right, keep straight on through the gate ahead and up the right side of the field, turning right along a fenced track about half way up the hill. Follow this track to the lane at the far end. As

you follow the track, look south to your right, down the Devil's Brook, with Henning Hill on one side and Hewish Hill and Gallows Corner on the other. The track ends at the lane you walked down before (K).

(K) Turn left and follow lane to the road at the top of the hill, turn left along this for about 200 yards and then go through the gate on your right. Walk straight across the field to a gate into the wood. Go through this and follow the track to the gate at the bottom by which you entered the wood earlier. Retrace your steps to the interesting church at Hilton (H). Take the narrow footpath ahead, between iron railings and a hedge, passing to

the left of the church. Turn left onto the road at the end and, after 200 yards take the right turn and follow the road back round behind the houses for about 100 yards.

(P) Turn left up a farm road signposted 'Manor Farm' and follow it for about a mile to a barn, stopping to admire the landscaped lake on the way.

(Q) On reaching the barn, pass around it on your left. Watch out for a green track going half right uphill about 50 yards past the barn. Follow it to the gate at the top, then cross the field to pick up Ice Drove again and return to the starting point (A), thus completing Walk 8.

Walk 9
Lawrence of Arabia's Heathland Country

Allow 4 hours

This walk over country much loved by T.E. Lawrence in the closing years of his life, gives a variety of scenery — woodland, field and heathland and pleasant riverside views. In spring there are bluebells and anemones, followed by wild rhododendrons and, in late summer, the heather is in flower everywhere.

The gradients are easy but there is some difficult walking on the edge of Bovington's tank training area and later over rough ground which may be boggy. The best view point is from the car park, looking south over descending woods to high ground beyond.

(A) Start from Cull-peppers Dish Car Park (194) (SY 816-925) in Wareham Forest, which is close to the village of **Briantspuddle**, and which is on our **Tour 5**, and our **Tour 8**. Cull-peppers Dish, the deepest of a number of natural hollows in the ground, is on the opposite (north) side of the road. From the car park return to the road and walk left (westwards) along the same side of it for a

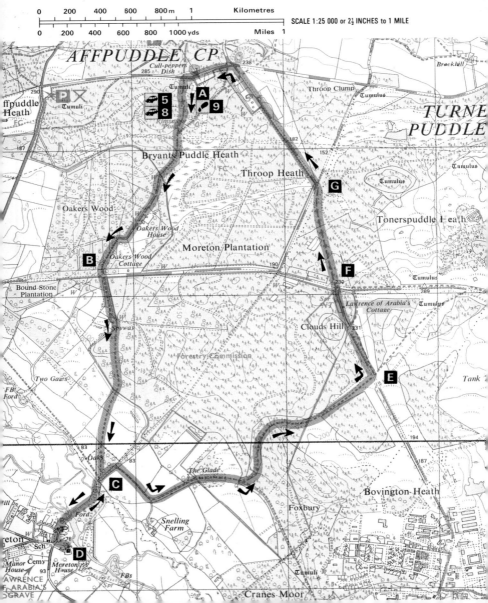

SCALE 1:25 000 or 2½ INCHES to 1 MILE

Post Office Stores at Moreton.

little way and watch for a blue bridleway sign on the left. Take the path into the woods downhill, across a wide dirt track, following the blue arrows until you reach another wide track. Join this and continue right along it. Look for Rimsmoor Pond below you on the left. Walk along the woodland path until reaching a minor road.

(B) Cross this road and walk along a track until you reach some ruined buildings at Spyway. Turn left along a track and almost at once right on to a path into the woods. The path is clear at first and, though it becomes less so, it is well marked by yellow arrows on the trees and presents a challenge to the pathfinder. The path emerges from the woods by a stile into a field. Look for another stile in the same line across the field and after crossing that slant left, skirting a clump of trees, to come to a gate and stile into a lane.

(C) Turn right along this lane which leads to a long footbridge over a ford (the River Frome) . This is a beautiful place with swans and ducks in the water and wild flowers in the hedgerows. On the far side of the bridge, is a pleasant picnic spot. Continuing from the footbridge is a lane to **Moreton** village, the church with the windows engraved by Laurence Whistler, and the nearby cemetery where T. E. Lawrence (of Arabia) is buried.

(D) Returning from the village recross the footbridge and walk up the lane a little way past **Point C** and turn right along a farm road. When the road forks to right, turn left and walk along a track between trees for about ¼ m. At a meeting place of tracks turn left and go through a gate waymarked with a yellow arrow. Follow this track uphill and just before two posts at the beginning of woods turn right as waymarked onto a woodland path. This is a delightful area of mixed

woodland with wild flowers in season. At what appears to be the end of the path there is open ground ahead, but turn left along the remains of the woodland track. This area is now a tank training ground and the alignment of the path has been altered. At the end of the path keep left along the edge of the training ground. Walking may not be easy but is better close to the fence. This leads out to a minor road.

(E) Turn left and walk up the road towards a T-junction **(F)**. There is a wide verge on each side of the road. On the right, just before the T-junction, is T. E. Lawrence's cottage, **Clouds Hill**. This is in the care of the National Trust, and if open, it would be well worth visiting.

(F) At the junction just beyond **Clouds Hill**, cross the road and on the signpost immediately opposite a painted blue arrow indicates a bridle path directly ahead. At first it is overgrown by rhododendrons but passable. When you come into the open go to the right of a row of dead trees ahead and look for and join a track between posts with M.O.D.' Out of Bounds' notices. The ground may be boggy in places. Walk left down the track which is later joined by a wider one coming in on the right. Continue down this in the same direction. This is typical sandy heath country and walking may be difficult but before long the track bends round to the right and, just past a M.O.D. 'Out of Bounds' notice in red, go straight ahead down a fairly clear track out to a minor road.

(G) Turn right onto this road and then quickly left at a signpost to Briantspuddle. Walk up the road which leads to a cross roads at which you turn left to arrive at the Cull-peppers Dish Car Park **(A)**, thus completing Walk 9.

Walk 10
Corfe Castle and the Purbeck Ridgeway

Allow 3 ½ hours

Corfe Castle is one of the Dorset's major attractions and this includes both the castle itself and the village. This walk to the west of the village takes you along the popular Ridgeway and up on to Creech Barrow. This is one of the highest points of the Purbeck Chalk Hills and provides magnificent views on every side. Ball clay is mined in the area north of the ridge, and it is only in recent years that a drift mine under Creech Barrow itself was closed, most of the workings nowadays being opencast. The minor road passes through the Domesday settlement of East Creech with cottages and a farm built in the 17th and 18th centuries. After leaving the road our path enters a unique area that owes its present interest to past clay working; here and there pools have formed in old clay pits and trees have colonised the rough ground of the spoil heaps in between. The path here can be muddy and slippery in wet weather.

(A **Corfe Castle** is on our **Tour 9.** Park in car park off West Street (195)(SY 95-81) (free in winter, charge in summer) and start by climbing the stile nearest to the ticket booth and drop down slightly right to the concrete bridge over the Corfe River. As you go look across to a rough area on the far slope — these are the Castle Rings, a ring and bailey

castle which was possibly a siege castle used by King Stephen in 1139 when he unsuccessfully beseiged Corfe, and which was probably also used in the Civil War. After crossing the bridge bear left across the narrow field to a gate and stile in the right-hand fence, over the stile keeping the hedge on your right. Walk up the field to the road, over which the path continues across a stile slightly to the left (not through the gate directly opposite). Continue uphill to another stile.

(B) Turn left along a bridleway, but after 300 yards this forks and you walk to the right uphill onto the top of Knowle Hill, continue in the same general direction for the length of the ridge, meanwhile enjoying the view to the left across the farming valley to the limestone hills of Purbeck stretching away in the distance to Tyneham Cap, with **Kingston** on the skyline and **Church Knowle** nestling in the valley. As the path starts to dip a large chalk quarry comes into view on the right.

(C) A metal gate leads onto a narrow road (beware of vehicles) and follow this uphill until it swings to the right at a gateway. Through the gate onto a stony track continuing straight ahead.

(D) *It is possible to go straight ahead (westwards) along the Ridgeway to visit the Grange Arch, now in the care of the National Trust. It was built in the first half of the 18th century as an 'eye-catcher' by the owner of nearby Creech Grange.* But for the main route — at the stile in the right hand fence (D) — cross the downs diagonally left, downhill, then up and down again to a stile onto a stony track.

(E) Through the gate the track forks, take the left fork onto the road and straight across

SCALE 1:25 000 or 2½ INCHES to 1 MILE

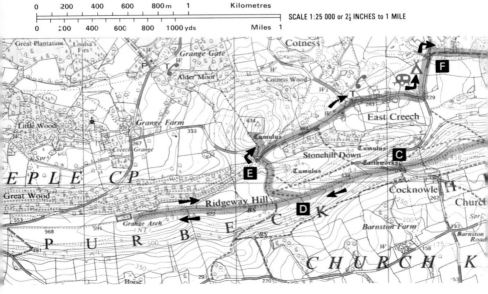

Corfe Castle ... a dramatic ruin with dark memories.

onto a flat, grassy area. This is the site of the mine that went under Creech Barrow. Walk up the Barrow (marked 'Tumulus' on our map) and back by the clear path winding its way to the top from the far side of the flat area. This path is not a public right of way but the owners have no objection to its use. There was once a medieval hunting lodge at the top and the views from its site are spectacular. Returning to the road at **(E)**, turn left, past a turning to the left, and through East Creech Farm with its duckpond. At the T-junction turn left until the road swings left.

(F) Now leave the road on a bridleway to the right, taking you through the old clay workings. Keep straight ahead along this.

(G) Where the path goes straight ahead and is marked with a yellow arrow, turn right to follow the blue arrow and wind through the wooded area until reaching a stile into the field on the right.

(H) Walk up the fields towards the trees, to a gate into a rough area at the top. Now turn left through the gate and continue eastwards as straight as possible with the field boundary on your left. This path tends to be hidden under bracken in the summer, but it is there. Further on there are muddy patches where the clay lies on the surface. As you come out of the tree canopy, **Corfe Castle** comes suddenly into sight and you cross a stile and turn right **(J)**, round the end of West Hill past a barn to the road. Turn left, cross the bridge and immediately right onto the footpath between the castle mound and the river. Now enter the Square and go beyond to the starting car park in West Street, **(A)**, thus completing Walk 10.

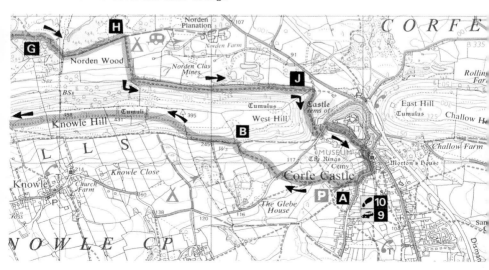

Walk 11

Worth Matravers, Dancing Ledge and the Coast Path

Allow 2¾ hours, or longer if you wish to explore cliff ledges

This walk takes the rambler through an area that has traditionally been used for farming and quarrying, though the latter is now less intensive. The first section is along the Priest's Way, reputedly the route along which the priest from the mother church of Worth Matravers travelled to say Mass at Swanage. This journey took place up to the latter part of the 15th century when Swanage grew in importance and became the more dominant partner. Much of the land here is now owned by the National Trust, being part of the largest legacy the Trust has ever received, that of the late Mr Ralph Bankes of Kingston Lacy, near Wimborne.

The return route along the Coast Path gives views of the spectacularly sheer cliffs of Portland limestone, much of which has been shaped into 'ledges' and 'caves', not only by the forces of the sea, but also by quarrying in days gone by, when stone was taken from here and lowered into boats to be shipped away to London and other ports. Dancing Ledge is one such quarried area with a wide platform where in rough weather the waves come dancing over — could this be the derivation of its name? The final section takes walkers up the Winspit Valley, flanked by East Man and West Man, hills on whose slopes are displayed some of the best examples of strip lynchets in the country.

(A) This walk starts from **Worth Matravers**, which is on our **Tour 9**. Set out from car park (195) (SY 97-77) (a small charge is made by the Parish Council for upkeep). Turn right, out of car park, and at the road junction turn left uphill — from this road there is a good view of the strip lynchets on the hillside towards the sea.

(B) Fork right off minor road at a finger post, cross a stile and continue over two fields to a field gate. Now join the Priest's Way at Eastington Farm, originally built in the 17th century and now sympathetically converted to a complex of dwellings. The path is now a clear stony track between stone walls

Dancing Ledge ... the Dorset Coast at its very best.

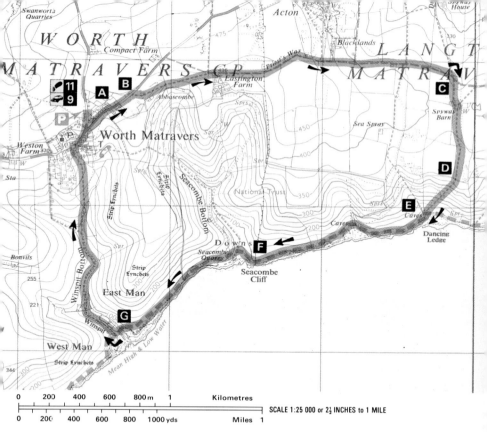

and hedges. Over to the left is the hamlet of Acton, a settlement recorded in Domesday book, surrounded by opencast quarries. Traditionally quarrying and farming have gone on hand in hand in this area, with exhausted quarries have been filled in and returned to rough grazing land. See also the information board. Stone markers show where footpaths cross the track, ignore the first one indicating 'Dancing Ledge ¾ — No Cars', and continue straight ahead between Purbeck stone gate-posts, and —

(C) — At the second stone marker, turn right along the access to Spyway Barn. Turn in front of the buildings and through the car park into the field behind, bearing slightly left to the gate and stone stile into the next field.

(D) At the end of this field, go through another pair of Purbeck stone gateposts, this time with the traditional slots for sliding bars, onto the wares, the grassy slopes dropping down from the cultivated fields to the cliff edge. This is usually a mass of flowers, changing according to the season — in spring and early summer orchids of several varieties, with cowslips and violets, these being followed by a wide variety of summer flowers including field scabious, horseshoe and kidney vetch, knapweed, sheep's bit, dwarf thistle, wild thyme and the delightfully named squinancywort. Drop down the slope slightly to the right and Dancing Ledge is visible ahead.

(E) Join the Coast Path and follow it with the sea on your left and the downs on your right — all along there is evidence of the old cliff quarries and at Seacombe where a path comes down the valley to the coast you can divert to explore the ledges over-looking the sea, but do take special care.

(F) To rejoin the Coast Path it is necessary to walk up the valley for 200 yards or so to where a stone sign points you up a set of steps. At the top turn seawards along the edge of the field and continue on the Coast Path to Winspit.

(G) At Winspit it is again possible to explore the ledges left by the old quarrying after which the walk continues up the valley, forking right at the sewage plant to **Worth Matravers**. A short cut through the Percy Wallace Memorial Garden opposite brings you to the village green and pond providing a picturesque setting for the village's surrounding stone cottages. **Worth Matravers** has retained its post office and stores, and there is also a very welcome tearoom. After visiting the interesting Norman church (to the left) bear right up the hill to return to the starting-point car park **(A)**, thus completing Walk 11.

Walk 12
Ancient Earthworks and Downland Vistas

Allow 4 hours

This walk, in the north-east of the county, is mostly over open downland, providing good all-round views and taking in a length of Bokerley Ditch (or Dyke), a defensive Romano-British earthwork built in the 4th century to repel Saxon invaders from the north and east. Turning south-west, the route follows the ridge of Pentridge Down which, although only six hundred feet above sea level, is the highest point in the area and affords magnificent views. The walk descends to the isolated village of Pentridge, which has connections with Robert Browning's family, before returning to to the Dyke by quiet lanes. In spring and summer there is a wealth of chalk-loving wild flowers to be seen on this route.

(A) Start from the layby near the 'County of Dorset' entry sign, at Bokerley Junction, on the west side of the A354 Blandford-Salisbury road, approximately halfway between the two towns (184) (SU 03-19), and which can easily be reached from our Tour 7. From the layby, cross the road (beware of fast traffic), turn left and walk along the wide green verge for a few yards to a rusty iron gate on your right. Go through this, scramble across the ditch to the top of **Bokerley Ditch** (or Dyke) and walk along it, watching out for rabbit holes underfoot. After about half a mile cross over the collapsed barbed wire fence and walk along the south side of the dyke, on the edge of a field. There is an impressive long barrow in the middle of the field and views of the ridge you will be walking on later. Shortly after a track comes in from the right. This is the track we shall be walking up from Pentridge later on.

(B) Go through the dyke at this point by the 'Martin Down Nature Reserve' signboard, and continue with the dyke on your right. Our way continues uphill still with the dyke on our right. At first its bank is

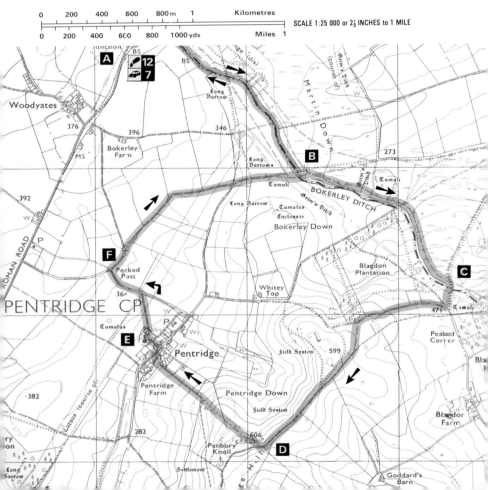

Downland country from Bokerley Ditch.

overgrown but further on the scrub has been cleared (at the time of writing) and is very impressive, stretching away into the distance. There are good views on our left looking across Martin Down to the downs of Hampshire and Wiltshire, The wooded clump in the foreground is Windmill Hill three miles to the east (184) (SU 08-19) and the similar one on the far north-eastern horizon is the Iron Age settlement of Clearbury Ring (184) (SU 15-24) about seven miles away.

(C) Now leave the dyke, turning right where the chalk track cuts through the dyke by the Nature Reserve's map and information board. Walk up the track for about sixty yards, then turn right on to another track and after another hundred yards turn left off this and through a hunting gate. With a fence on your right, walk through trees and the path soon emerges into the open, with a good views of the dyke on your right, winding its way across the edge of Martin Down. Continue with the fence on your right until, after about three hundred yards, the path emerges onto a field. Aim for a group of ash trees, taking you across the middle of the field, but if there is a crop growing you may find it preferable to walk round the left-hand edge of the field. Go through the hunting gate and over the rise, keeping the hedge on your left. There are now fine views on your left, ranging from the New Forest in the south-east, the tower-blocks of Bournemouth to the south, with the line of the Purbeck Hills beyond You are now on Pentridge Hill and the pine-clad rise that comes into view is Penbury Knoll.

(D) Turn right off the track here, wander through the pine trees, and you will see the steeple of **Pentridge** church nestling amongst trees below. From the knoll make your way down the steep hill to the corner of the fence, keeping the church directly ahead. The ridges in the field to your right are all that remain of an ancient field system. Go over the stile in the bottom left hand corner of the field onto a narrow grassy lane. The fields on the right are beautiful in late spring with massed cowslips. The stile at the end of the lane brings you onto the road in the centre of the **Pentridge** village by two large trees, one chestnut, one maple. Walk a few yards up the road to the right before turning left onto the lane to St Rumbold's Church.

(E) Cross the green in front of the brick and flint cottage to find a stile in the top corner, go over, and follow the hedge on your left to the road. Where the path emerges onto the road it crosses the course of the Dorset Cursus, a Neolithic earthwork of which all trace has been ploughed out. Turn left and walk down the road until it turns left at Peaked Post.

(F) Turn right here onto a grassy enclosed lane and keep on this for about half a mile, ignoring another track on your left soon after leaving the road. Where another track joins in from the right continue in the same direction, once more over downland. This track takes you back to the Dyke. Go through the gap at the Nature Reserve board **(B)** as before, but this time turn left and walk along the down with the Dyke on your left. After about half a mile look for a suitable spot to climb the bank and return along its top to the rusty gate you passed through at the start of the walk, to return to the layby on the A354 **(A)**, thus completing Walk 12.

131

CONVENTIONAL SIGNS
1:190 080 or 1 INCH to 3 MILES

ROADS
Not necessarily rights of way

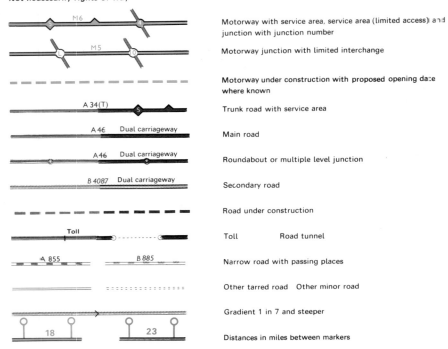

Motorway with service area, service area (limited access) and junction with junction number

Motorway junction with limited interchange

Motorway under construction with proposed opening date where known

Trunk road with service area

Main road

Roundabout or multiple level junction

Secondary road

Road under construction

Toll   Road tunnel

Narrow road with passing places

Other tarred road   Other minor road

Gradient 1 in 7 and steeper

Distances in miles between markers

The representation of a road is no evidence of the existence of a right of way

PRIMARY ROUTES

These form a national network of recommended through routes which complement the motorway system. Selected places of major traffic importance are known as Primary Route Destinations and are shown thus POOLE Distances and directions to such destinations are repeated on traffic signs which, on primary routes, have a green background or, on motorways, have a blue background.
To continue on a primary route through or past a place which has appeared as a destination on previous signs, follow the directions to the next primary destination shown on the green-backed signs.

RAILWAYS

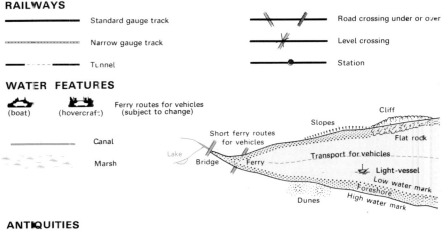

Standard gauge track

Narrow gauge track

Tunnel

Road crossing under or over

Level crossing

Station

WATER FEATURES

(boat)   (hovercraft)   Ferry routes for vehicles (subject to change)

Canal

Marsh

Short ferry routes for vehicles

Lake   Bridge   Ferry

Cliff
Slopes
Flat rock
Transport for vehicles
Light-vessel
Low water mark
Foreshore
Dunes   High water mark

ANTIQUITIES

※ Native fortress   Site of battle (with date)   Roman road (course of)   CANOVIUM ·   Roman antiquity

Castle ·   Other antiquities

Ⓜ   Ancient Monuments and Historic Buildings in the care of the Secretaries of State for the Environment, for Scotland and for Wales and that are open to the public.

BOUNDARIES

+ — + — + — + — National

— — — — — — — { County, Region or Islands Area }

GENERAL FEATURES

 Buildings

 Wood

Lighthouse (in use)

Lighthouse (disused)

Windmill

Radio or TV mast

▲ Youth hostel

⊕ Civil aerodrome { with Customs facilities / without Customs facilities }

✈

Ⓗ Heliport

☏ Public telephone

☏ Motoring organisation telephone

+ Intersection, latitude & longitude at 30' intervals (not shown where it confuses important detail)

TOURIST INFORMATION

† Abbey, Cathedral, Priory

🐟 Aquarium

⋀ Camp site

🚐 Caravan site

🏰 Castle

Cave

Country park

Craft centre

❀ Garden

▷ Golf course or links

🏛 Historic house

ℹ Information centre

Motor racing

🖼 Museum

👣 Nature or forest trail

🦆 Nature reserve

☆ Other tourist feature

✕ Picnic site

Preserved railway

Racecourse

Skiing

Viewpoint

Wildlife park

Zoo

WALKS, CYCLE & MOTOR TOURS
Applicable to all scales

 Start point of walk

➡ Route of walk

Featured walk

 Start point of tour

➡ Route of tour

Featured tour

FOLLOW THE COUNTRY CODE
Enjoy the countryside and respect its life and work

Guard against all risk of fire

Fasten all gates

Keep your dogs under close control

Keep to public paths across farmland

Leave livestock, crops and machinery alone

Use gates and stiles to cross fences, hedges and walls

Take your litter home

Help to keep all water clean

Protect wildlife, plants and trees

Take special care on country roads

Make no unnecessary noise

Reproduced by permission of the Countryside Commission

CONVENTIONAL SIGNS 1:25 000 or 2½ INCHES to 1 MILE

ROADS AND PATHS

Not necessarily rights of way

M I or F6(M)	M I or A5(M)	Motorway	
A 31 (T)	A 31(T)	Trunk road	Narrow roads
A 35	A 35	Main road	with passing places are
B 307~	B 3074	Secondary road	annotated
A 35	A 35	Dual carriageway	

Road generally more than 4m wide

Road generally less than 4m wide

Other road, drive or track

Unfenced roads and tracks are shown by pecked lines

Path

RAILWAYS

Multiple track } Standard gauge

Single track

Narrow gauge

Siding

Cutting

Embankment

Tunnel

Road over & under

Level crossing; station

PUBLIC RIGHTS OF WAY

Public rights of way may not be evident on the ground

Public paths { Footpath / Bridleway

+ + + + + Byway open to all traffic

Road used as a public path

DANGER AREA

MOD ranges in the area
Danger!
Observe warning notices

The indication of a towpath in this book does not necessarily imply a public right of way
The representation of any other road, track or path is no evidence of the existence of a right of way

BOUNDARIES

— · — · — · — County (England and Wales)

— — — — District

—•—•—•— London Borough

·········· Civil Parish (England)* Community (Wales)

— — — — — Constituency (County, Borough, Burgh or European Assembly)

} Coincident boundaries are shown by the first appropriate symbol

*For Ordnance Survey purposes County Boundary is deemed to be the limit of the parish structure whether or not a parish area adjoins

SYMBOLS

Church or chapel { with tower / with spire / without tower or spire

Glasshouse; youth hostel

Bus or coach station

Lighthouse; lightship; beacon

Triangulation station

Triangulation point on { church or chapel / lighthouse, beacon / building; chimney

Electricity transmission line

pylon pole

VILLA Roman antiquity (AD 43 to AD 420)

Castle Other antiquities

Site of antiquity

✕ 1066 Site of battle (with date)

Gravel pit

Sand pit

Chalk pit, clay pit or quarry

Refuse or slag heap

Sloping wall

Water | Mud

Sand; sand & shingle

National Park or Forest Park Boundary

NT National Trust always open

NT National Trust opening restricted

FC Forestry Commission

VEGETATION Limits of vegetation are defined by positioning of the symbols but may be delineated also by pecks or dots

Coniferous trees

Non-coniferous trees

Coppice

Orchard

Scrub

Bracken, rough grassland

In some areas bracken (⌂) and rough grassland (······) are shown separately } Shown collectively as rough grassland on some sheets

Heath

Reeds

Marsh

Saltings

HEIGHTS AND ROCK FEATURES

50 } Determined by { ground survey / air survey
285 ·

Surface heights are to the nearest metre above mean sea level. Heights shown close to a triangulation pillar refer to the station height at ground level and not necessarily to the summit

Vertical face

Loose rock Boulders Outcrop Scree

75
60
50

Contours are at 5 metres vertical interval

ABBREVIATIONS 1:25 000 or 2½ INCHES to 1 MILE also 1:10 000/1:10 560 or 6 INCHES to 1 MILE

BP,BS	Boundary Post or Stone	P	Post Office	A,R	Telephone, AA or RAC
CH	Club House	Pol Sta	Police Station	TH	Town Hall
F V	Ferry Foot or Vehicle	PC	Public Convenience	Twr	Tower
FB	Foot Bridge	PH	Public House	W	Well
HO	House	Sch	School	Wd Pp	Wind Pump
MP,MS	Mile Post or Stone	Spr	Spring		
Mon	Monument	T	Telephone, public		

Abbreviations applicable only to 1:10 000/1:10 560 or 6 INCHES to 1 MILE

Ch	Church	GP	Guide Post	TCB	Telephone Call Box
F Sta	Fire Station	P	Pole or Post	TCP	Telephone Call Post
Fn	Fountain	S	Stone	Y	Youth Hostel

Maps and Mapping

Most early maps of the area covered by this guide were published on a county basis, and if you wish to follow their development in detail R. V. Tooley's *Maps and Map Makers* will be found most useful. The first significant county maps were produced by Christopher Saxton in the 1570s, the whole of England and Wales being covered in only six years. Although he did not cover the whole country, John Norden, working at the end of the 16th century, was the first map-maker to show roads. In 1611-12, John Speed, making use of Saxton and Norden's pioneer work, produced his *'Theatre of the Empire of Great Britaine'*, adding excellent town plans, battle scenes, and magnificent coats of arms. The next great English map-maker was John Ogilby, and in 1675 he published *Britannia, Volume I*, in which all the roads of England and Wales were engraved on a scale of one inch to the mile, in a massive series of strip maps. From this time onwards, no map was published without roads, and throughout the 18th century, steady progress was made in accuracy, if not always in the beauty of presentation.

The first Ordnance Survey maps came about as a result of Bonnie Prince Charlie's Jacobite rebellion of 1745. It was, however, in 1791, following the successful completion of the military survey of Scotland by General Roy that the Ordnance Survey was formally established. The threat of invasion by Napoleon in the early 19th century spurred on the demand for accurate and detailed mapping for military purposes, and to meet this need the first Ordnance Survey one-inch map, covering part of Essex, was published in 1805 in a single colour. This was the first numbered sheet in the First Series of one-inch maps.

Over the next seventy years the one-inch map was extended to cover the whole of Great Britain. Reprints of some of these First Series maps incorporating various later 19th-century amendments, have been published by David & Charles. The reprinted sheets covering most of our area are Numbers 84, 85, 92 and 93.

The Ordnance Survey's one-inch maps evolved through a number of 'Series' and 'Editions', to the Seventh Series which was replaced in 1972 by the metric 1:50 000 scale Landranger Series. Between the First Series one-inch and the current Landranger maps many changes in style, format, content and purpose have taken place. Colour, for example, first appeared with the timid use of light brown for hill shading on the 1889 one-inch sheets. By 1892 as many as five colours were being used for this scale and at one stage the Seventh Series was being printed in no less than ten colours. Recent developments in 'process printing' — a technique in which four basic colours produce almost any required tint — are now used to produce Ordnance Survey Landranger and other map series. Through the years the one-inch Series has gradually turned away from its military origins and has developed to meet a wider user demand. The modern detailed full colour Landranger maps at 1:50 000 scale incorporate Rights of Way and Tourist Information and are much used for both leisure and business purposes. To compare the old and new approach to changing demand, see the two map extracts of Dorchester on the following pages.

Modern Ordnance Survey Maps of the Area.

Dorset is covered by Ordnance Survey 1: 50 000 scale (1 ¼ inches to 1 mile) **Landranger** map sheets 183, 184, 193, 194 and 195. These all purpose maps are packed full of information to help you explore the area. Viewpoints, picnic sites, places of interest, caravan and camping sites are shown, as are public rights of way information such as footpaths and bridleways. To look at the area surrounding Dorchester, the Ordnance Survey 1 inch to 4 miles **Routemaster** Sheet 8 (South West England and South Wales) and Sheet 9 (South East England) will prove most useful. An alternative will be found in the form of the **OS Motoring Atlas** of Great Britain at the larger scale of 1 inch to 3 miles.

To examine Dorset in more detail and especially if you are planning walks, Ordnance Survey 1: 25 000 scale (2 ½ inches to 1 mile) **Pathfinder** maps which include public rights of way information are ideal. There is a special **Outdoor Leisure Map**, also at 1:25 000, of the Purbeck area of the county.

To place the area in an historical context the following Ordnance Survey **Archaeological and Historical Maps** will also be found useful: **Ancient Britain, Roman Britain, Britain before the Norman Conquest,** and **Monastic Britain.**

Ordnance Survey maps are available from officially appointed agents (local agents are shown on page 21, under 'Useful Addresses'), and from most booksellers, stationers and newsagents.

See following pages for map extracts relating to the Dorchester area taken from a First Series One-inch map, and a recent Landranger map.

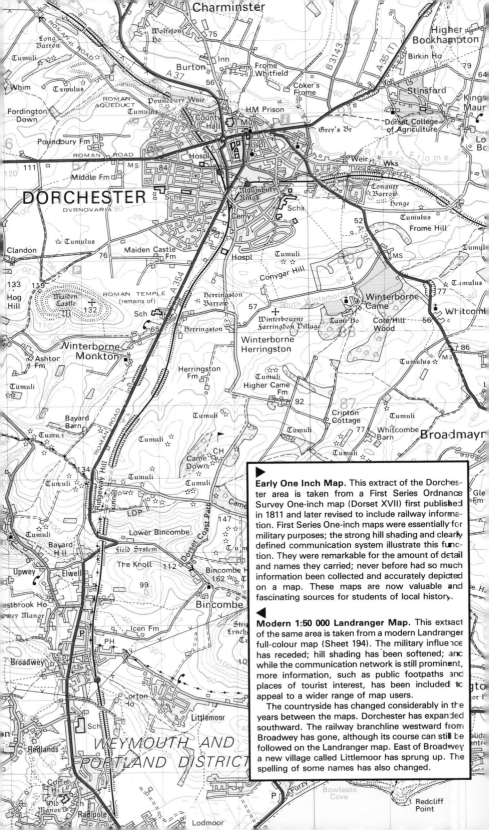

▶ **Early One Inch Map.** This extract of the Dorchester area is taken from a First Series Ordnance Survey One-inch map (Dorset XVII) first published in 1811 and later revised to include railway information. First Series One-inch maps were essentially for military purposes; the strong hill shading and clearly defined communication system illustrate this function. They were remarkable for the amount of detail and names they carried; never before had so much information been collected and accurately depicted on a map. These maps are now valuable and fascinating sources for students of local history.

◀ **Modern 1:50 000 Landranger Map.** This extract of the same area is taken from a modern Landranger full-colour map (Sheet 194). The military influence has receded; hill shading has been softened; and while the communication network is still prominent, more information, such as public footpaths and places of tourist interest, has been included to appeal to a wider range of map users.

The countryside has changed considerably in the years between the maps. Dorchester has expanded southward. The railway branchline westward from Broadwey has gone, although its course can still be followed on the Landranger map. East of Broadwey a new village called Littlemoor has sprung up. The spelling of some names has also changed.

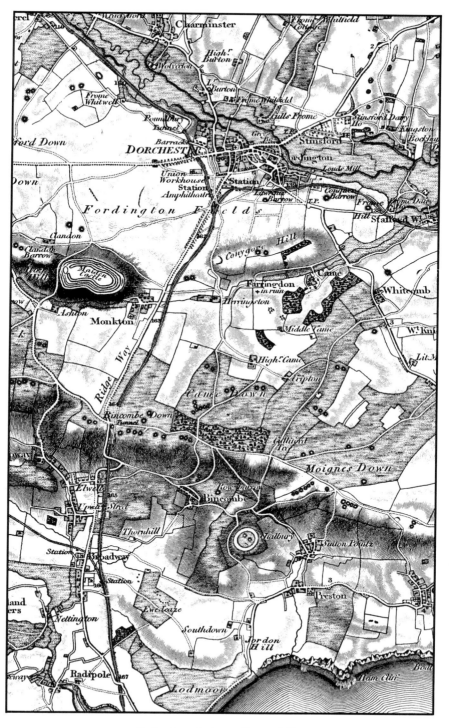

Scale of one Inch to a Statute Mile

0   1   2   Miles 3

Index

Name	Map No.	Map Ref.	Page No.
Charmouth	193	SY 36–93	36,91
Chedington	193	ST 48–05	36
Cheselbourne	194	SY 76–99	99
Chesil Beach	194	SY 60–80	22,36,46,89,96
Chetnole	194	ST 66–07	95,
Chettle	195	ST 95–13	37,103
Chettle House	195	ST 95–13	37
Chideock	193	SY 42–92	37,91,110,111
Chilcombe	194	SY 52–91	37
Chilcombe Fort	194	SY 53–92	37
Child Okeford	194	ST 83–12	48
Christchurch	195	SZ 15–92	37–39,107
Christchurch Castle	195	SZ 15–92	38
Christchurch Harbour	195	SZ 17–91	39,48,60
Church Knowle	195	SY 93–81	39,104,126
Church Ope Cave	194	SY 69–70	65
Churchill Family			59
Clarkham Cross	194	ST 55–07	92
Clavell Family			40
Clavell's Tower	195	SY 90–79	51
Claysmore School	194	ST 86–14	51
Clearbury Ring	184	SU 15–24	131
Clifton Maybank	194	ST 57–13	40
Closworth	194	ST 56–10	92
Clouds Hill	194	SY 92–90	40,60,105,125
Clubmen, The			50
Clyffe House	194	SY 78–92	78
Coach House Museum	195	SY 99–78	53
Coade, Mrs Eleanor			56
Cobb, The	193	SY 33–91	55
Cobham, Sir Alan			78
Colehill	195	SU 02–00	103
Colmer's Hill	193	SY 44–93	77,111
Common, The	194	ST 78–10	100
Comper, Sir Ninian			86
Compton Abbas	183	ST 87–18	40,100
Compton Abbas Airfield	183	ST 88–18	40,100
Compton Acres Gardens	195	SZ 05–89	40
Compton House	183	ST 59–16	61,95
Compton Valence	194	SY 59–93	115
Coney's Castle	193	SY 37–97	89,90,108,109
Constable's House, The	195	SZ 15–92	38
Constable, John			61
Corfe Castle	195	SY 96–81	40–41,52,67,106,126,127
Corfe Mullen	195	SY 98–97	41
Corscombe	194	ST 51–05	41
Cosmore	194	ST 67–05	95
Cote Hill	194	SY 71–88	84
Cranborne	195	SU 05–13	41,103
Cranborne Chase	184,195		23,29,37,41,45,61,72,80,88
Crawford Bridge	195	ST 91–02	73,101
Creech	195	SY 91–83	42,105,126
Creech Barrow	195	SY 92–82	127
Creech Grange	195	SY 91–82	126
Crichel House	195	ST 99–08	59,103
Crickmay, G.R.			79
Cross and Hand, The	194	ST 62–03	25
Crown Court Room (Dorchester)	194	SY 69–90	43
Culpeppers Dish	194	SY 81–92	31,99,105,124,125
Damer, Joseph			58,59
Dancing Ledge	195	SY 99–76	53,129
Dean's Court	195	SU 01–00	86
Defoe, Daniel			27
de Montfort, Simon			26,60
Dewlish	194	SY 77–98	42,99
Digby Family			59,72
Dinosaur Museum, The	194	SY 69–90	44
Dodington, Sir George			77

Name	Map No.	Map Ref.	Page No.
Dogbury Down	194	ST 66–05	118
Dogbury Hill	194	ST 66–05	59,118
Doghouse Hill	193	SY 43–91	110
Dorchester	194	SY 68–90	42–44,96,97,98,99
Dorset Coast Path			23,25,34,44,51,54,67,74,76,96,129
Dorset County Museum	194	SY 69–90	43
Dorset Cursus, The	195	ST 98–13	48,62,131
Dorset Heavy Horse Centre	195	SU 08–10	80
Dorset Military Museum	194	SY 68–90	44
Drimpton	193	ST 41–05	90
Dungeon Hill	194	ST 69–07	47
Durdle Door	194	SY 80–80	36,44,54,105
Durlston Country Park	195	SZ 02–77	44,76,106
Durlston Head	195	SZ 03–77	76
East Chelborough	194	ST 55–05	44
East Creech	195	SY 93–82	127
East Lulworth	194	SY 86–82	44,73,105
East Stour	183	ST 79–22	45
Eastbury House	195	ST 93–12	77,101
Edmondsham	195	SU 06–11	45
Eggardon Camp	194	SY 54–94	24,45,65,93
Encombe House	195	SY 94–78	52
Evershot	194	ST 57–04	45,58,93,112,113
Eype	193	SY 44–91	45
Eype Down	193	SY 44–92	45,110
Eype's Mouth	193	SY 44–90	45,91
Farnham	184	ST 95–15	45,103
Faulkner, J.Mead			46,68
Ferrey, Benjamin			62
Fiddleford	194	ST 80–13	45,94
Fiddleford Mill & Mill House	194	ST 80–13	45,94
Fielding, Henry			45,55
Fifehead Magdalen	183	ST 78–81	46
Fifehead Neville	194	ST 76–10	46
Fishpond Bottom	193	SY 36–98	90
Flambard, Ranulf			37
Fleet	194	SY 63–80	46
Fleet, The	194	SY 59–82	
etc			23,96
Flower's Barrow Fort	194	SY 86–80	45
Folke	194	ST 65–13	46
Folly	194	ST 72–03	99,120,121
Fontmell Down	183	ST 87–17	40,46
Fontmell Magna	183	ST 86–16	46,100
Forde Abbey	193	ST 35–05	46,90
Fortuneswell	194	SY 68–73	65
Fox-Talbot, Henry			77
Frampton	194	SY 62–95	46
Friar Waddon	194	SY 64–85	117
Friar Waddon Hill	194	SY 64–85	80
Frome St Quintin	194	ST 59–02	47
Furzey Island	195	SZ 01–86	64
Gadd Cliff	194	SY 88–79	79
Garnett, Edward			36
Giant Hill	194	ST 66–02	35
Gilbert Scott, Sir George			35,59
Gill, Eric			31
Gillingham	183	ST 80–26	26,47
Glanvilles Wootton	194	ST 67–08	47
Goathorn Pier	195	SZ 01–86	67
Godlingston Heath	195	SZ 01–82	74
Godlingston Manor	195	SZ 01–80	76
Godmanstone	194	SY 66–97	47,60
Gold Hill	183	ST 86–22	70
Golden Cap	193	SY 40–92	36,45,47,60,68,91,110,111
Goodden Family			61
Gore Heath Picnic Place	195	SY 92–91	106
Gore Hill	194	ST 63–03	25,49

142

143

Further Reading ...
A List of Books.

General:

Ashley, H. *The Dorset Village Book.* Countryside Books

Billet, M. *Thatched Buildings of Dorset.* Hale

Bond, L. *Tyneham, a Lost Heritage.* Dovecote Press

Gant R. *Dorset Villages.* Hale

Harfield, A. *Blandford and the Military.* Dorset Publishing Co.

Hawkins, D. *Cranborne Chase.* Gollancz

Hyams, J.H. *Dorset.* Batsford

Hyland, P. *Purbeck, the Ingrained Island.* Gollancz

Legg R. *Purbeck Island.* Dorset Publishing Co.

Mee, A. *Dorset (King's England Series).* Hodder & Stoughton

Pitt-Rivers, M. *Shell Guide to Dorset.* Faber & Faber

Russell, N. *Guide to Wessex Museums.* Gasson

Sale, R. *Dorset.* Hutchinson

Treves, F. *Highways & Byways in Dorset.* Macmillan

Wansborough, R. *The Tale of Milton Abbas.* Humphreys

Wightman, R. *Portrait of Dorset.* Hale

Art, Architecture & History

Cecil D. *Some Dorset Country Houses.* Dovecote Press

Dyer J. *Prehistoric England & Wales.* Penguin

Grinsell, L.V. *The Archaeology of Wessex.* Methuen

Hawkes, J. *Guide to Prehistoric & Roman Monuments in England and Wales.* Cardinal

Margary, I.D. *Roman Roads in Britain.* Phoenix House

Morris, J (Ed) *Domesday Book: Dorset.* Phillimore

Newman & Pevsner *Dorset. Buildings of England Series.* Penguin

Osborne, G. *Exploring Ancient Dorset.* Dorset Publishing Co.

Pevsner, N. *Hampshire. Buildings of England Series (for Bournemouth & Christchurch).* Penguin

Royal Commission for Historical Monuments. *Dorset.* H.M.S.O.

Street, S. *Tales of Dorset.* Countryside Books

Tooley, R.V. *Maps and Map-Makers.* Batsford

Wood, E.S. *Field Guide to Archaeology in Britain.* Collins

Fiction, Literary Interest and Early Travellers

Austen, J. *Persuasion.* Penguin

Defoe, D. *A Tour Through England and Wales.* Penguin

Drewitt, B. *The Heart of Hardy's Wessex.* (An invaluable map based on O.S. Landranger Sheet 194) Wessex Heritage Tours

Faulkner, J.M. *Moonfleet.* Penguin

Gibson, J. *The Complete Poems of Thomas Hardy.* Macmillan

Gittings, R. *The Young Thomas Hardy.* Heinemann

Gittings, R. *The Older Thomas Hardy.* Heinemann

Halliday, F.E. *Thomas Hardy; His Life and Work.* Granada

Hardy, T. *All his Wessex Novels.* Penguin

Hardy, T. *Thomas Hardy; Selected Stories.* Macmillan

Hutchins, J. *History & Antiquities of the County of Dorset*

Kay-Robinson, D. *Hardy's Wessex Re-appraised.* David & Charles

Jones, B.(Ed) *The Poems of William Barnes.* Centaur

Lea, H. *The Hardy Guides.* Penguin

Morris, C. (Ed) *The Journeys of Celia Fiennes.* Macdonald

Pinion, F.B. *A Hardy Companion.* Macmillan

Stevens Cox, J. *Hardy's Wessex.* Toucan Press

Railways

Atthill, R. *Somerset & Dorset Railway.* David & Charles

White, H.P. *Southern England. A Regional History of the Railways of Great Britain.* David & Charles

Walks and Walking

Dacombe & Legge, *The Dorset Walk.* Dorset Publishing Co.

Gant, R. *A Guide to the South Devon & Dorset Coast Paths.* Constable

Jackman, B. *Dorset Coast Path.* H.M.S.O.

Jesty, C. *Dorset Town Trails.* Gasson

Legge, R. *Purbeck Walks.* Dorset Publishing Co.

Legge, R. *Hardy Country Walks.* Dorset Publishing Co.

Proctor, A *The Wessex Way.* Thornhill Press

Stoker, H. *South Dorset Walks.* Mill House Publications

Stoker, H. *West Dorset Walks.* Mill House Publications

Westcott, H.D. *The Dorset Coast Path.* Penguin

Follow the Country Code

- Enjoy the countryside and respect its life and work
- Guard against all risk of fires
- Fasten all gates
- Keep your dogs under close control
- Keep to public paths across farmland
- Use gates and stiles to cross fences, hedges and walls
- Take your litter home
- Help to keep all water clean
- Protect wildlife, plants and trees
- Take special care on country roads
- Make no unnecessary noise